W9-CMF-215

Crime, Anti-Social Behaviour and Schools

*Also by Carol Hayden*

IMPLEMENTING A RESTORATIVE JUSTICE APPROACH IN CHILDREN'S
RESIDENTIAL CARE (*co-authored*)

CHILDREN IN TROUBLE

OUTSIDE LOOKING IN: Families' Experiences of Exclusion from School
(*co-authored*)

STATE CHILD CARE POLICY: 'Looking After' Children? (*co-authored*)

CHILDREN EXCLUDED FROM PRIMARY SCHOOL: Debates, Evidence, Responses

# Crime, Anti-Social Behaviour and Schools

Edited by

Carol Hayden
*University of Portsmouth, UK*

Denise Martin
*University of Brighton, UK*

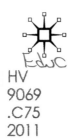
First published 2011 by
PALGRAVE MACMILLAN

Palgrave Macmillan in the UK is an imprint of Macmillan Publishers Limited,
registered in England, company number 785998, of Houndmills, Basingstoke,
Hampshire RG21 6XS.

Palgrave Macmillan in the US is a division of St Martin's Press LLC,
175 Fifth Avenue, New York, NY 10010.

Palgrave Macmillan is the global academic imprint of the above companies
and has companies and representatives throughout the world.

Palgrave® and Macmillan® are registered trademarks in the United States,
the United Kingdom, Europe and other countries.

ISBN 978–0–230–24197–8 hardback

This book is printed on paper suitable for recycling and made from fully
managed and sustained forest sources. Logging, pulping and manufacturing
processes are expected to conform to the environmental regulations of the
country of origin.

A catalogue record for this book is available from the British Library.

A catalog record for this book is available from the Library of Congress.

10  9  8  7  6  5  4  3  2  1
20  19  18  17  16  15  14  13  12  11

Printed and bound in the United States of America

# Contents

# List of Figures and Tables

## Figures

## Tables

# Notes on Editors and Contributors

## Editors

**Dr Carol Hayden, Professor in Applied Social Research, University of Portsmouth**
Carol has worked as a researcher and lecturer at the University of Portsmouth since 1989, following a ten-year teaching career working in school, college and community settings. She worked at the Social Services Research and Information Unit (SSRIU) for 14 years, including managing the unit for the last two years. Carol joined the Institute for Criminal Justice Studies (ICJS) in 2003 and has the responsibility for over-seeing the teaching of research methods, as well as conducting applied research. She has undertaken or managed around 40 funded research projects. Her research experience is wide-ranging, crossing services and service sectors; however, her particular expertise focuses broadly upon children in trouble. Much of her work to date at a national and international level has been conducted in collaboration with agencies (social services, education, children's departments, the police and charitable organisations). Recent books include: *Children in Trouble* (2007) and *Implementing Restorative Justice in Children's Residential Care* (2010, with co-author Dennis Gough).

**Dr Denise Martin, Senior Lecturer in Criminology, University of Brighton**
Denise has been a researcher and teaching for a number of years. Her work focuses on several key areas within criminology: including prisons, police and youth offending and victimisation. In recent years she has been conducting research in school environments. This has included research into young people's experience of crime and victimisation in schools in an inner London borough and more recently an ESRC-funded project. In the latter project Denise was the Principal Investigator exploring the nature of violence against teachers in schools. She has also, with colleagues from the University of Portsmouth, completed an evaluation of the UK case study of a European Safer School initiative. Her current interests include the growing levels of surveillance and policing in the school environment.

## Contributors

**Dr Andy Briers, Police Sergeant and Senior Lecturer, Middlesex University**
Andrew is a police officer in the United Kingdom, the first police officer to be placed in a school on a full-time basis and former coordinator for the Safer Schools Programme. He is also a former schoolteacher who has devoted much of his time to working with disaffected young people. He runs a Juvenile Mixed Attendance Centre for the Home Office. He also serves as a foundation governor at a local school in London where he assists with the development of school policies. He was awarded the Fulbright Police Fellowship Award and travelled to the USA to study the role of law enforcement agencies in schools as part of his PhD research with Middlesex University. He was also awarded the National Training Contract for Safer School Partnerships (SSPs) which was supported by the Home Office, Youth Justice Board, DfES, ACPO and CONFED. He is a senior lecturer at Middlesex University, Centre of Excellence for Work Based Learning. He was awarded the Fulbright Alumni Initiative Award which enabled him to set up an exchange programme between UK and US school-based police officers; which has led to the creation of the Centre for Excellence for International School/Community Safety at Colorado State University, USA, where Andrew is an Adjunct Professor.

**Dr Caroline Chatwin, Lecturer in Criminology, University of Kent**
Dr Caroline Chatwin contributes to the core criminology undergraduate teaching programme and specialises in the fields of drug use and young people and crime. She has recently been involved in researching crime against young people and is a co-author of a report on young people and victimisation in the London borough of Newham.

**Dr Ellyn Dickmann, Associate Dean, University of Wisconsin, USA**
Ellyn became Associate Dean in the School of Education and Professional Studies at the University of Wisconsin in August 2010. Prior to that she was Associate Professor of Educational Leadership, Renewal and Change at Colorado State University. She completed her PhD at Colorado State University in 1999 with a focus on interdisciplinary studies and youth violence. Her dissertation examined the culture of police in schools. Dr Dickmann also studied and worked for one year (1989–1990) at the University of Michigan. She is also a recognised international speaker in the area of school resource officers and school safety.

**Jane Healy, Research Fellow and Lecturer, Middlesex University**
Jane has a BA in Psychology, an MSc in Criminology & Forensic Psychology and a Postgraduate Certificate in Higher Education. Her Masters dissertation explored young people's experiences of victimisation in two schools in Ireland. She has worked on two research projects: Experiences of Violence by Secondary School Teachers in London, Hertfordshire and Essex, funded by the ESRC; and Adolescent Drinking Cultures: Peer Influence and Ethnicity, funded by the Joseph Rowntree Foundation. She has been teaching part-time since September 2006 and runs a number of seminars, lectures and workshops in victimology and forensic psychology. She is currently studying for her PhD and exploring the treatment of disabled victims.

**Dr Amanda Holt, Senior Lecturer in Criminal Psychology at the Institute of Criminal Justice Studies, University of Portsmouth**
Amanda teaches across a range of undergraduate and postgraduate programmes within psychology, criminology and forensic studies. Her research interests include youth justice, crime within families, and qualitative methods. She has a particular interest in the use of transdisciplinary theoretical approaches in addressing these topics.

**Dr Belinda Hopkins, Director of 'Transforming Conflict'**
Belinda carried out research on restorative justice in schools for her PhD, which was completed in 2006. She runs her own training company, writes and teaches in the area of restorative approaches to conflict. She has had wide experience in developing policy and practice in the field of restorative justice, particularly in school settings, for over a decade. For example: various roles with the Restorative Justice Consortium (RJC); Member of the Home Office Committee that developed National Practice Guidelines for Restorative Justice Practitioners; Member of the Winchester Restorative Justice Group and responsible for planning and coordinating several successful international Restorative Justice conferences; Organiser of an annual conference on Restorative Justice in Educational and Residential Settings in partnership with Public Sector Strategies (PSS); Chair of European Forum for Restorative Justice Education Committee.

**Dr Nicola Mackenzie, Senior Research Officer at the Department for Education, Schools Research Team.**
The Team cover research on all aspects of schools, from ages 5–16. Nicola has previously worked on various research projects, including an

ESRC-funded project looking at Secondary School Teachers' Experiences and Perceptions of Violence.

**Dr Andrew Millie, Senior Research Fellow, University of Glasgow**
Andrew is probably best known for his work on anti-social behaviour leading to the publication of numerous articles and two recent books: *Anti-Social Behaviour* (2009) and *Securing Respect* (2009). Andrew has also researched and published on issues of policy, policing, criminological theory and criminal justice. He has an evolving research agenda that integrates elements of policy, theory and philosophy in order to understand better processes of criminalisation, ideas of order and the creation of urban civility.

**Dr Stephen Moore, Reader in Social Policy, Anglia Ruskin University**
Stephen has written numerous textbooks of sociology and social policy, as well as journal articles on anti-social behaviour and offending. He is currently leading a cross-European project on the victimisation of school-age children.

**David Porteous, Principal Lecturer in Criminology, Middlesex University**
David teaches criminological theory and research, international comparative criminology and youth crime and youth justice. His recent research has focused on violence involving young people as perpetrators and victims and on the effectiveness of the youth justice system in meeting their needs.

**Dr Dawn E. Stephen, Principal Lecturer, University of Brighton**
As an academic determined to work across disciplinary boundaries, Dawn's primary interest is promoting justice for children and young people and she has published several works in pertinent areas, including: critiques of the progressive criminalisation of youth, understanding marginalised young people's transitions to adulthood and students' experiences of higher education. In each of these areas, the frequently troubling accounts of children and young people's experiences of schooling provided the impetus to contribute to this edited collection.

**Dr Peter Squires, Professor of Criminology and Public Policy, University of Brighton**
Peter has worked at the University of Brighton since 1986. He has wideranging research interests in the field of criminology and social policy, that include young people and anti-social behaviour. He is well known for his research and publications on anti-social behaviour, and gun and knife crime.

**Professor John Visser, University of Birmingham and Visiting Professor, University of Northampton**
John is prominent in the United Kingdom as a trainer of professionals who work with children with Social, Emotional and Behavioural Difficulties (SEBD) and as a researcher. He has produced wide-ranging publications in this field. He has been involved in research projects for English government bodies, including the 2003–05 Ofsted investigation into challenging behaviour in schools.

# 1
# Crime, Anti-Social Behaviour and Schools – Key Themes

*Denise Martin, Peter Squires and Dawn E. Stephen*

## Behaviour and schools: educational and criminological perspectives

> Poor behaviour in schools cannot be tolerated. To do so is to harm the interests of pupils, staff and the perpetrators of the bad behaviour. Children have a right to attend school in safety and to learn without disruption. Parents are entitled to expect that their children have the best possible learning experience and one that will allow them to fulfil their potential. Teachers have a right to work in an environment that allows them to use their skills to the full for the benefit of all their pupils.
>
> (Steer, 2009, p. 18)

How children and young people behave in and around schools is an issue of enduring public and policy interest. Most people are likely to have a view on the matter, including a view about whether the behaviour of young people is changing (Hayden, 2010). Educationalists and criminologists have a different, but overlapping, concern in this respect. For educationalists the main focus is on 'pupil' behaviour and whether it gets in the way of other pupils' learning and teachers doing the job of teaching (as the above quotation illustrates). Government enquiries (DES/WO, 1989) and reviews (Steer, 2009), as well as most academic education research in the United Kingdom on behaviour in school concludes that it is the low-level disruption and general rudeness that saps the energy of teachers and gets in the way of children learning (Hayden, 2009). Criminologists, by definition, generally focus on the most problematic behaviour, which may be seen as 'anti-social' or is clearly 'criminal' (in the sense that it breaks the law). For criminologists (and criminal justice agencies), schools are often the site on which data are collected from young people (see, for example, Smith and McVie, 2003; MORI, 2005; YJB, 2009a, b), with the focus being on victimisation and offending. However, since the late 1990s schools have explicitly become part of a wider crime prevention project, in which the psychological discourse of 'risk' and 'protective' factors is liberally used as justification for a range of interventions focused on pupil behaviour. The interests of educationalists and criminologists now overlap more explicitly than previously in the United Kingdom. At the same time, this difference in disciplinary focus inevitably means some tension in how the two disciplines construct the problem and the language they use to do this (Hayden, 2010).

The opening quotation from the Steer Committee utilises 'poor', 'bad' and 'disruption' in relation to pupil behaviour in just one short paragraph. Even the choice of referring to young people as 'pupils' is not without its critics, with some arguing that 'students' is a preferable term. Add to this our decision to include 'crime' and the much-contested term of 'anti-social behaviour', and we have a complex terrain that needs further explanation. An area of contention in relation to the behaviour of children and young people in and around schools is how we understand why people behave in a particular way. For example, 'bad' behaviour implies a clear moral judgement that the behaviour is wrong; whereas 'social, emotional and behavioural difficulties' is a recognised category of special educational need (SEN), which should be met by the appropriate teaching strategies in school. 'Anti-social' and its opposite term 'pro-social' have their origins in psychological concepts about behaviour. These terms, too, imply a judgement about behaviour, with the promotion of 'pro-social' behaviour being the explicit aim of some work with children and families. This approach inevitably presumes agreement about social norms and the behaviour wanted from children and young people (Hayden, 2010).

Contributors to this volume have different ways of conceptualising behaviours in and around schools, which reflects the key tensions between criminological and educational perspectives. However, we agree about some key issues – such as the way the media tends to amplify adult concern about the behaviour of young people, and that most behaviour causing concern in schools is neither 'anti-social' nor 'criminal'. That said, it is clear that some highly problematic behaviour happens from time to time, and the evidence suggests that this is concentrated in schools in already adverse circumstances (see Neill, 2008). The connection between patterns of inequality, particularly as this relates to boys, is expanded upon in Chapter 4.

Schools and education as a way of responding to various social ills was a feature of the New Labour administrations (1997–2010). 'Education, education, education' was said to be the priority of New Labour from the outset. This priority was set alongside a broader goal of clamping down on crime and anti-social behaviour (ASB), which was epitomised by the Crime and Disorder Act (1998) and later the 'Respect' agenda (Home Office, 2006b). The emphasis on individual rights and responsibilities as the route to gaining collective entitlements was also evident. These key themes have been consistent in legislation over the past few years, and much criminal and social policy has been aimed at reducing the seemingly problematic behaviour of young people and their families. The school as an institution has long been seen as having a primary socialising role (Hendrick, 2006) and has increasingly also been seen as having a primary crime prevention role (Hayden, 2005). This chapter begins by exploring how crime and ASB came to be seen as relevant to what happens in the education system. It will critically examine definitions of anti-social and other forms of problem behaviour and the complexities involved in the use of terminology across disciplines. The chapter refers to the wider context of ASB legislation and recent criminal justice and social policies, identifying key themes that emerge as an underlying thread throughout this volume.

## Schools and problem behaviour

A wide range of problematic behaviours are likely to be found in any school, partly because of the very large number of young people concentrated under the supervision of a relatively small number of adults. Not everyone wants to be in school, or at least not for all the activities on offer. The opportunities for conflict are numerous, as are the sources of stress. Children and young people have relatively little control over how they spend a large proportion of their day throughout their childhood. They have to learn how to get on with others under the close supervision of adults who are greatly outnumbered. Teachers are also heavily monitored by the state; so, this combination of being outnumbered and heavily monitored can lead to concerns about maintaining order (Hayden, 2010).

Problem behaviour in schools is not new. Hayden (2007) has documented how adult concern is evident wherever there are written records about schooling. Chapter 3 documents how schoolmasters historically were depicted with birches or rods. Riots and other incidents of violence were recorded at schools, even well-known public schools such as Eton. The language used has shifted in recent years, with some researchers using the word 'violent' to describe certain behaviour in schools. In part, this started in the United Kingdom with surveys undertaken by criminologists (Gill and Hearnshaw, 1997) but is also due to the more generic use of the term 'violence' by European researchers (Hayden and Blaya, 2001) and the establishment of an International Observatory of Violence in School (see http://www.ijvs.org/). Hayden and Dunne (2001) have also argued that the word 'violence' began to appear more frequently in the language of schools when the guidelines about exclusion from school allowed for exclusion after a 'one-off incident of violence', following a period when schools were under pressure to reduce exclusions. In other words, the choice of language is important and has consequences for our response to young people's behaviour. Nor should we underestimate the wider influence of incidents of school shootings, most famously Columbine High School in the United States, and in other countries (see Chapter 5). Such events inevitably receive massive media coverage, arguably adding to adult concerns about risk and safety at school.

## Defining terms: 'crime', 'anti-social', 'violent' and 'problem' behaviours

Significant consideration needs to be given to how we attach certain labels to behaviour and what we mean by these definitions. In the United Kingdom, under the first New Labour Government, the emerging definition of ASB became an umbrella term that could include any number of incidents (Millie, 2009a). The 1998 Crime and Disorder Act (s.1(1a)) defines ASB as acting:

> in a manner that caused or was likely to cause harassment, alarm or distress to one or more persons not of the same household as the perpetrator.

This definition is problematic because of its subjectivity and because it includes behaviour 'perceived' to be a threat rather than actual threatening behaviour (see Chapter 2). This can mean that behaviour previously viewed as unwanted now becomes criminalised or anti-social (Squires and Stephen, 2005). Squires and Stephen (2005) suggest that this is reminiscent of Cohen's (1985) perspective on net-widening (an issue to which we will return). A common example of this is young people 'hanging out' together as part of their everyday routine. Where previously local residents and authorities may have not appreciated this type of activity, under the above definition of ASB the meaning of this action is altered and some young people have found themselves on the wrong side of the law; for example, where part of their anti-social behaviour order (ASBO) is not to congregate with other young people (Stephen, 2006, 2009). Young people congregating can now become subject to dispersal orders and can then be required to move on by the police. The elasticity of the ASB definition is something else that Millie refers to, since to allow subjectivity means that discretion can be used to address local issues. However, this elasticity can be problematic. A loose definition means that action that would normally be viewed as criminal can be defined as anti-social. This allows for interventions such as the ASBO that does not require the level of evidence needed in a full criminal conviction. Furthermore, an ASBO can be sought quickly, subverting the rights of the individual and compromising principles of justice (Ashworth, 2004; Von Hirsch and Simester, 2006; Stephen, 2008, 2009). There are similar complexities in defining behaviour as 'anti-social' in the context of the school.

Figure 1.1 illustrates some of the key problematic behaviours in schools and, as shown, most of this behaviour is not 'anti-social' or 'criminal' or 'violent'. Some of these behaviours can overlap, such as 'mental health' and 'disaffection', 'special educational need' and 'testing the boundaries'. In other words, understanding young people's behaviour in schools is not straightforward. Furthermore, there is ample evidence that individual teachers, as well as schools, have an influence

---

*Naughtiness and disruption* – talking out of turn, not responding to teacher's instructions

*Testing the boundaries/adolescent behaviour* – challenging adult authority

*Special educational needs* (such as Social, Emotional and Behavioural Difficulties, (SEBD) such as impulsivity and attention problems

*Distressed behaviour* – indicative of abuse or neglect, family problems and mental health

*Disaffected behaviour* – *poor attendance, more serious disruptive behaviour*

*Bullying* and other forms of *aggression and violence* – very varied cyber-bullying, physical and psychological bullying; playground fights, assaults and 'gang' or group-related aggression and violence. May also be seen as 'anti-social behaviour'?

*Criminal behaviour* – behaviour that breaks the criminal law

---

*Figure 1.1* The range of problem behaviours in schools
*Source*: Hayden (2010, p. 3).

on how children behave and how well their behaviour is understood. Moreover, much of the focus is on what constitutes a problem *for adults*, as in behaviour that makes the teaching and other adult roles in schools more difficult (Hayden, 2010).

General 'naughtiness' or 'testing the boundaries' is to be expected in any group of children and young people. SEN affects around one in five children at some point during their schooling. Although most SEN is not SEBD (see Chapter 10), children having trouble with aspects of their schooling can behave in a problematic way. Identifying distressed behaviour and its myriad causes is another important consideration in relation to understanding behaviour that can pose a problem for adults in schools. Disaffected behaviour is equally complex: lack of affection for school can arise because of SEN, bullying, home- or community-based problems, as well as a range of other specific issues such as particular relationships with teachers or other young people. Non-attendance is a common indicator of disaffection, which in turn is associated with an increased likelihood of offending behaviour (Stephenson, 2007). When it comes to conceptualising bullying, aggressive and violent behaviour, it is clear that such behaviour could be seen as 'anti-social' and might sometimes be serious enough to be criminal. In Chapter 3 (Table 3.1), Millie and Moore consider the similarities and differences between bullying and ASB, noting that repetition and cumulative effect are generally agreed to be characteristic of both. It has been argued that some forms of bullying can be seen as a form of 'hate crime' (Hall and Hayden, 2007), whilst Furniss (2000) argues that some forms of more serious bullying are criminal offences and should be seen as such. However, language is important here – given that a playground fight might be referred to as 'assault' and minor 'theft' is not uncommon in schools, and that adults in schools can (and do) exercise choice and discretion about how they view a particular behaviour or incident (Hayden, 2010).

Table 1.1 maps ASB in an attempt to distinguish its potential relevance in the school context. It illustrates some of the complexities of the language we use in relation to children's behaviour in schools, linking this to debates about the criminalisation of social policy (see also Squires, 1990). The table illustrates how the boundaries are blurring between some problem behaviours that break social norms or rules and behaviours that are increasingly viewed as 'anti-social' and sometimes 'criminal'.

The term 'violence' is also problematic, as already intimated. There is a lack of consensus in how various countries and researchers define what

*Table 1.1* Conceptualising 'problem', 'anti-social' and 'criminal' behaviour

| Problem behaviour | | Anti-Social Behaviour (ASB) |
|---|---|---|
| *Breaks social norms or rules* | B O U | *Breaks more serious social norms or rules and often (but not always) involves physical threat or contact* |
| Behaviour that is described by teachers as 'disruptive', 'challenging', 'disaffected', 'inappropriate' or 'unacceptable' | N D A | Behaviour that is described by teachers as 'anti-social', 'violent' or 'threatening'; tends to be repeated and cumulative |
| Some forms of bullying (non-physical) | R | Bullying that involves threats of or actual violence/physical contact |
| Some forms of non-attendance | I | Pushing, touching, unwanted physical contact |
| Offensive language | E S | Offensive language (with threats of violence) |

**BOUNDARIES BLURRING**
*The criminalisation of social policy?*

| ASB and criminal behaviour | | Criminal behaviour |
|---|---|---|
| *ASB often (but not always) breaks the law – often referred to as delinquent in the past* | B L | *Breaks the law* |
| Behaviour that is threatening to the sense of security, physical and mental health of others; ASB tends to be repeated and cumulative | U R R | Behaviour that is seriously threatening to the sense of security, physical and mental health of others; some behaviour is repeated and cumulative |
| Serious bullying involving social exclusion and humiliation | I | Assault and other specific crimes, such as Actual Bodily Harm (ABH) |
| Theft, robbery and break-ins | N | Some forms of bullying as 'hate crime' |
| Vandalism and criminal damage | G | Theft, robbery and break-ins |
| Weapons-carrying (for 'protection') | | Vandalism and criminal damage |
| | | Weapons-carrying (for 'threats' or 'attack') |

*Source*: Hayden (2010, p. 4), adapted from Hayden (2009).

is meant by the term. Osler and Starkey (2005) identify different 'vocabularies of violence'. They use the example of France, which often refer to 'incivilities' – a term inferring ASB, whereas in England the term applied is often 'disaffection'. Similarly, Smith (2003) discusses some of the key issues identified with defining the term violence and whether narrow or broader definitions should be applied in the school context. Narrow definitions such as that applied by Olewus (1999, cited in Smith, 2003, p. 4) defines violence as 'aggressive behaviour where the actor or perpetrator uses his or her own body or an object (including a weapon) to inflict (relatively serious) injury or discomfort upon another individual'. This type of definition refers to actions that are purely physical. However, as in other research on violence, more recent definitions and policy responses to violence have tended to expand beyond physical acts to include a range of behaviours (Waddington et al., 2006). While an inclusive definition can mean acknowledging the harm caused by non-physical action, it does mean that any action (no matter how minor) can be defined as violence, and this does not necessarily provide an accurate picture of what is occurring. In relation to schools, there has been an attempt to distinguish different forms of or the severity of violence, for example Debarbieux (2006) refers to 'micro-violence'. The importance here lies not on the act itself, or the seemingly minor nature of that act, but rather the accumulation of a series of acts, that can have harmful effects for the victim (see Chapter 2, where ASB and bullying behaviour are compared). Despite these ongoing debates there is still no agreement on how violence in the context of schools should ultimately be defined (Smith, 2003). Stanko (2003) argues that, when investigating violence, there are a number of considerations to make, including the act of violence itself, the relationship of the participants to each other, the location of the act and the resultant damage caused by that act. Chapter 7 illustrates that these were certainly key factors in how teachers conceptualised their own experiences of violence in the workplace (see also Martin et al., 2008). Their perceptions of their role within the school and the context surrounding the act framed how they interpreted their experiences.

## ASBO nation?

In *ASBO Nation*, Squires (2008) presents a collection of perspectives on 'the criminalisation of nuisance'. In this volume, various writers note how rapidly the ASB problem came to be defined and the ASBO solution adopted. The ASBO is a key example of the potential for criminalising young people, through a civil order that if breached can lead to a criminal justice sanction. Anti-social behaviour as a phenomenon, while not new (Burney, 2005; Squires, 2006b; Millie, 2009a) took a new ideological shape when it was driven forward by New Labour and more specifically Tony Blair (Squires, 2006a). It was then presented as a social problem that 'encompasses civic renewal, economic regeneration, personal morality, new forms of governing and the elimination of criminal and public nuisance' (Squires, 2008, p. 11). This broad spectrum of discourses indicates how the response to ASB was not just about reducing the behaviour itself but also the wider benefits that this could bring to society, such as more cohesive communities and opportunities to 're-generate' communities, while also rebalancing rights and responsibilities (Stephen, 2006). For Blair, social cohesion was a personal crusade to mend a perceived moral decline that had occurred over a period of time, with the result that:

> Family ties were weakened. Communities were more fractured, sometimes as a result of desirable objectives like social mobility or diversity, sometimes as the consequence of mass unemployment and failed economic policies. Civil institutions such as the church declined in importance. At the start of the 20th century, communities shared a strong moral code. By the end of the century this was no longer as true.
>
> (Blair, 2005)

To resolve this moral decline, the solution was to adopt an approach that favoured enforcement. This was evident in Blair's earlier 'tough on crime, tough on the causes of crime' approach, where there would be a balance of hard-hitting measures for those who stepped out of line, but promised the rewards of social inclusion for the law abiding. The language of 'zero-tolerance' was adopted, informed to some extent by the now well-known 'broken windows thesis' (Wilson and Kelling, 1982) This suggests that a window that is broken and left unfixed sends a message of neglect and abandonment, which, in turn, allows the escalation of further incivility that leads to the disintegration and segregation of communities; when left to escalate, minor incivilities are then followed by more serious crime. Fixing the metaphorical 'broken window' suggests that someone does care and demonstrates that graffiti or similar minor incivilities will not be tolerated. According to this view, stamping down on the minor incivilities will have a positive upward spiral affect, reducing crime and generally improving high crime neighbourhoods.

The approach that emerged from this was 'zero-tolerance' policing (see Dennis, 1997; Burke, 1998). Zero-tolerance policing associated with Mayor Guliani and Chief of Police William Bratton was seen as a key strategy in the 'great-American crime drop' (see Levitt, 2004). It targeted even minor offences and promoted visible reassurance policing. It was exported worldwide as an effective means of tackling crime and disorder. For New Labour, particularly the former Home Secretary Jack Straw, this type of approach was one way to deal with what was seen as the 'justice gap' (Home Office, 2002) or the deficit between the crime committed and those brought to justice. Zero-tolerance approaches have also increasingly been linked to the educational environment (see Chapter 5). As identified by Simon (2007), following the Safer Schools Act 1996 in the United States (originally introduced to prevent weapons and drugs being brought into school) zero-tolerance has been used to deal with a widening range of 'disciplinary' problems. Any form of behaviour by young people viewed as unacceptable by the school authorities can result in young people being subjected to intervention by the authorities, mostly the police or juvenile justice system.

Squires and Stephen (2005) discuss the concept of a perceived 'enforcement deficit'. The first characteristic of this is described by Hansen et al. (2003, cited in Squires and Stephen 2005, p. 3), who argue that criminal justice sanctions have tended to be individualistic in nature and ignore the collective harm that crime and disorder can cause. In contrast, the ASB framework has tended towards resolving ASB as a community issue and formed a key part of a wider community safety agenda operated under New Labour. The problem here is that the attempt to deal with 'crime and disorder' to improve communities has led to a shift away from dealing with other welfare issues that impact on communities, such as poverty (Crawford,1997). A second characteristic of this enforcement deficit involves responding to young people who are often seen as the primary perpetrators of anti-social acts, and in the first half of the 1990s there was a growing sense that young peoples' levels of 'delinquency' were increasing with apparent impunity (Campbell, 2002 cited in Squires and Stephen, 2005). This perception is not new, and young people have recurrently been the focus of criminal justice attention (Pearson, 1983). However, in late modernity feelings of insecurity have made us wary of particular 'risky' populations (Hudson, 2003). This has led in the past 20 years to changes in how young people are perceived and how they are dealt with in the youth justice system in the United Kingdom, where an increasingly punitive approach has seemingly been taken towards young offenders (Muncie, 2004; Pitts,

2008). The final characteristic of this enforcement deficit has been the focus on the family (Stephen and Squires, 2003) and their responsibility to adhere to certain rules of engagement, for example ensuring that children attend school and behave sensibly. Failure to adhere to these obligations can result in penalties and restrictive orders being placed on them (for example, curfew orders, parenting orders, ASBOs, eviction notices). This process of disciplining the family has also been linked to a wider phenomena of the criminalisation of social policy.

## The criminalisation of social policy

In recent years social policy and crime have become inextricably linked (Crawford, 1997; Rodger, 2008). Rodger (2008, p. 3) states, 'the notion that social policy and criminality are closely tied together has moved from an assumption to a phenomena that must be named and understood more rigorously.' The connections between these two strategies of governance have been driven by changes to the way in which welfare and crime and disorder have been conceptualised. Rodger suggests that rather than welfare being based on a system that provides for the disadvantaged who have reached that state primarily because of social injustices (poverty, unemployment, ill-health or as a results of the gaps in the welfare net), benefits are now conditional on the applicant adhering to a certain set of rules and perspectives. Those who do not adhere to the conventions of the 'moral' and 'law-abiding' majority are then constructed as 'anti-social'. Moreover, this ASB is not perceived as a result of social injustice; rather, it is seen as attributable to individual pathology (Rodger, 2008). This perspective begs the question how such behaviour is then tackled. As pointed out by Squires (2006a), the dominance of division and fear generated by the belief in the 'Criminology of the other' (Garland, 2001) signalled a shift in priorities which focused more on 'enforcement' than support. At first this was particularly evident within the benefit system, poverty becoming a question of 'fault' rather than of 'need' (Squires, 1990). A number of authors have also illustrated how the progressive 'criminalisation of nuisance' was initially pursued in the (social) Housing Policy field, in part consequent upon the wholesale residualisation of the housing sector (Burney, 1999; Flint, 2006) where the pejorative labelling of 'neighbours' or 'families from hell' were used as a means of making it easier for local authorities (and social landlords) to evict 'anti-social' tenants.

The 'dysfunctional' family has been a key focus of recent criminal and social policy. In contrast, the 'stable' family is viewed as critical to producing 'law-abiding' young people. Some of the main variables identified as being influential in creating ASB among young people include poor parental supervision, socially disorganised communities, living in social housing in the inner-city, family dependence on social security and marital separation (Farrington and Welsh, 2007). Muncie (2006, p. 781) argues that this has led to a 'remoralisation agenda' that includes strategies of surveillance and regulation of families and communities that:

> rests crucially on the identification of a feckless, 'at risk' underclass which through a combination of refusal to work, teenage parenthood, single parenting and lack of respectable adult role models threatens to undermine the entire fabric of society. What may previously have been an indicator of the need for family welfare support is now read as a precursor to criminality.

The perceived deficiencies affecting family life led to the adoption of a particular strand of polices (such as parenting orders) aimed at trying to re-train families in order to draw them back into the acceptable community (see Chapter 8). Enforcement policies have been supplemented by inclusionary policies such as Sure Start which aim to tackle the 'risk factors' identified above. While the benefits of such programmes have been highlighted (see Chapter 12), Rodger (2008) emphasises their success is measured not on the improvement to family life or social mobility but on whether they can contribute to the reduction of crime. As with many of our recent socially inclusive policies, the aim of improving the lives of the poorest has been subordinate to regulating their outward behaviour. Schools have not been immune from this agenda. Furedi (2009, p. 6) argues that schools are seen as playing a part in the 'salvationist perspective' and as having a role in the socialisation of children as good citizens, particularly where parenting is lacking. It is also believed that young people with the 'correct' values can then socialise parents into the 'correct' way of thinking and behaving. Furedi refers to this as 'socialisation in reverse', where, rather than adults socialising their children, the opposite occurs. Similarities can be seen in relation to responses to problem behaviour in school; for example, parents can be punished by fines (and even imprisonment) when their children truant 'persistently' (see Chapter 3).

## Responsibilisation

This process of remoralisation can be linked to a wider process of responsibilisation, which has underpinned much recent criminal justice and welfare reform (Garland, 1996, 2001; Squires, 2006b). Responsibilisation strategies work at two levels. The first focuses on making individuals face up to their actions and ensuring their liability. This idea of individual responsibility has featured in youth justice policy (Stephen, 2008) and has also filtered into schools, most notably through the introduction of Restorative Justice (RJ), usually known as Restorative Approaches (RAs) in schools (see Chapter 11). Within the context of Youth Justice a key aim of RJ has been for young people to face up to what they have done and meet the victim of their act in order to understand the affects of their actions and to elicit an apology. In the school context RJ has developed and been adapted as a way of responding to the full range of problematic (and even criminal) behaviour in schools. As with RJ in the criminal justice system, RAs are generally presented as a paradigm shift, in which punishment is replaced by making amends for the harm done and taking responsibility for one's actions.

The second aspect of this process of responsibilisation is related to community. As Garland (1996) has pointed out, certain western governments have attempted to devolve some responsibility for crime to local residents and other non-state organisations, such as businesses and voluntary agencies. These agencies are seen as having an essential social and crime control role. This type of strategy was implicit in the Crime and Disorder Act (1998), which was influenced by the earlier Morgan Report (1991) in which local authorities, police authorities and other agencies (including health and education) were tasked with working in partnerships to resolve local crime and disorder issues. Responding to justice issues became the role of all agencies who worked with young people (see Smith, 2007). This convergence of criminal justice and social welfare agencies through such partnerships further blurs the boundaries between welfare and justice strategies for responding to young people, for example, Safer Schools Partnerships (SSPs), which originally focused on high crime areas, are now 'mainstreamed'; that is, they are available to any school (see Chapter 9).

## Young people and risk

As mentioned above, the young people or families targeted by much of the recent public policy are typically characterised by a number of negative attributes or 'risk' factors (Farrington and Welsh, 2007). This dominant construction suggests young people are a 'dangerous' group and that they have been simultaneously constructed as both 'risk' to the 'law-abiding majority', and 'at risk' of developing more serious offending practices. These constructions have profound consequences for perceptions of the levels of youth offending and ASB, but, more significantly, for the way in which we as a society respond to young people (Brown, 2005; Case, 2007; France, 2008; Stephen, 2009). The term 'risk' has increasingly been used as an analytical tool across various disciplines. The key proponent, Beck (1992), advanced the concept of in 'Risk Society' to describe the nature of the contemporary epoch whereby, he argued, that we are exposed to a number of global threats including terrorism, war and environmental disasters. These wider risks have an impact on our world view, making individuals feel less secure and more susceptible to risks or threatening events, including crime. As some theorists (such as Garland, 1996, 2001) have argued, crime has become part of our daily routine, so it becomes not a case of avoiding it but managing the likelihood that we will become a crime victim. As Feeley and Simon (1992) argued in their analysis of penology (particularly in the United States), assessing risk and conceiving justice in a more actuarial sense (management by probability) had become a dominant aspect in the development of penal policy. Penal systems, the argument goes, now work on the basis of 'actuarial justice' and risk calculation where there is less concern about treating or reforming individuals; on the contrary, more attention is paid to managing what are considered to be unruly groups. Furthermore, this has to be achieved within the limited resources available (Brownlee, 1998).

Within the discourse of risk and unruly groups, young people have increasingly been identified as one of these 'unruly' groups that needs to be managed and controlled (Stephen, 2006; Martin et al., 2007). This has been witnessed in a number of ways, first in attempting to make the youth justice system more 'efficient'. In the Audit Commissions report of 1996, Misspent Youth, the cost of dealing with the problem of youth crime was seen as excessive, especially in the time and cost taken to process young people through court. The Audit Commission therefore recommended quicker, more cost-effective measures that diverted young people away from the expensive court system and offending. This report and other subsequent policy documents such as No More Excuses (Home Office, 1997) encouraged strategies that aimed at intervening with children at an earlier stage in the development of their criminal behaviour, the aim being to 'nip crime in the bud' and divert young people way from the end (and more expensive) stages of the criminal justice process. The underlying message was that engaging young people in 'constructive activities' (Audit Commission, 1996, p. 96) in order to prevent crime was more cost-effective. This led to programmes such as 'caution plus'. In this particular programme, young people were not prosecuted as offenders but were sent to a youth offending team (YOT), who would then refer them to a programme of activities aimed at targeting the 'offending behaviour' (Muncie, 2002). Other early interventions, such as child curfews, child safety orders and ASBOs, were aimed at targeting the 'at-risk' or 'unruly' groups of young people. Squires and Stephen (2005) argue that much of these diversionary or lower level policies introduced by New Labour Governments can be explained by the ideas of the 'dispersal of discipline' thesis outlined by Cohen (1985). This 'contends that as crime control strategies are increasingly dispersed into the community they penetrate more deeply into the social fabric' (Jamieson, 2005, p. 186). The dominance of crime control also neglects young peoples' experiences as victims; as Hudson (2003) suggests, once identified as an 'other' you lose your victim status. The problem here is that this ignores the realities of crime and ASB, where young people are often subject to high levels of victimisation. It is important to note that young people have their own conceptions and experiences of risk and victimisation, as we will explore in Chapters 5 and 6.

This chapter has aimed to explore some of the background to the developing debate on and response to crime, ASB and schools. It illustrated how the boundaries of behaviour that are problematic in school (and are often simply part of growing up) have gradually become part of a wider debate about behaviour that may lead to criminality in wider society. The consequences of this shift will be discussed throughout this book. Schools do not operate in a vacuum, and, as with other areas of the public sector, cannot escape wider economic, social and political processes. In recent years it could be argued that the school (and other agencies) have a key role in addressing societies' ills. The danger comes when we expect too much of the school system and of education as a way of altering or changing the behaviour of individuals, families and communities. As Furedi (2009, p. 19) has argued:

> The tendency to confuse the problem of society with education creates the risk that schools become distracted from getting on with the

task of cultivating the intellectual and moral outlook of children. A classroom that is subjected to the dictates of a policy agenda is very different from one devoted to inculcating a love and habit of learning. When education is perceived as providing an answer for everything, its distinct meaning and role become unclear.

# 2
# Crime, Anti-Social Behaviour and Education: A Critical Review

*Andrew Millie and Stephen Moore*

## The discourse about crime and anti-social behaviour in schools

In this chapter we consider the relevance of a discourse of crime and anti-social behaviour (ASB) for an educational setting. Our focus is on schools although much of what we discuss is also starting to permeate further and higher education sectors as well. We are interested in the interplay between discipline and criminalisation, and the place of increased securitisation and policing within schools. The language of 'risk' is often used to justify increases in controls (controls on 'at-risk' children thought likely to behave anti-socially and criminally, and on adults for fear of what they might do to children). We question the use and accuracy of this risk paradigm and the connection to the increased criminalisation of education policy.

But first we start with an anecdote. Early in 2009 one of the authors visited his mother in a town in the east of England where her home backs onto the grounds of a local comprehensive school. The author grew up there and went to the school. The school grounds at the end of the garden have been used for a school chicken run, for tennis courts, and is now a multi-sports area used for anything from a kick-about to basketball. While in the garden the author and his mother saw a group of three or four boys from the school trying to climb the boundary fence into the garden. When confronted the boys said they were looking for a ball. A fairly unremarkable event in itself, yet the language used by the boys was offensive and challenging (and quite upsetting). This had happened before so the author went to the school with the hope of talking to someone in authority to highlight the problem. But rather than talking to a teacher or head teacher, the author was directed to an on-site police officer who had an office just off the school lobby.

What was a minor issue and, at most, a community relations or discipline concern was being elevated to something that would interest the police. It clearly wasn't criminal or an issue of ASB, yet for the school the first response was the police. When asked, the officer said part of his remit was discipline. Whether he was correct in this assessment is another matter, but it seemed that the emphasis of the school had changed fundamentally from when the author was a student. Furthermore, a glass screen had been inserted bisecting the lobby and restricting access to the school's corridors to only those with a pass. Drawing on experiences in the United States (see Casella, 2006; Simon, 2007) such securitisation is now common across many British schools following panics about adult strangers, students carrying knives and guns and – more mundanely – about school equipment 'walking' out the front door. And following the development of Safer Schools Partnerships (SSPs) (Bowles et al., 2005), police officers are now routinely based in many British schools (see Chapter 9). But having such an emphasis on crime and ASB in the school context is both problematic and controversial; it can raise anxieties for parents and children and create image problems that schools have to manage.

A central focus of this chapter is the criminalisation of education policy, which is part of a wider process of the criminalisation of social policy more broadly (Crawford, 1997; Hughes, 2002; Giroux, 2003). In an educational context, the defining quality of schooling becomes crime control rather than learning and teaching. In this chapter we argue that in Britain ASB is taking over discourses about behavioural acceptability within schools, where previously the language was of discipline and truancy control. This is not to say that crime and ASB do not occur. Clearly, criminal and anti-social activities occur within schools (Rutter et al., 1979; Boxford, 2006; Hayden, 2009) as they do in any other location. And the unique nature of the schooling environment can increase opportunities for crime and ASB. Yet it is possible that (mis)behaviour that had previously been regarded as disciplinable within school can instead be regarded as requiring police intervention. The reasons for, and consequences of, such a shift can be discussed in relation to a narrative of risk. In line with Hirschfield (2008) we use the term 'criminalisation' to mean:

> ...the shift toward a crime control paradigm in the definition and management of the problem of student deviance. Criminalisation encompasses the manner in which policy makers and school actors think and communicate about the problem of student rule-violation

as well as myriad dimensions of school praxis including architecture, penal procedure, and security technologies and tactics.

(p. 80)

## Schools, control and ASB

Schools have always been controlling environments through both overt and less obvious methods. And while more extreme methods of control – that come under the umbrella of corporal punishment – have (thankfully) been largely consigned to history in Britain, other less obvious methods continue. For instance, drawing on Foucault's (1977) influential work on discipline and punishment, Cladis (1999, p. 5) compares the disciplinary structure of schools to prisons; that: 'In schools and in prisons, time and space are divided by ringing bells and painted lines that weld disciplining power, socially constructing individuals' (we expand on this idea in Chapter 3, Table 3.1, p. 49). But in the contemporary British school such *informal* methods of ensuring normative compliance are being supplemented by more *formal* – and criminalising – methods (and language). As with much social policy in Britain, these developments have been influenced by experiences in the United States (see Jones and Newburn, 2007). According to Jonathan Simon's (2007) influential study of US policy making, the situation in US public schools is reflective of a wider meta-narrative of governance through crime. For Simon (2007, p. 4), as well as being seen as a 'significant strategic issue' in itself, and something that can be deployed for 'legitimate interventions that have other motivations', the category of crime becomes pervasive through much social policy:

> ... the technologies, discourses, and metaphors of crime and criminal justice have become more visible features of all kinds of institutions, where they can easily gravitate into new opportunities for governance. In this way, it is not a great jump to go from (a) concern about juvenile crime through (b) measures in schools to treat students primarily as potential criminals or victims, and, (c) later still, to attacks on academic failure as a kind of crime *someone* must be held accountable for....
>
> (Simon, 2007, pp. 4–5, emphasis in original)

This 'governing through crime' narrative has overlap with the notion of a dispersal of (state) discipline (Foucault, 1977; Cohen, 1979; Bottoms, 1983). In the British context, Crawford (2009, p. 817) has identified a process of 'governing through anti-social behaviour', where 'ASB has come to constitute an organizing concept central to the exercise of contemporary authority.' In an educational context, running parallel to this is a narrative of powerlessness, that teaching staff are powerless to intervene and that the students know this. In some ways the increasing use of 'technologies, discourses, and metaphors of crime and criminal justice' (Simon, 2007, p. 4) – and of ASB – are a response to this perceived, and in many cases actual, lack of power. The result is that student misbehaviour is rebranded as ASB, and the role of educators becomes ever more entwined with issues of community safety and crime control – a situation enhanced by the physical presence of school-based police officers.

Over the past decade ASB has grown to prominence in British politics and policy. The legal definition, drawn from the 1998 Crime and Disorder Act, is that it is: '[acting] in a manner that caused or was likely to cause harassment, alarm or distress to one or more persons not of the same household as himself'. By excluding domestic incidents this makes ASB something that occurs in public spaces. But beyond this the definition is entirely subjective – one person's 'harassment, alarm or distress' can be quite different to the next. And by including behaviour 'likely to cause' such concerns, the subjectivity is reinforced (Millie, 2009a). The characteristics of behaviour usually defined as ASB are shown in Table 2.1, alongside the more established concept – at least in an educational context – of bullying. An important difference between the two concepts is in terms of intentionality. ASB does not have to be a deliberate act, but bullying is usually associated with intentional harm.

*Table 2.1*   Characteristics of anti-social behaviour and bullying

| Anti-social behaviour | Bullying |
| --- | --- |
| Harassment, alarm or distress | Aggressive behaviour/intentional harm |
| Can be interpersonal (e.g. vandalism directed at someone) | Power imbalance |
| Can be environmental (e.g. litter, fly tipping, graffiti) | Often without provocation |
| Restricts use of shared public spaces (e.g. young people congregating are frequently given as an example of ASB) | Negative actions carried out though contact (physical or otherwise as with cyber-bullying) |
| Repetition and cumulative effect | Repetition and cumulative effect |

*Source*: Derived from Millie et al. (2005) and Smith et al. (2002).

What they have in common is that both ASB and bullying are usually seen as cumulative actions, or the result of the effects of repetition. The classic example for ASB is a ball being bounced against the wall of someone's house. If it happens occasionally, it is annoying. If it happens every day, then this can become something given the ASB label.

In a school setting, ASB and bullying both lie at the boundary between criminal and lawful – yet disciplinable – behaviour. But in terms of policy, ASB is becoming an all-encompassing term for unwanted behaviour.

The shifting and expanding boundary of what is understood as ASB, and where the responsibilities of the school authorities finish, make any discussion of ASB within schools more complex. Virtually, all behavioural matters within school (and committed by schoolchildren outside school) now fall within the broad remit of ASB. Inter-agency working and ASB legislation have made discussion of the division between youth misbehaviour in school and in the community more fluid. There has also been an expansion of the notion of ASB to incorporate a range of behaviours which had previously been seen through an educational perspective. For instance, truancy may previously have been seen as solely an educational problem, but is now often viewed in terms of the truant's increased opportunity to commit crime and ASB. Examples of policy and practice where schooling is increasingly seen through an ASB lens are outlined below.

## School policy and practice and ASB

Responsibilities attributed to schools have expanded. For instance, not only are schools responsible for educating children and young people, they are now also typically concerned with health and citizenship (Reid, 2003; DCSF, 2007a). Added to this is schools' increased role in relation to crime and crime prevention. Alongside these changes of expansion and penetration has been a shift from the perception of school students' *mis*behaviour to *anti-social* behaviour, justifying the introduction of criminal justice agencies along with youth, health and social service agencies into the school.

These changes are evidenced by new legislative power, for instance parenting orders for cases of truancy or exclusion from school (Anti-Social Behaviour Act, 2003). A large number of government 'action plans' and policy guidelines have also been introduced, which blur the boundary between traditional educational issues and criminal or ASB concerns. The most important of these are Every Child Matters (2003), Youth Matters (2005) and The Children's Plan (2007). Further guidance was provided through the Respect Action Plan (2006) (see also

Millie, 2009b) and the Youth Crime Action Plan (2008). Throughout these documents, professionals from a range of agencies are encouraged (and sometimes required) to work together in order to bring about changes in the behaviour of young people. It is not our intention here to provide a full account of policy changes towards young people and the consequent impact upon schools. However, it is useful to use examples to illustrate the way schools and criminal justice policies have moved together. We will look at three examples: the National Behaviour and Attendance Strategy (DfES, 2005), the response to the first Steer Report (DfES, 2006) and the Youth Taskforce Action Plan (Youth Taskforce, 2008).

## The National Behaviour and Attendance Strategy

In 2002 the Department for Education and Schools (DfES) introduced a Behaviour Improvement Programme, which evolved into the National Behaviour and Attendance Strategy. The aim was to adopt a partnership approach to improve poor behaviour and attendance in schools in locations deemed to have particular educational and social problems. Yet, though introduced under the auspices of the government department responsible for educational policy, the programme initially emerged as part of the Government's Street Crime Initiative. (The SSPs similarly emerged as part of the Street Crime Initiative in 2002, see Chapter 9.) A range of initiatives emerged, including: Behaviour and Education Support Teams (BESTs); a 'Police in Schools' initiative (a forerunner to Safer Schools); the development of 'extended' schools to cater for pupils outside 'standard' school time; and a range of strategies for tackling truancy, extending electronic registration and increasing 'truancy sweeps' (Haydn, 2008). Each of these initiatives claims to be both educational and behavioural in scope. Indeed the evaluation of the SSPs conducted for the Youth Justice Board (YJB) (Bowles et al., 2005) actually sought to measure the impact on GCSE results of the introduction of police officers into schools. Interestingly, the impact was mixed, with some schools improving, but a significant number of the schools involved in the evaluation actually falling behind similar schools without SSPs.

## The Steer Report 2005–2009

A second example of the relationship between ASB/crime control measures and educational matters is the early response in the Steer Report

(DfES, 2006) written by a working party headed by Alan Steer, a prac-
tising head teacher – which was itself an update of earlier reports on
school behaviour. The original brief for the working party was to promote 'practical examples of good practice that promote good behaviour
and that can be adopted by all schools' (p. 2). In the original report
there was little mention of police involvement with just one quoted
example included. Yet, for the 2009 update (Steer, 2009), police involvement was mentioned throughout, and the report spoke approvingly of
the usefulness and relevance of police officers in schools.

## The Youth Taskforce Action Plan 2008

The aim of the Youth Taskforce Action Plan (Youth Taskforce, 2008)
was to focus on 'a minority [who] can get into serious trouble, including anti-social behaviour' (p. 4). The plan put forward a triple-track
approach – also adopted by The Youth Crime Action Plan (HM Government, 2008). The three strands were tough enforcement, non-negotiable
support and better prevention. It was encouraging to see a focus on
prevention, but tough enforcement remained a priority, and support
offered to young people and their families was coercive, or 'non-
negotiable'. The targets for preventative action were to be identified
using a risk paradigm (of more later) – for instance through the use of
Family Intervention Projects (FIPs) (see, for example, Parr and Nixon,
2008). Of direct relevance to the current chapter, it was claimed that
FIPs work: 'to reduce problem behaviour and get vulnerable children
back in school, improving their key skills and physical and mental health' (Youth Taskforce, 2008, p. 5). Better behaviour is seen as
linked to school attendance and, like the SSPs, also to 'key skills'
(as well as physical and mental health). Furthermore, parental support advisors were to be provided within schools, further blurring the
boundaries between student education, parental support and behaviour
improvement.

In an age of partnership working, schools have had to adopt multiple
foci on health, citizenship, parenting, crime and ASB – all in addition to
the day job of teaching and learning. From these three examples (and
others), we can witness how a discourse of ASB has grown in importance.

## School pupils and ASB

We should note the obvious fact that young people in school reflect the
general pattern of offending of their age group. According to the Youth

Justice Board (MORI, 2010), about a quarter (23 per cent in 2008) of young people in mainstream education admit to committing offences, including ASB, with the peak age of offending being between 15 and 16. When asked to complete a self-report study on the type of offending behaviour they are most likely to commit, 79 per cent of offences are categorised as ASB. However, given the wide and ambiguous definition of ASB this would be expected. Interestingly, of those who offend, 33 per cent admit to having stolen something at school, suggesting a high rate of theft within schools. However, the general pattern of youth crime that emerges from research for the YJB tells us relatively little about crime or ASB within, or related to, schools. Indeed, information on offending within or against schools is relatively difficult to come across in Britain.

## School vandalism as ASB

There are some forms of student misbehaviour – now labelled as ASB – that are aimed at the school itself; that is, the school as an institution is often the target or victim. One such example is vandalism, including various forms of destruction of school property and graffiti, ranging from the occasional scribble on a desk through to more serious and malicious messages. Writing in the 1970s, Cohen (1973) regarded a great deal of school vandalism as occurring under conditions of 'walling-in' – in other words, it occurred within a 'fairly closed setting such as a factory or a school' (p. 30). According to Cohen, in this setting '[t]he act of rule-breaking is rarely processed as a conventional vandalism offence...[as] the damage is too trivial or occurs too routinely to be taken much notice of' (p. 30). When notice is paid, it is dealt with internally. The types of vandalism that Cohen (1973) regarded as routine included the following:

> Examples are legion and part of the unwritten folklore of the school: graffiti on the lavatory walls; scratching names and slogans on desks; flooding the changing rooms or cloakrooms by plugging the sinks and turning the taps on; defacing textbooks; breaking various items of sports equipment; tearing off coat hooks from cloakroom walls, etc.
>
> (p. 31)

Such examples were 'rationalised as play activity' and 'just put up with and accepted as normal' (Cohen 1973, p. 31). Times have clearly changed and, whilst some low-level vandalism is still dealt with through internal discipline procedures, much is regarded as an anti-social or criminal concern.

Dedel Johnson (2005) has suggested that the underlying motivations for vandalism of schools by school students are rather complex. She suggests a number of motivations specific to schools, including: *tactical* vandalism, used to accomplish goals such as getting school cancelled; *ideological* vandalism which is 'social or political protest' against school rules; and *malicious* vandalism where students express their anger or frustration with school life. Johnson also suggests there may be *acquisitive* vandalism, *vindictive* vandalism and *play* vandalism. Drawing on Cohen's work (1973), *ritual* vandalism can be added to this list, for instance when vandalism occurs at the end of term or by school leavers.

While much vandalism is low level and it is debateable whether it should be accepted as normal, dealt with internally as a discipline issue or regarded as a form of ASB, some more serious instances are clearly criminal. The obvious example here is arson, where fires are started within the school or school grounds. According to the Arson Prevention Bureau (2002) there are about 800 fires each year in schools (attended by fire brigades) which are started deliberately. One-third of these fires occur during school hours, suggesting that this proportion at the very least are likely to be carried out by pupils. These figures do not include any of those unknown number of fires put out by school staff.

## Attacks on school staff as ASB

A second form of behaviour sometimes regarded as anti-social, that is unambiguously aimed at the school and its authority, consists of actions directed against teaching staff. As with vandalism, the use of the label ASB is not necessarily always appropriate. In this case, the existing language of bullying and violence against staff may be more suitable. The extent of the problem is difficult to quantify, as there are few academic studies of the issue (see Chapter 7). However, in a survey of 300 teachers (Wright and Keetley, 2003), two-thirds claimed to have been 'verbally or physically assaulted' by a pupil in the previous year (and a fifth said they had been verbally or physically assaulted by a parent or guardian in the last year). In a self-selected online survey by the Teacher Support Network (2007), of those teachers who claimed to have been physically attacked, 53 per cent had been assaulted with a thrown object, 26 per cent with a 'weapon' such as furniture or equipment, 2 per cent with a knife and 1 per cent with a gun. These figures are very different from those released by the Department of Children, Schools and Families, which indicate that in 2007/08 in England and Wales there were a total of 176 teachers who suffered injuries as a result of violence in schools (HSE, 2008). Nevertheless, according to results from the On Track studies (based in schools with a higher proportions of 'at-risk' pupils in poorer areas) conducted on behalf of the Department for Children, Schools and Families (DCSF) (Bhabra et al., 2006), 29 per cent of pupils from secondary schools in On Track areas claimed to have seen a teacher attacked by a pupil at school.

## Bullying as ASB

School pupils not only engage in ASB (and crime) against the school and teachers but also against each other. The lack of reliable statistics concerning the extent of ASB between pupils is similar to that concerning arson and other forms of vandalism, and physical or verbal abuse against teachers. This may seem puzzling at first, as school comprises the one place where most young people spend the majority of the time during the day in term time, and it would seem that research into the safety of young people would be a priority for the education authorities. However, as Hayden and colleagues (2007) point out, it is not in the interests of either the schools or the DCSF to emphasise the nature of the problem:

> These issues are not part of the way individual schools present themselves to the public... managing difficult behaviour and crime prevention are hardly likely to be selling points in a public sector that has to meet consumer demand as well as performance targets. Schools have to be conscious of their public image and, specifically, parents as consumers.
>
> (p. 293)

One area where there has been a great deal of research is the subject of bullying (see Chapters 5 and 12). A number of studies have sought to distinguish between bullies and victims. However, a recent Ipsos MORI study for the Youth Justice Board (2009a) shows that pupils who engage in a range of anti-social activities in schools, and who may be involved in bullying, also self-report being the victims of bullying. This fits in with the work of Wolke and colleagues (2000) who suggest that drawing a clear distinction between the victims of bullying and the bullies is too simplistic and that bullies can also be the bullied, depending upon different contexts and different times. The complexity of roles surrounding bullying is illustrated by Salmivalli (1999) who suggests that apart from the two roles of bully and victim, there are a variety of intermediate participant roles involved in bullying, ranging from *assistants* to the bully, through *reinforcers* providing an audience and *outsiders* who avoid becoming involved, to *defenders* who take the side of the victim.

The types of activity regarded as bullying have expanded with advances in technology, for instance with the recording and online distribution of bullying instances, ranging from the minor where the victim is made to look foolish, to more serious assaults (known collectively as 'happy slapping'), and other forms of online or cyber-bullying (Smith et al., 2008), for instance through social networking sites such as Facebook, Bebo, Twitter and so on. Whilst a lot of this activity can have very serious consequences for the victim, a critical perspective is provided by Waiton (2008) who argues that too wide a range of behaviours have been incorporated under the heading of bullying. Waiton gives the example of his own son's primary school. His son had been reprimanded (and Waiton himself had received a letter from the head teacher), for 'teasing' a friend about his crush on Waiton's daughter (also attending the school). According to Waiton a mild form of 'normal' behaviour amongst young children had been drawn into the wider bullying agenda and, instead of an informal approach from the teacher, a formalised process (a formal letter and record) had been instituted.

According to Waiton, a process is occurring where an ever-widening range of behaviours – including bullying – fall within the ambit of ASB and this has led to increasingly formalised responses by schools, police and other agencies of control. Waiton suggests that, as these controlling agencies increase the scope of their activities, so informal control by communities declines.

## Truancy as an issue of ASB

Attacks on the physical structure of the school, on teachers and on other pupils are all clear examples where school pupils are the perpetrators. However, as the ASB net has been drawn more widely, truancy has also come to be redefined, not solely as non-attendance at school, but in terms of its links to offending. For instance, in 2002, Estelle Morris (then education secretary) claimed that: 'figures show that 40% of street robberies, 25% of burglaries, 20% of criminal damage and a third of all car thefts are carried out by 10–16 year olds during school hours.' It was unclear whether these were London or national figures – either way, when reported in the press they made persuasive reading. Morris also claimed '[t]he link between truancy and crime is too great to ignore' (Cassidy, 2002, para. 8). According to this way of thinking, truanting therefore becomes an anti-social activity and can be seen as an 'offence' against the community. Truancy is tackled, not just because it is an educational issue, but because it is assumed to increase the risk of crime being committed.

This is not a new assessment. Over 50 years ago Albert Cohen (1955) was of the opinion that anti-social attitudes were linked to truancy and failure at school. For Mannheim (1965), truants had greater opportunity and were therefore more likely to get into trouble. By the 1970s there was talk of a 'truancy crisis' (Pratt, 1983). More recently, findings from the 1998/99 Youth Lifestyle Survey showed that almost half of boys aged 12–16 who persistently truanted were also offenders, whereas the figure was around 10 per cent of those who truanted less frequently or not at all (Flood-Page et al., 2000). But, as Flood-Page and colleagues (2000) comment: 'while there is a clear link between truancy and delinquency, attributing cause and effect remains an area of debate' (p. 37). Others have questioned direct causality between absence from school and anti-social and criminal behaviour (May, 1975; Graham and Bowling, 1995; Millie, 2009a). According to May (1975): 'it is only a minority of boys with a record of irregular school attendance who subsequently make a juvenile court appearance' (p. 106). Similarly, according to a small study by Hodgson and Webb (2005) with young people who had experience of exclusion from school, these young people were no more likely to offend post-exclusion than they were pre-exclusion. Some were less so due to being 'grounded' by their parents on being excluded (see Chapter 8, for parents' perspectives on their child's exclusion from school).

It seems that, while truancy is identified as a 'risk factor' (see Farrington, 2002), direct causality between truancy (and exclusion) and crime and ASB is not established. Nevertheless, it was declared in the Youth Taskforce Action Plan (Youth Taskforce, 2008, p. 9) that: 'We *know* that risk factors – including school exclusion, poor parental discipline, and drug and alcohol misuse – can be major contributory factors for a young person, getting involved in anti-social behaviour and disorder' (emphasis added) (p. 9). Such claims ought to be questioned. Yet, despite a muddled picture, the identification of 'risk factors' and the role of school attendance as a preventer of youthful ASB is assumed. It is to the focus on risk that we now turn.

## Schools and the risk paradigm

That we now live in what has been termed a 'risk society' has been well documented (Beck, 1992): that there is an actuarial focus on calculating the risk of some future calamity or problem (Farrington, 2002), and that people are frequently fearful of intervening or getting involved in such issues for fear of any legal or other repercussions. Within the current context, there is a focus on tackling factors that have been identified as associated with future offending and ASB, such as poor parenting skills and truancy. Similarly, adults are increasingly seen as a threat to schoolchildren and controls are put in place to restrict adult access in an attempt to mitigate danger. One way of doing this is through physical exclusion from the school – there has been a move to introduce strict controls of entry to school buildings – and also strict controls on the contact of adults (except immediate family) with children of school age. This culminated in the 2006 Safeguarding Vulnerable Groups Act, which requires most adults having regular contact with children to register with the Independent Safeguarding Authority. In short, school pupils are seen as both *at* risk and *as* risk (Valentine, 2004). Furthermore, adults are recast around what they might do to children.

Parents have arguably always considered potential risks to their children from contact with other adults, to falling over while playing or crossing the road safely. However, the increased awareness and focus on risk in contemporary Britain has, according to some academics (see Valentine, 2004; Woolley, 2009), resulted in a privatisation of children's play – so that children are more 'battery-reared' than 'free range' (McNeish and Roberts, 1995). With the current policy focus on risk these concerns are transferred to the school setting. And one group that has been increasingly excluded from entry to the school has been adults – following a precautionary principle that it is better to restrict all adults in order to stop the few who are a genuine threat. For instance, a spokesperson for the National Association of Head Teachers was quoted as saying: 'Visitors are the most obvious threat to schools, and the biggest [threat among] them are parents.' In the same article it is claimed that, '[h]aving an entry control system that allows only limited public access – for example, into a reception area where staff can assess the situation before deciding whether or not to allow the person any further – is a clear benefit here' (NAHT, 2008, para. 10). True, knowing who is in, or who is out, of a school building is going to be beneficial; however, the danger is that increased securitisation will result in crime and security being the defining quality of a school, and that this will be seen as the norm by students. It is debatable whether this is healthy in the long term. According to Hirschfield (2008), the situation in the US public school system is that: 'the gated community may be a more apt metaphor to describe the security transformation of affluent schools, while the prison metaphor better suits that of inner-city schools' (p. 84). It is a question of who is seen as the greater risk: adults for what they might do to school pupils, or school pupils for what they might do if allowed to leave the confines of the building.

The factors that are often linked to a child committing ASB and crime include family, community and individual risk factors. There is also a set of school-related risk factors, which include poor achievement at school, aggression (including bullying), poor commitment (including truancy) and 'school disorganisation' (Beinart et al., 2002). These concerns are not new (see Millie, 2009a). For instance, it has long been recognised that schools can and do have a major impact on the way young people behave, their aspirations and achievements (Rutter et al., 1979), and that poor engagement with schooling is likely to have a negative impact, contributing to later anti-social and criminal behaviour. But, as with the evidence of links between truancy and ASB, causality is not always apparent, or is disputed. For instance, a link between poor academic performance and delinquency was identified by Maguin and Loeber (1996), yet a more recent longitudinal study in America only found a 'spurious, not causal relationship' (Felson and Staff, 2006, p. 312).

There is also a danger that a focus on risk factors can lead to the labelling of school pupils as potentially anti-social or criminal, or of adults as potential paedophiles, drug dealers or other threats to children. We would argue that, while some risks are genuine, by having such a focus on the potential for ASB and crime the focus of the school shifts from education to community safety. This cannot be good for learning and teaching in the long run.

The school has also become increasingly involved in work with parents – including the disciplining of parents who are seen as failing to control their children. Continuing with the risk paradigm, poor parenting is tackled, not because of its impact on student learning, but because of its assumed impact on ASB and crime. For instance, Flint and Nixon (2006, p. 948) recount a case of a 43-year-old mother given a parenting order with the condition that she made her children go to school. She was later: 'jailed for 60 days in 2002 after breaching the terms of her order and failing to ensure that her children attended school' (see also Arthur, 2005; Cohen 1973). One might comment on the irony of this situation; a jail sentence ensured that the parent was not available for her children – whether in terms of getting them to school, or otherwise.

It has always been the case since the introduction of compulsory schooling that parents had the responsibility to send their children to school, but the problem was tackled as an educational problem; it is only recently that the parent has been recast as deviant. From 1998 onwards, as truancy and misbehaviour at school came to be reframed in terms of a problem of anti-social and criminal behaviour, a plethora of measures were introduced which focused on parenting skills. The introduction of parenting orders linked to truancy has already been mentioned. But under a series of provisions (for instance, 2003 Every Child Matters, 2006 Education and Inspections Act, 2009 Your Child, Your Schools, Our Future) schools, through their multi-agency partnerships, have become increasingly able to impose contractual and civil controls on parents – such as parenting orders, parenting contracts and penalty notices. The number given out is quite significant; for instance, from September 2004 to August 2008 an astonishing 55,107 parenting contracts were given related to attendance issues, and 7752 contracts were issued for behaviour. The use of more formal parenting orders were fewer: 2048 in comparison with 48,549 penalty notices for unauthorised absence (Teachernet, 2009).

As misbehaviour in school and truancy are correlated with ASB outside school, and as research points to the role of parenting skills in generating or restraining these behaviours (see Gillies, 2005), so interventions to change parenting styles have come to be seen as the answer. This means that the parents of children who are causing problems at school are categorised with the parents of children engaging in ASB in the wider community. Often, but not always, these are the same children. The result is that parents of children with school behavioural problems become drawn into the general net of the 'anti-social behaviour' family. An example of just how wide this 'net' is becoming can be seen from the following quotation from an evaluation of the Parenting Early Intervention Pathfinder, a government initiative targeting schools with particular behaviour issues:

> Since parents are fundamental to their children's development there has been considerable interest in the development of programmes that support the parent role including those that are intended to enhance the understanding and skills of parents through direct training. There is now considerable evidence to suggest that such

programmes do have benefits in improving antisocial behaviour in children and the psychological and social functioning of parents.

(Lindsay et al., 2008, p. 3)

The extent of these parenting interventions and the degree of compulsion varies. There are compulsory parenting orders and (effectively) compulsory Family Intervention Projects, as well as entirely voluntary parenting classes offered by schools. Lister (2006) has suggested this emphasis on the parental deficit indicates an expansion of the state into the sphere of the family. This expanded involvement outwards, from the school into the family, has been the subject of some debate. For instance, Goldson and Jamieson (2002) see these involvements as evidence of an increasingly interventionist and punitive approach by government. Holt (2008) and Nixon and Parr (2009) take rather more ambivalent positions about these types of work with parents, arguing that where parents wish to change their behaviour and receive positive support to do so, then there are benefits from parenting interventions. However, they call for greater debate on how to measure 'success', questioning the 'white, nuclear family parenting norms'. Nixon and Parr argue that parenting interventions should be regarded as 'complex and contradictory.... in which regulation and coercion sit side by side' (2009, p. 51).

## Conclusions

Schools' responsibilities have expanded to include health, citizenship, parenting, crime and ASB, in addition to teaching and learning. In this chapter we have argued that a discourse of crime and ASB has increased in significance, to the extent that it now dominates talk of behaviour standards, discipline and truancy. But, as noted, the processes involved in the criminalisation of education policy are not unique to Britain. For instance, Simon (2007), Hirschfield (2008) and others have investigated how crime has become a dominant discourse in public schools in the United States. Yet the language here is specifically British, with talk of anti-social school pupils and anti-social parents. Much of this discourse is predicated on a risk paradigm that justifies increases in controls on at-risk children thought likely to behave anti-socially and criminally, and on adults for fear of what they might do to children.

While there are clear benefits from improved parenting, tackling truancy and poor behaviour in school, or even from having controls on adults entering school premises, we argue that the defining quality of such action should not be ASB or crime, but should be learning and teaching, alongside student and staff safety. The danger of focusing too much on ASB or crime risk is that some of the assumptions of the risk paradigm can be questioned, and those targeted by ASB-reducing initiatives can be labelled as potentially anti-social. If a risk paradigm must be used, then school policy should not be centred on the risk of crime and ASB, but on the risk of educational failure. In effect, education policy would become *de*criminalised. This may be an optimistic position to take. And clearly there will always remain a role for the police within schools; as we stated earlier, crime and ASB occurs in schools and some serious incidents will need criminal investigation. Yet there is a lot of lower level (mis)behaviour that does not need police involvement or criminalisation – for instance, the boys climbing the fence in the anecdote at the start of the chapter, or Waiton's (2008) example of teasing being treated as a more serious case of bullying. Furthermore, by having police officers stationed within schools, the message to students, parents (and maybe also to teachers) is that the officer's role is to step in with *all* behaviour issues – as the officer in the earlier anecdote saw it, discipline was his responsibility. While there may be advantages in young people 'getting to know' their local officer, we argue that the benefits of having on-site police officers may be oversold, and may also run the risk of crime control being seen as the central element to education.

Much of the policy outlined in this chapter came into being under a New Labour government and at the time of writing there is a relatively new government. However, it appears that a continuation of a criminalising narrative for behaviour policy in education is likely. For instance, Michael Gove as secretary of state for education for the incoming Conservative/Liberal Coalition in 2010, said:

> It is because we want to attract more talented people into the classroom that we will also remove the biggest barrier to people entering or staying in the teaching profession; we will focus relentlessly on improving school discipline. We will change the law on detentions so that teachers will no longer have to give parents 24 hours' notice before disciplining badly behaved pupils. We will change the law on the use of force and enhance teachers' search powers so that they will be able to prevent disruptive pupils from bringing items into school that are designed to disrupt learning. We will change the law to enhance teacher protection by giving teachers anonymity when they face potentially malicious allegations, and we will insist that allegations are either investigated within a tight time period or dropped.

We will also change the law to ensure that heads have the powers that they need on exclusions, and we will ensure that there is improved provision for excluded pupils to get their lives back on track.

(para. 64).

The talk is certainly tough. While Conservative policy includes more traditional school discipline measures such as detentions, talk of searches, confiscation and removal of rights continues the criminalising discourse. We believe a more progressive education policy would be to *de*criminalise school safety and discipline issues.

# 3
# Schools and Social Control

*Carol Hayden*

## Schools as custody: the rise of compulsory school attendance

Schools are inherently about controlling the behaviour of large groups of children and young people who are confined in a relatively small space for several hours a day in school term time, throughout their childhood and adolescence. Control in the history of schools has often been explicitly about discipline and punishment. Contemporary schools can seem much more liberal but they are no less controlling.

Contemporary society has a range of (sometimes) competing needs from its schools, ranging through childminding, before and after school care and activities, breakfast clubs, academic, vocational, social, sporting and leisure-orientated education, through to the promotion of active citizenship and crime prevention. However, an overarching requirement from schools is that they keep children and young people occupied and promote compliant and conforming behaviour. Keeping children off the streets and in school is often equated with keeping them out of trouble; this has been a longstanding aspect of compulsory schooling, as has the notion that education more broadly is a civilising force. Engagement in education (and sometimes schooling specifically) is often put forward as a solution to all kinds of social problems. For example, education within penal institutions is provided as part of the prisoners' rehabilitation and the crime prevention remit; with young offenders' institutions referring to education as 'purposeful activity'.

Schooling and education are not the same thing. Education is often viewed as part of the socialisation process for children, an adjunct to the work of the family and community (as well as other agents of socialisation). Education occurs both formally in institutions, such as schools, as well as informally in a range of settings. Education is also part of a lifelong process that involves the acquisition of knowledge and skills, shaping beliefs and moral values. In sum, education can be an empowering process and as such can lead to individual development and advancement. It is often said that 'knowledge is power' and power is knowledge (in a Foucauldian sense): the acquisition of knowledge through education can be seen as a potential threat to any established order, and what knowledge is available through schooling is decided upon by those with power. On the other hand, being 'educated' has long been seen as a preventative measure against unwanted and criminal behaviour – or the growth of 'the criminal classes'.

The earliest attempt to bring about universal schooling in England was a bill in 1819, but this bill failed to get parliamentary support (Carlen et al., 1992). The competing views of public officials, politicians, philanthropists and employers in the first half of the nineteenth century meant a long debate before universal schooling became available for children up to the age of 10 years, after Forster's Education Act 1870. At this time education was also made compulsory, with enforced attendance being progressively applied. Before Forster's Act, school was a privilege for the minority and much of it was either provided by the church and monasteries, or paid for privately by those who could afford it. In the monasteries of the Middle Ages, physical punishment was routine and was passed on to the emerging church schools of that time. McManus (1989) observes that most sixteenth- and seventeenth-century pictures of teachers showed an adult with a birch or rod. Serious riots in schools are documented, some of which involved shootings and even deaths, and included intervention from the army. In 1818, in Eton (the well-known English public school), for example, a riot amongst pupils occurred in which pupils smashed the desk of their headmaster. This headmaster has been described as a 'champion flogger' who, even in his 60th year, found the energy to 'flog' 80 boys in 1 day (Tubbs, 1996). Lawrence and colleagues (1984) confirm these types of stories and observe that canings and beatings were the only way that some level of order was maintained in schools in the past.

Very early on in the introduction of universal schooling the imperative to enforce school attendance was apparent – the 'payment by results' system was predicated on the crucial importance of pupil numbers and their levels of attendance. For example, in 1883 over a fifth of an assistant teacher's salary and one-third of a head teacher's salary depended on government grants given on the basis of attendance and examinations (Rubenstein, 1969). School boards were expected to oversee compulsory attendance and they appointed school attendance visitors. However, these 'school board men' or 'truant catchers' were hampered by the relaxed attitude of landowners and industrialists who employed children. Furthermore, magistrates often held the view that some young people (and their families) would be better off working if it relieved their material poverty. Thus from the start there was a tension between compulsory school attendance and the needs of poor families, as well as the needs of employers. According to Johnson (1976), working people tended to use schools at the end of the nineteenth century in an instrumental fashion, despite the legislation; using them for the acquisition of skills such as literacy and then withdrawing their children once these skills were acquired. Over the last century the school-leaving age has risen progressively from 14 in 1918, to 15 in 1947 and 16 in 1972; contemporary plans include education and training in a variety of settings, up to the age of 18 years. Extending the period of time that young people spend in schools and other forms of educational institutions has broadened the range and nature of behavioural and control issues presented to adults.

Rather than view schools as a potential solution to various social problems, radical criticisms of the school system (see Illich, 1971) have argued that schools are at the root of many of these problems. Illich starts with an ideal about what education should be, which involves both the acquisition of specific and needed skills and education as a liberating experience. Education as a liberating experience would allow individuals to explore, create and use their own initiative and judgement, developing their faculties and talents to the full. Subsequent criticisms of schooling agree that schools are not particularly effective at teaching some needed skills and that there are major limits to education in schools as a liberating experience (Dale et al., 1976; Giroux, 2001). According to Illich, the solution would be the abolition of schools as the means by which we educate young people. It is interesting now to reflect on this seminal text on schools in relation to contemporary concerns. In more recent decades the emphasis on 'skills' and measurable achievement through qualifications has greatly increased; with the notion of education as a liberating experience rarely given a mention, at least in policy and popular discourse. Indeed the control *of* schools (as well as control *in* schools) is very much a function of the emphasis on increasing measurable achievement.

The connection between education, schooling and the needs of the workplace illustrates a particular aspect of the social control function of schools. This connection was increasingly recognised in nineteenth-century Britain, and for some the concept of 'enlightened self-interest' through education was believed to be in the interests of employers. At the same time, keeping children off the streets and occupied, whilst their parents were at work was part of the equation. Parsons (1999) writes of the custodial function of schools and reminds us that this function changes as children get older. Childminding and socialising are an important part of what schools do with younger children. School as a safe place to grow up and socialise with one's peers becomes more important as children get older. And, in the teenage years especially, school can be a place that helps keep young people out of trouble. However, Parsons (1999) goes on to say that:

> At its most benign and unprison like, school is a healthy place for associating and growing. It is a place of safety and is resourced for young people in a way that the home and street cannot be......[But]......Most schools do not seem like places designed to satisfy children's expressed wishes. Edward Blishen, reading children's competition essays on 'the school I'd like,' admits 'the image of the prison returned to me again and again' (Blishen, 1969:14). A sad truth?
>
> (pp. 7–8)

Clearly the essays referred to were written decades ago, but does this make them any less relevant today? It depends on what the reader perceives as happening in the intervening decades. Table 3.1 takes a look at some key features of schools and prisons suggesting that schools can be compared with custody, or seen *as* custody, in many ways. Schools are essentially controlled and controlling environments that are focused

*Table 3.1*   Schools as custody?

|  | Schools | Prisons |
| --- | --- | --- |
| Compulsory 'attendance' | Parents fined; can be imprisoned. Education Welfare Service dedicated to promoting school attendance. | Sentence decided by the courts. |
| 'Attendance' and crime prevention | Explicit in truancy sweeps involving the police; implicit in programmes promoting attendance. | Incarceration as crime prevention. |
| 'Sentence' | Compulsory from 5 to 17 (as of September 2008); plans to extend to 18. No time off for good behaviour! | Sentence decided by the courts. Time off for good behaviour. |

| | | |
|---|---|---|
| Designated space and time for particular activities | Both types of institution work to clear timetables, with pupils/prisoners expected to be in a particular space at the designated time. | |
| Governed by rules, regulation and inspection | Both types of institution are rule bound and explicitly focused on a small number of people controlling the movement and behaviour of a larger group. | |
| Uniforms | Usual in both types of institution. Some evidence of the increased use of uniform in schools. Increases visibility and identifiability in situations outside the institution. | |
| Education and qualifications as crime prevention | Increasingly explicit since the mid-1990s. | Education and training through 'purposeful activity' part of prison regimes; varies in quantity and quality. |
| Education as preparation for the 'outside' world (outside the institution) | An explicit function of school-based education. | Connected to crime prevention through promoting alternative futures (and thinking); possibility of employment. |
| Discipline and punishment | 'Discipline' and 'punishment' are less popular concepts in schools in the twenty-first century. 'Behaviour management', 'rewards' and 'sanctions', 'conflict resolution' and so on, more common. | Discipline an essential part of prison regimes. Loss of freedom as punishment; restrictions and deprivations of prison regimes. Punishment a more explicit part of prison regimes. |
| Role of professionals | Teachers as educators, childminders and *safe*guarders. | Education provided by dedicated staff. Prison officer's role more focused on surveillance. |
| Surveillance | CCTV commonplace in both institutions. | |

as much on ensuring predictable and conforming behaviour and the smooth running of the institution, as they are on education. Furthermore, both the content and context of education have become more prescribed and regulated in recent decades. The belief that engagement in education can lead to reduced crime has been an increasingly explicit aspect of social policy from the late 1990s onwards, to the extent that it has been argued that social policy has been 'criminalised' (Crawford, 1997; Rodger, 2008). It is in this focus on education and schools within the broader remit of crime prevention that schools can most clearly be seen as a form of custody. Indeed the development of extended schools, where children and young people may breakfast at school and be occupied in a variety of activities at the end of the school day, could also be seen as part of this custody role.

The concept of the 'hidden curriculum' is highly relevant to the issue of social control and schools. As well as teaching a formal curriculum, schools transmit the hidden curriculum through the attitudes and values promoted in the way the school is organised, in the expectations about how people relate to each other and by the achievements recognised and rewarded. In other words, the hidden curriculum consists of what young people learn by the experience of attending school, rather than the openly stated aspects of the formal curriculum (the subjects and activities on the school timetable). It is argued here that some aspects of this hidden curriculum are in increasing evidence in contemporary schools.

Part of the Illich (1971) criticism of schooling is the role of schools in creating conforming and easily manipulated citizens. Conformity is learned in schools as part of the hidden curriculum. Conformity includes the imperative towards passive consumption and deference to authority. Bowles and Gintis (1976) also argue that the hidden curriculum shapes the workforce in a number of ways: by producing a subservient workforce, by encouraging the acceptance of hierarchy, by motivation through the external rewards in the form of qualifications and promise of employment as well as in the fragmentation of knowledge. However, Bowles and Gintis differ from Illich as regards to his focus on schools as the problem; they see the capitalist system as the driving force behind how and why we organise social relations and schools in particular. Bowles and Gintis (2002) have revisited this latter thesis, concluding that they now see little alternative to some form of the capitalist system in democracies and that:

> Today, no less than during the stormy days when Schooling was written, schools express the conflicts and limitations as well as the hopes of a heterogeneous and unequal society. Schools continue to be both testing grounds and battlegrounds for building a society that extends its freedoms and material benefits to all.
>
> (p. 18)

They argue (and provide evidence) how inequality in parental status and income in the United States is still crucial in explaining economic success and how the contribution of schooling to individual success is only partial. In contemporary Britain the way schools prepare young people for, and replicate aspects of, the workplace can be seen in the target-setting culture and focus on measurable achievements in schools, as preparation for the controls exercised by performance-management targets in the workplace. For example, university education is often explicitly linked with the extrinsic rewards of better pay and work prospects, rather than the intrinsic rewards of being 'educated' (Greenaway and Haynes, 2003). This latter view can also be seen as clearly linked to arguments justifying increasing university fees.

## Schools: pupil and adult behaviour

Adult concern about children's behaviour in schools is a longstanding issue and probably endemic to the nature of childhood and schools as mass institutions. The focus is often on 'pupil' rather than adult behaviour. From the point of view of factors in the control of teachers and schools a great deal is known about the labelling process in relation to academic expectations of pupils (Ball, 1981) and in relation to school ethos and its effect on pupil behaviour (Rutter et al., 1979) as well as the effectiveness of various behaviour-management approaches (see examples in Chapter 12). However, whether or not pupil behaviour is actually getting worse is difficult to establish for a host of reasons, including changing behavioural norms over time, different school 'cultures' and a lack of reliable and comparable monitoring systems.

What has gradually changed is the length of time young people spend in formal education and thus the potential time for conflict when the expectations of the institution are at odds with those of the individual, the home and/or the community. One response in the school system has been to segregate and send the badly behaved children somewhere else. This latter tendency became more apparent from the 1970s onwards in England, with debates about 'disruptive' and 'disaffected' pupils becoming increasingly common. Following the raising of the school leaving age in 1972, from 15 to 16 years, there was a marked growth in off-site 'special units'. Many schools also developed on-site withdrawal rooms or on-site units in the 1970s. Off-site units were aimed at pupils who (it was believed) could not be contained in mainstream schools because of their behaviour or because they regularly truanted (chose not to attend school). The first 'special unit' for disruptive and truanting pupils was established in 1961, but by 1969 there were still only 20 nationally. Rapid growth came in the 1970s so that by 1977 there were 239 special units. Two-thirds of all local education authorities (LEAs) in England and Wales had these special units; they were spread throughout the country and not confined to inner city areas. However, London could still be viewed as the *capital of the disruptive industry* with, by 1980, over half the units that were available nationally (Basini, 1981, p. 192). Essentially special units were where pupils went following exclusion from school. The use of these units was criticised for segregating pupils, for the limited role models they could provide and for the content and breadth of the curriculum. The over-representation of black pupils was also noted (Basini, 1981).

Parallel to the growth in special units for disruptive and truanting pupils, there was a growth in residential and day schools for 'maladjusted' children, especially in the 1970s. The distinction made between 'disruptive' children and those deemed 'maladjusted' is an interesting one, not least because it brought with it a different response; although Laslett et al. (1998) comment that *while maladjusted children are not the same as disruptive children, they resemble them in many ways* (p. 12). From 1945 to 1970 it was common to use medical terminology in relation to maladjusted children, with a tendency to see them as ill or sick in some way. Gradually, a distinction was made between emotional maladjustment and social maladjustment. In relation to the latter group, home and community conditions were believed to explain their behaviour. Laslett (1998, p. 13) estimates that around 8000 children attended day or residential state schools for 'maladjusted' children in 1980. However, around a third of this type of provision came from the independent sector, which then (as now) made it difficult to garner accurate estimates of how many children are educated in these types of school. Grimshaw with Berridge (1994) cite an estimate of 12,609 'maladjusted' children resident in special boarding schools and community homes with education in England in 1983. The Warnock Report (DES/WO, 1978) is often seen as the watershed in relation to the concept and use of the term 'maladjusted'. The report replaced the concept of 'handicap' with 'special educational needs' and 'educationally subnormal' was replaced with the term 'learning difficulty'. The report also marks a move away from separate and specialist provision for such children.

General concern about pupil behaviour continued to grow throughout the 1980s, culminating in the government enquiry, known as the Elton Report (DES/WO, 1989). The teaching profession at the time was of the view that disruptive, even violent, behaviour was becoming more apparent in schools (see Chapter 7). However, a key finding from this enquiry was that the biggest problem for teachers was the cumulative effects of everyday minor acts of misbehaviour. The growth of whole school behaviour policies (now expected in all schools in Britain) and training in pupil behaviour management can be seen as developing from the recommendations of the Elton Report (see Chapter 12).

Important to the emerging educational policy context of the late 1980s was the Education Reform Act 1988, which introduced the national curriculum, which was linked with attainment targets and testing. This led to a more competitive and image-management-driven ethos developing in schools. The Office for Standards in Education (Ofsted) inspection system, with its publication of reports further added to the pressure on schools to focus on measurable results. The pace of change and pressures to perform and 'deliver' the national curriculum helped to create behaviour problems in the classroom, as well as limit the possibility of more flexible responses to them. Many of these pressures have continued to intensify to date, although there is a great deal more attention paid to behaviour management, conflict resolution and safety in schools, as we shall see in later chapters.

Chapter 2 introduced the Steer Committee, which at the time or writing is the most recent government enquiry into behaviour in schools (Steer, 2009). In many ways it reaches very similar conclusions to the Elton Report (DES/WO, 1989) about the overall pattern of problem behaviour in schools. The Steer Committee produced a series of reports between 2005 and 2009. The initial assessment was that:

> It is often the case that for pupils, school is a calm place in a disorderly world. We realise that this is not the case in every school, but in our experience, where unsatisfactory behaviour does occur, in the vast majority of cases it involves low level disruption in lessons. Incidents of serious misbehaviour, and especially acts of extreme violence, remain exceptionally rare and are carried out by a very small proportion of pupils.
>
> (Steer, 2005, p. 5)

This view was endorsed in the final report where it was also acknowledged that surveys by teaching unions show that teachers perceive the behaviour of a minority of pupils to have got worse:

> (the) behaviour of a minority of pupils had got worse. This perception that schools are facing greater problems dealing with the behaviour

of a small number of pupils, rather than experiencing problems with pupils as a whole is found in other teacher surveys.

(Steer, 2009, pp. 23–4)

The Steer Committee Reports emphasise the connection between pupil behaviour and the quality and appropriateness of teaching, whilst recognising that certain problematic aspects of pupil behaviour in schools are new. For example, the general availability of technology to pupils such as mobile phones, which are used in new forms of bullying and to record assaults and humiliations (such as 'happy slapping') or to summon angry parents into the school at the behest of a pupil who has been disciplined. Further, Steer highlights the uncertainty about the meaning and application of *in loco parentis* (which gives teachers the same authority over their pupils as parents have over their children) for contemporary teachers. Both Steer and the earlier Elton Committee in 1989 remind us that the legal judgements supporting this concept are very old and that the principle is based on an ancient doctrine of common law (p. 79). This is seen as problematic in a context in which *the trend for parents to challenge schools at law, noted in the Elton Report, has continued and intensified* (Steer, 2005, p. 80). Steer (2009) is critical of media treatment of young people and behaviour in schools and notes the gap between representations in the media and the reality in schools.

## Changing disciplinary practices in schools

As we have seen earlier in this chapter, the physical threat of corporal punishment was ever present in early schooling and much used in some institutions. Although the various methods of corporal punishment were steadily outlawed throughout the twentieth century in Britain, it was not until after the Plowden Report, Children and their Primary Schools (Plowden Committee, 1967), that the abolition of corporal punishment in state schools was treated as a major issue, and it was not until 1986 that it was outlawed altogether in state schools. Corporal punishment was outlawed in 1998 in those independent schools that still retained the practice. This is still relatively recent history for many adults and leads to great differences of opinion when the official views of most public servants and politicians (anti-corporal punishment) are compared with those of the general public (opinion divided). It is not uncommon for opinion polls to show that around half of the general public are in favour of a return to corporal punishment and that many connect the lack of this option to a perceived lack of discipline in schools (BBC, 2000). At the same time, this latter survey, in common with many similar surveys, showed that parents were more positive about their own child's school and education. In other words, the process of 'othering' is very apparent in this debate, with other people's children and other schools being the problem (not one's own).

Foucault's (1977) analysis of how the move away from punishment focusing on the body has led to the dispersal of disciplinary powers is highly relevant to how responses to 'discipline' in school have evolved. This dispersal of disciplinary powers has led to a range of professionals being involved in the behaviour and security management industry: Safer Schools Partnerships (SSPs) (see Chapter 9) can be seen as one example of this trend. CCTV is another, as we outline later in this chapter. Accompanying these professional and technological changes is an increased rhetoric about the responsibility of parents in relation to their children's behaviour in school (see Chapter 8). Schools have always had rules and punishments but since the publication of the Elton Report on Discipline in Schools in 1989 the emphasis has been on 'managing behaviour' and there has been a growth in training in particular approaches (we review the evidence about different approaches to managing pupil behaviour in Chapters 9–12). The Elton Report found that schools that relied on a long list of rules that were prohibitions and that did not have consistent behaviour policies were more likely to have increased levels of troublesome behaviour. Research had already confirmed these patterns (Rutter et al., 1979; Mortimore et al., 1988). The Elton Report advocated the development of 'whole school behaviour policies' so that the boundaries of acceptable behaviour were not left to the individual teacher. This report advocated that parents and children should be involved in discussion about the development and review of such policies.

At the same time as there was increasing discussion of behaviour management strategies in schools, the first national figures on exclusion from school were published (DfE, 1992). The use of exclusion from school (considered in more detail in the next section) can be seen as a paradox: has the child lost a right or received a punishment? (see Parsons, 1999). In law a child has a right to education (but not schooling) and a parent (or carer) has the legal responsibility to ensure that their child goes to school – unless they can satisfy the local authority that they can provide the education themselves. Thus, technically, the exclusion of a child from school does *not* involve the removal of a right – so perhaps it is a punishment? The effect of exclusion from school is punitive (whether or not it is immediately experienced as such), involving as it does the exercise of adult and institutional power over a child and the enhancement of any existing (and highly likely) disadvantages through the withdrawal of schooling for a period. Parents (and carers) are also explicitly punished in relation to their child's attendance at school (by fines and even imprisonment) and implicitly when their child is sent home from school and they are expected to ensure they are supervised, whether or not they are in paid employment themselves.

The growth in recent years of specific 'security' and 'crime prevention' concerns in and around the school environment has already been noted above: the use of CCTV in schools might be understood with reference to Foucault's writings on the panopticon. The panopticon was Bentham's design for a prison (published in 1791) which used visibility as a trap, with the 'inmate' subject to the possibility of constant surveillance. The use of CCTV in all kinds of environment in Britain is so common that it has developed with relatively little comment or question in the school environment. The initial implementation of CCTV in schools can be connected to high-profile incidents in the 1990s, such as the murder of head teacher Philip Lawrence outside his school in 1995 and the Dunblane 'massacre' in 1996, in which 16 people (mostly primary-age children) were killed by a lone gunman. In other words, the initial use of CCTV was protection from outsiders, rather than surveillance of insiders. Hope (2009) argues that there has been 'function creep' in the use of CCTV in schools, so that this initial use of *protection from* 'outsiders' has moved to a more routine surveillance device used to monitor and gather *evidence on* pupil behaviour. This in turn can be seen as an example of an important underlying shift in values in schools, wherein some level of disorder is viewed as inevitable, with the response moving to the situational control of this disorder (Hope, 2009). Hope's (2009) research found that 'disciplinary action' in schools is often dependent on the production of evidence and that CCTV was often used retrospectively to produce evidence, sometimes as proof of behaviour to parents. Whether this use of CCTV simply replaces the informal controls and guardianship previously provided by adults and children in schools, or is a more insidious and problematic development is highly debatable. It is possible to have sympathy with the idea that the use of CCTV in schools may well be evidence of the 'morality of low expectation' (Furedi, 1997). However, other developments in schools, such as peer mediation and restorative approaches present an alternative and value-based response to problematic or 'anti-social' behaviour in schools (see Chapter 11).

## Contemporary schools: exclusion and attendance

National data on school exclusion first became available in England and Wales in 1992 but are still not nationally available in many countries. In common with many issues that are officially recognised and recorded, the figures initially increased to the level shown in 1995–96 in Table 3.2. The election of the first New Labour government in 1997 saw a major push to promote educational opportunity as the way to combat social exclusion. Reducing official records of permanent school exclusion was an important policy focus and led to the reduction in these *official* records as shown in Table 3.2. Official records show that permanent exclusion reduced by almost half, from 1995–96 to 2008–09. Behind this official data there is of course a more complex picture, not least because it is possible to send children home for up to 45 days in any school year, and through the use of withdrawal units and rooms within or on the school site.

There has been a massive amount of research on exclusion from school, since the early 1990s when government monitoring data became available (see, for example, Hayden, 1997; Parsons, 1999). When permanent exclusion figures are compared with surveys of teacher experience like those reported in later chapters, one might be surprised by the relatively small proportion of children who are permanently excluded, according to official statistics. Permanent exclusion from school might be viewed as an indicator of teachers' limits to tolerance in relation to pupil behaviour.

Although the official figures for permanent exclusion represent a very small proportion of the school population (the rate of permanent exclusion was 9 per 10,000 school population in England or 0.09 per cent in 2008–09) they are the tip of the iceberg in terms of problem behaviour in schools. Fixed period exclusions (a matter of days usually) have been monitored since 2003–04 and are much more numerous, as Table 3.2 illustrates. Fixed period exclusions represent 4.89 per cent of the school population in 2008–09. The most common single reason

*Table 3.2*   Permanent exclusions from school

|                     | 1995–1996     | 2008–2009 |
|---------------------|---------------|-----------|
| Permanent           | 12,500        | 8130      |
| Fixed period (days) | Not collected | 363,280   |

*Source of figures*: Available at www.dcsf.gov.uk; see, for example, DfE (2010a).

given for both permanent and fixed period exclusions is 'persistent disruptive behaviour' (29.6 per cent of all permanent and 23.3 per cent of fixed period exclusions). Physical assault against an adult accounted for 11.1 per cent of permanent and 4.7 per cent of fixed period exclusions (DfE, 2010a). Physical assault against a pupil was more common and accounted for 15.7 per cent of permanent and 18.6 per cent of fixed period exclusions in 2008–2009 (DfE, 2010a).

The social pattern of exclusion from school reflects other differences and inequalities in society. Children from poorer families (eligible for free school meals) are more likely to be permanently excluded (28 in 10,000) as are children with special educational needs (33 in 10,000 with statements; 38 in 10,000 without statements), travellers of Irish heritage (53 in 10,000), black pupils (24 in 10,000) and pupils of mixed ethic origin (20 in 10,000) (DCSF, 2009a). This disparity is even more noticeable within particular ethnic groups: for example, the permanent exclusion rate of Asian boys is ten times that for Asian girls and, within this group, Pakistani boys are 15 times more likely to be excluded, compared with girls (DCSF, 2009a). Overall, boys are around three times (13 in 10,000) as likely to be permanently excluded as girls (4 in 10,000). Academies have higher rates of exclusion than other state schools (31 in 10,000), as do special schools (13 in 10,000). The overall trend in rates of exclusion is that the more deprived a school is, the higher the rate of exclusion (DfE, 2010a).

Much has been written about exclusion from school and its association with criminal activity. As Chapter 8 highlights, the evidence points to a complex association between offending behaviour and the type of behaviour that results in some exclusion from school (Berridge et al., 2001). More generally, exclusion from school has become an important indicator or predictor of the likelihood of other problems in a young person's life, as well as poor prospects following exclusion. Surveys such as those carried out for the Youth Justice Board (YJB) by MORI (see YJB, 2009a, b) organise their sampling and comparison on the basis of excluded and non-excluded children. The Youth Cohort Study (see, for example, DfES, 2003b) has also produced comparative data on excluded and non-excluded children, as well as on regular truants; the results show worse outcomes for excluded and truanting pupils in terms of qualifications achieved, likelihood of being in work, education or training at 17 and so on. More broadly, longitudinal analysis of the Offending, Crime and Justice Survey (OCJS) highlights decreasing levels of school discipline as associated with an increased likelihood of an offending or drug-use trajectory (Hales et al., 2009).

A larger proportion of children self-exclude or are absent from school for various reasons. The terminology around this issue is as complex as the underlying reasons. Schools, and the education system, refer to 'authorised' or 'unauthorised' 'absence' (or sometimes 'non-attendance'). The reasons for pupil absence are varied, but in some cases they represent disaffection or disinterest in schooling, while certain other cases may be explained by avoidance of work pressures or bullying, or by the fact that the non-attender is a young carer. Table 3.3 shows that the proportion of children missing school because of authorised (e.g. by parent or carer) absence has improved, whilst unauthorised absence (where no reason is supplied by parents/carers) has got slightly worse.

Other estimates for children not attending school include: 0.5 million schoolchildren engaged in illegal work, of whom 100,000 are believed to 'truant' from school daily in order to work (TUC/MORI, 2001). The term 'truant' is usually used to refer to children who chose not to go to school, rather than those who do not attend because of family pressures and responsibilities, or for medical reasons (including school phobia). The most commonly quoted figure in government announcements on children 'truanting' on any school day is 50,000 (NAO, 2005).

'Persistent' absence from school is an increasing focus in Britain. This is defined as absence during 20 per cent or more of the school week. It is estimated that there are over a quarter of a million (272,950) persistent absentees – 4 per cent of all enrolments (2 per cent primary, 7 per cent secondary and 11 per cent at special schools). It is known that persistent absence increases with age, is slightly higher with boys than girls and is higher amongst pupils on free school meals. More broadly, higher levels of deprivation in an area or school intake are associated with higher levels of absence from school. Persistent absence is highest amongst travellers of Irish heritage, followed by those who are Gypsy/Roma. Young people of mixed white and black heritage also have higher rates of persistent absence. Other minority ethnic groups have lower rates of persistent absence than white pupils (DCSF, 2009b).

*Table 3.3*  Pupil absence (% half days missed)

| Whether authorised | 1995–1996 | Spring term 2010 |
|---|---|---|
| Authorised | 6.9 | 4.81 |
| Unauthorised | 0.7 | 1.12 |
| Total non-attendance | 7.6 | 5.92 |

*Source of figures:* Available at www.dfes.gov.uk; see, for example, DfE (2010b).

In sum, there are a complex set of circumstances and reasons by which children are not benefiting from school. Each set has their behavioural manifestations, although it tends to be the 'acting out' child that causes most consternation amongst teachers because such behaviour demands attention.

## Schools and enforcement

Contemporary schools exercise control in a number of ways. Officially, the main emphasis, as we have seen, is on regular attendance and conforming behaviour and in the overall imperative to achieve and make a positive contribution to society. These priorities are bolstered by a range of sanctions; many focused primarily on the parent, some primarily on the child. This occurs alongside the language of consumerism, choice and parental participation.

The role of parents in relation to the life of the school and specifically their own child's participation in school has changed rapidly in recent decades. In the post-war period parents were generally kept at a distance from schools and the process of schooling. Gradually things began to change with the common belief expressed in a range of reports in the 1960s and 1970s that parents' involvement with and support of their child's education and school was likely to reap positive benefits for all concerned. Participation and active citizenship were key underpinning principles to this change. All of this focused on the positive aspects of parents in contact with schools and their child's education. However, the 1980s brought in the different emphasis of the parent as a consumer, in common with changes across the public sector and associated more broadly with New Public Sector Managerialism. Parental 'choice' of school became a dominant discourse. However, with this emphasis on choice came a realisation that choices were limited and in some cases entirely absent. In part this was due to whether or not parents perceived they had a choice and were motivated to exercise this choice, and, in part, it was due to increased awareness of 'failing' or 'sink' schools and limited or no choice in some areas.

The connection between increased expectations and school performance information available to parents is part of the backdrop to increased formality about the response to infringements in school expectations about behaviour and attendance, as well as a way of managing expectations. Home-School Agreements (sometimes referred to as contracts) became increasingly common in the late 1990s. Originally, these formally written and signed understandings between parents and schools were seen as a two- (parent and school) or three-way (parent, school and pupil) understanding of the obligations of each party to the other. Such agreements were meant for everybody and sought to make explicit common expectations about behaviour and other issues. However, in the climate of rising official records of school exclusion in the early to mid-1990s (and attempts by government and a range of agencies to challenge these actions) such written agreements would soon be differentially used in the battle against non-conforming and 'disruptive' pupils (Vincent and Tomlinson, 1997).

Parallel to the emphasis on education as crime prevention, as well as a solution to a myriad of other social ills, improving parenting 'skills' for similar reasons has been a familiar part of policy development since the late 1990s. As with other New Labour developments this was characterised by a strong emphasis on the enforcement of participation and improvement. The parenting order was introduced in section eight of the Crime and Disorder Act 1998, becoming operational in 2000. Prior to this time other legislation had expressed the concept of parental responsibility in relation to parents exercising control over their children and in relation to the payment of fines. Burney and Gelsthorpe (2008) argue that what is different about the parenting order is the assumption that parents are unable to exercise control over their children and need to be taught how to do so. The parenting order (like the anti-social behaviour order (ASBO)) is a civil order, but if the parent fails to comply without a reasonable excuse, s/he commits a crime (as with the breach of an ASBO).

Parenting contracts for truancy and misbehaviour, parenting orders for truancy and exclusions and serious misbehaviour in schools and penalty notices for truancy and in relation to the responsibility for the 'whereabouts' of excluded pupils have been introduced to reinforce parental responsibility for school attendance and behaviour. Parenting contracts are formal agreements between parents and a school, or parents and a local authority, in which each side sets out the steps they will take to secure an improvement in the child's attendance and behaviour. Parenting orders can be used with parents prosecuted and convicted of a school attendance offence. New parenting orders for behaviour complement this by enabling local authorities and schools to apply to the courts for civil parenting orders for parents whose child is excluded from school or for serious misbehaviour. These provisions are supposed to complement parenting contracts and orders arranged by youth offending teams for problem behaviour in the wider community. Failure to secure regular attendance of a registered pupil is already a criminal offence for parents. Penalty notices provide an *alternative* to prosecution and are justified as a much quicker and cheaper way of sanctioning parents who are not hard-core offenders. Designated local education authority officers (typically education welfare officers), head teachers (and deputy and assistant head teachers authorised by them), police officers and community support officers can issue fixed penalty notices. All prosecutions must be brought by the local authority.

The emphasis on attendance and achievement also relates to concerns about early 'drop out' from education and training and associated issues to do with citizenship, the reduction in the availability of unskilled work and the perceived risk of social exclusion for those who drop out early. As it has become less and less common for young people in rich countries to get full-time employment at the age of 16, youth transitions have become more protracted. Ending education and training at 16 can now be seen as a form of early 'drop out'. Not staying in education or training beyond the age of 16 will, in some cases, follows a longer period of disengagement with and poor attendance in compulsory schooling. Early drop out and lack of qualifications and training is strongly associated with unemployment. In Britain those not in education, employment or training ('NEET') at age 16 make up about 8–10 per cent of their age group. Young people entering secondary education (age 11 years) from September 2008 cannot leave education or training before the age of 17 years. There are proposals that this age is further raised to 18 years, with a requirement to participate. This requirement to participate will be enforced by an attendance order, if a young person who drops out of education or training refuses to take up other offers. A breach of an attendance order may be a civil or criminal offence (DCSF, 2007b).

## Fear, 'failing' schools and inequality

A range of socio-economic and policy changes have come together to make the fears and anxieties of adults about the future focus ever more strongly on children, young people and their schooling. These fears might be seen as part of the more generalised fears and conceptions of risk in late modernity that are already well documented (see Beck, 1992; Giddens, 1999), and are highlighted in Chapter 2. There is also an increased appreciation that educational qualifications are a critical part of individual success in 'knowledge economies'. Widening participation to higher education has increased the competition around access to professional and well-paid jobs. This situation is coupled with continuing and marked inequalities in relation to income and life chances. These inequalities are played out in services like schools, where geographical location interrelates with social and economic capital, which disadvantage the poor. Performance management and, specifically, school inspections have made available a wealth of data to the discerning parent that further advantages and privileges their access to popular (usually high-achieving) schools. The wide availability of such data and the media treatment of it enhances the climate of fear in relation to access to popular state schools. As with 'fear of crime', the available evidence about direct experiences of the state education system is more positive than public fears (as expressed in everyday discourse and media representations) might suggest.

Sammons (2008) reviewed the impact on school standards of ten years of Labour administrations (1997–2007). She concluded that there was evidence of significant and sustained improvements in overall pupil attainment levels for the majority of schools but that relative inequality has not been successfully tackled. A 'zero-tolerance' approach to new conceptions of 'failure' has meant that the continuing drive to improve standards has tended, whatever the initial intention, to 'name and shame' schools. For example, the launch of the 'National Challenge' in 2008 was followed by the publication in the national media of a list of 638 schools in England that did not have 30 per cent or more of their pupils achieving five GCSE's A*–C, including English and Maths. This amounted to most local authorities (134 out of 150) having one or more secondary schools on this list that needed to improve to meet this 'challenge'. Such tactics remain highly contentious; with some head teachers claiming that identification as a National Challenge school is counterproductive, adversely affecting pupil and staff recruitment. Certainly the individual dynamics around schools in this situation may mean those teachers and families able to exercise choice may be less likely to 'choose' such a school. However, for most pupils and teachers there may be no option but to carry on working and attending what is often seen as a publicly named and shamed 'failing school', despite the more optimistic language of being a 'National Challenge' school.

The link between 'failure', poverty and inequality is well appreciated by many commentators on the issue. Indeed, a former inspector

(Blatchford) with responsibility for 'failing schools' is quoted as saying that:

> ... schools which struggle are nearly always on what the Americans call 'the wrong side of the tracks'. It is rare to find a school in difficulties serving a catchment area that is truly comprehensive – as opposed to being skewed towards the poorer families.
>
> (Richardson, 2008, paras 6, 7)

Harris and Ranson (2005) argue that part of being disadvantaged means ending up at poorer institutions, and that the promotion of 'choice' and 'diversity' is unlikely to break this link. Diversity of school provision changes the nature of control of state education and its purpose. Traditional forms of governance are being steadily eroded – religious denominational interests, as well as business and private sector interests are increasingly involved in the provision of state education. The involvement of private capital in the rebuilding and renovation of schools can enable such corporate sponsors to gain influence (even a controlling influence) over the ethos and accompanying practices of a school (Harris and Ranson, 2005).

## Social control and contemporary schooling

A focus on 'anti-social' and 'offending' behaviour and schoolchildren is potentially dangerous. It has already entered the common lexicon in relation to the overarching outcomes of all children's services, as outlined below in relation to the Every Child Matters (DfES, 2003a) agenda. Children are easy targets. This chapter has argued that in many respects schools already represent a form of custody that carries with it a high degree of adult surveillance and the associated power to do good or ill with the information available. A focus on a perspective influenced by the criminal justice system carries with it the risk of further demonising the behaviour of young people in general, as well as contributing to existing tendencies towards 'net-widening' or 'mesh thinning'. This is not to say that we should ignore the very real problems faced by adults and children in and around some schools. The most important issue is intention: what is the purpose of developing this focus in relation to schools? The tension between prevention and detection is particularly problematic for the police. It is important to differentiate between the behaviour associated with different stages of child and adolescent development, behaviour caused by poor adult management of children and behaviour that is serious and is causing harm to others. Adults always have the responsibility to respond in ways that reduce harm and promote positive behaviour, especially with young people who need help to change.

Contemporary social policy locates schools within 'Children's Services' in which there are five overarching outcomes, as part of the Every Child Matters (ECM) agenda:

*Being healthy* – enjoying good physical and mental health and living a healthy lifestyle.

*Staying safe* – being protected from harm and neglect and growing up able to look after themselves.

*Enjoying and achieving* – getting the most out of life and developing broad skills for adulthood.

*Making a positive contribution* – to the community and to society and not engaging in anti-social or offending behaviour.

*Economic well-being* – overcoming socio-economic disadvantages to achieve their full potential in life.

(DfES, 2003a, para 1.3)

Ensuring that children and young people in school are educated in an environment conducive to all of these outcomes necessarily involves a focus on behaviour and social relations. Child and adult experiences of behaviour within the school environment will be illustrated by original research in later chapters, as will examples of different ways of responding to these issues. Bailey (2009) writes of 'the new politics of behaviour' associated with a focus on well-being, and the development of emotional intelligence and interpersonal skills. Whether a focus on individual behaviour can address the issues of inequality and social justice referred to here is a question we consider in the next chapter.

# 4

# The Problem with Boys? Critical Reflections on Schools, Inequalities and Anti-Social Behaviour

*Dawn E. Stephen*

## Is there a 'problem' with boys?

In recent years there has been increasing popular and policy debate about 'the problem with boys'. Concern about boys and education has two main aspects: the achievement gap and concerns about behaviour. Most contemporary educational researchers would see achievement and behaviour as connected. It should be noted at the outset that this focus on boys' achievement has come after the relatively recent gains made by girls of school age and is happening alongside the ongoing inequalities women face in the workplace. In other words, there is a need for a more careful look at the evidence before we accept that there is a problem with boys, in general.

Martino and colleagues (2009) note how concern about boys' schooling has led to interventions such as a more 'boy-friendly' curriculum, single-sex classes and more male teachers and role models (p. xii). Martino and colleagues assert that such practices are being adopted in the United Kingdom, the United States, Canada and Australia in an unreflective way that does not take into account the complexities of the lives of boys and male teachers. They argue about the importance of culture, locality, sexuality, social class, ethnicity and disability in relation to the education of boys. Such a perspective reminds us that some caution is needed when trying to understand and respond to the needs of *all* boys in the education system.

Nevertheless, a focus on boys and young men can be seen as highly relevant to the issues of crime, anti-social behaviour and schools. More broadly, it is males who are more likely to be convicted of crime and the prison population is around 95 per cent male. Highly problematic 'acting out', and violent and aggressive behaviour is more common from boys than from girls. These behaviours demand the attention of teachers. Internalising behaviours (such as depression and self-harming) are more common with girls and can get ignored in the classroom. These gender differences in behaviour are reflected in the different types of bullying behaviour from boys and girls, as well as by the different rates of exclusion from school (see Table 4.1). However, these broad patterns overlay a complexity that reflects broader patterns of inequality. In particular, it is in some inner-city state schools that these inequalities are at their most severe. This chapter will focus on these issues, drawing on a range of previous research to do with anti-social behaviour (see Stephen and Squires, 2003, 2004; Squires and Stephen, 2005; Stephen, 2006, 2008, 2009). The key argument upon which this chapter is premised

*Table 4.1* Exclusion and absence from school

|  | Gender | Ethnicity | Free School Meals |
|---|---|---|---|
| **Exclusion from school** | **% of each type of exclusion** *Permanent* Boys: 78% Girls: 22% *Fixed period* Boys: 75% Girls: 25% | **Rate per 10,000 school population** *Permanent* Irish traveller: 0.38 Gypsy/Roma: 0.30 Black Caribbean: 0.30 White/Black Caribbean: 0.25 White British: 0.09 Indian: 0.03 Chinese: – All: 0.09 | **% school population** *Permanent* Yes: 0.22% No: FSM: 0.06% All: 0.09% *Fixed period* Yes: 11.10% No: FSM: 3.77% All: 4.89% |
| **Absence from school** | **% half days missed** Boys: 6.20% Girls: 6.33% | **% half days missed** Irish traveller: 24.44% Gypsy/Roma: 10.05% Black Caribbean: 5.09% White/Black Caribbean: 7.30% White British: 6.19% Indian: 5.32% Chinese: 3.59% All: 6.27% | **% half days missed** Yes: 9.09% No: 5.73% All: 6.27% |

*Sources:* DfE (2010a, b), data are for the 2008–09 school year.

is that the current educational system can be seen as anti-social in the way that inequality is entrenched and because the system is not based on the needs of all children.

There is a massive amount of educational research on gender and achievement, as well as on other factors affecting achievement such as poverty and ethnicity (see, for example, Gillborn and Mirza, 2000; Archer and Francis, 2007). Furthermore, since the late 1990s there have been numerous initiatives that have tried to develop more 'equality of opportunity', many specifically aimed at boys (see, for example, Sharp et al., 2001; Ofsted, 2003a). A great deal of official monitoring data about education and schooling are available by gender and ethnicity and by whether a pupil has free school meals (as a proxy indicator of low income). This monitoring data include a host of other indicators – such as special educational needs, age and relative deprivation of the whole school intake, as well as whether school is an academy. Academies are state schools but involve other supporters and backers and, important to the focus of this chapter, they exclude children at a higher rate than other state schools (DfE, 2010a). Some of the key official data on exclusion and absence from school are reproduced in Table 4.1.

We will concentrate here on the three main issues illustrated in Table 4.1 in relation to patterns of exclusion from school and attendance. We have referred to these issues elsewhere in this volume, so our main concern here is to focus on the gender issue and the extent to which it is mediated by other pupil characteristics, such as ethnicity and low income. Table 4.1 begins to illustrate some broad patterns that relate to gender, but also reflect other inequalities. Boys are more likely to be excluded from school than girls, but are equally likely to be absent from school. Some ethnic groups are more likely to be excluded from school than others and there are different ethnic patterns in relation to absence from school. The highest rates of exclusion (Irish travellers, Gypsy/Roma) are also reflected in absence from school in these groups. Black Caribbean pupils are more likely to be excluded from school, but are less likely to be absent from school. Within these broad ethnic patterns there are also gender differences. Pupils who take free school meals are more likely to be excluded from school and are also more likely to be absent from school.

Annual data produced by the Department for Education detail achievement and progress. In terms of the broad picture on gender, one of the common measures of achievement is the percentage of boys and girls achieving five or more GCSE passes (A*–C). In 2008–09: 65.8 per cent of boys achieved this and 75.4 per cent of girls (DfE,

2010c). Therefore the current achievement gap at age 16 is 9.6 per cent fewer boys than girls achieving these GCSE passes. We need to think about these figures carefully: there is this achievement gap, but 'the problem' isn't with all boys. It is crucial to remember that around a quarter of girls do not achieve five or more GCSE passes (A*–C) and, as Table 4.2 illustrates, 14 per cent of 18-year-old girls are estimated to be NEET (not in education, employment or training).

The Youth Cohort Study is another longitudinal survey that is useful in following through what happens to a cohort of young people over time. The sample is weighted to represent the key socio-economic characteristics of the whole population. Table 4.2 is a very small extract from some of the useful data collected by this survey. This study shows that women are more likely than men to be in full-time education at the age of 18 and are equally likely to be in a job without training at the same age but are a bit less likely to be NEET at this age (12 per cent of young women compared with 14 per cent of young men). The pattern in relation to ethnicity adds another layer to this picture, with 'White' young men and women at the age of 18 being less likely to be in full-time education than other ethnic groups, more likely to be in a job without training and equally likely to be NEET, compared with black Caribbean

*Table 4.2* Education, employment and status at age 18

| Main activity at the age of 18 | Gender | Ethnicity | Free school meals (in year 11, age 16) |
|---|---|---|---|
| **Full-time education** (All = 45%) | Men: 42% Women: 48% | Black African: 85% Black Caribbean: 57% Indian: 78% Mixed: 48% White: 41% | Yes: 41% No: 44% |
| **Job without training** (All = 22%) | Men: 22% Women: 22% | Black African: 5% Black Caribbean: 15% Indian: 8% Mixed: 21% White: 24% | Yes: 18% No: 23% |
| **NEET (not in education, employment or training)** (All = 15%) | Men: 16% Women: 14% | Black African: 7% Black Caribbean: 16% Indian: 9% Mixed: 16% White: 16% | Yes: 29% No: 13% |

*Source*: DfE (2010c, table 2.1.1, p. 6).

and mixed heritage young people. The data on free school meals illustrate the increased likelihood of being NEET amongst relatively poor young people.

What the official data increasingly illustrate is a number of very specific problems with different groups of boys. Ethnicity is important in relation to the choices made and the response of the system (notably in relation to exclusion) but a crucial issue is relative poverty. Increasingly it is (re-)recognised in official discourses that there is a particular 'problem' in relation to the aspirations and achievements of 'White' working-class boys (DCSF, 2008b). Nationally this latter group is the most numerous group of boys. This issue has been debated for some time by educationalists (see, for example, Gillborn and Kirton, 2000).

## Contemporary schooling and boys

Evans' compelling ethnography of inner-city state school life provides insight into the routine conflict and strain for pupils and their teachers as both groups struggle to make sense of, and operate within, the demands of contemporary schooling in this setting.

> The whole of the school day, as it unfolds in the various spaces of the building, becomes a virtual battleground in which the fight to inculcate in children a disposition towards formal learning is waged against their more fundamental desire to play, move about a bit and interact freely and noisily. The extreme expression of this conflict is witnessed in the teacher's outbursts of irritation and anger when she is distracted from teaching in order to have to continuously focus on managing the comportment and misbehaviour of the most disruptive boys.
>
> (Evans, 2007, p. 83)

The 'disruptive boy' is a problem in the large group setting and 'disruptive' is very much the concept used by many teachers (rather than 'anti-social' or 'violent', as we note elsewhere in this volume, for example Chapter 1). Evans' study is reminiscent of Willis' (1977) seminal work on how working-class boys get working-class jobs. In the school context their competing values are the weapons within the battle in schools, as working-class children learn what it is to be working class in unequal contemporary Britain (see Wilkinson and Pickett, 2010). The reduction in traditional manual occupations for men adds an additional pertinence, as Arnot (2004, p. 37) explains, in a *society in which qualifications matter even more than before and the social exclusion of the manual classes is even harsher* than at the time of Willis' research.

This chapter highlights the impact of inequality and the way in which contemporary school policy and practice not only goes against laudable liberal-humanist values but also serves to entrench inequality, disaffection and underachievement, despite the rhetoric of inclusion and meritocracy inherent in much of the official discourse about state education. Evans' analogy of a 'battleground' is useful in relation to the competing interests of the 'disruptive' or 'disaffected' pupil, other pupils and, of course, the teachers. The discursive frenzy that has developed around school violence, problem behaviour and discipline in schools has been alluded to by educational researchers (see, for example, Osler and Starkey, 2005; Watkins et al., 2007) and, as we know from Chapter 3 (also see Chapter 7), there is a long history of teacher and adult concern about the behaviour of young people (specifically in schools). However, to focus on this alone would be too narrow, for these concerns need to be located within the 'learner hostile' (Meighan, 2004, p. vi) and 'teacher-hostile' nature of managerialist-driven schooling. Contemporary state schooling places unrealistic demands on both teachers and pupils alike to meet performance targets, yet simultaneously expects them also to deliver on multiple social imperatives (Furedi, 2009).

The 'discursive conflation' of intentions (see Gillies, 2008) is reflective of society's *schizophrenic attitude towards education* (Furedi, 2009, p. 140) epitomised in the national curriculum, which has undermined teachers' professional creativity and commitment to learning and teaching (Barker, 2008) whilst simultaneously squeezing pupils into an inflexible system. This critique therefore challenges the discourse about violence within schools by drawing upon Brown and Munn's (2008) examination of this phenomenon. The authors chart how this discourse has developed and consolidated since the early 1990s and explain the way in which this has been related directly to renewed public and media interest in 'the youth problem', which they show is associated with *a particularly vengeful attitude towards disaffected pupils* (p. 222). Perhaps not by chance, this has proceeded against the backdrop of the neo-liberal inspired *anti-comprehensive assault* (Regan, 2007, p. 3) of the last two decades (see Barker, 2008), which is now developing apace with the prioritisation of academies and 'free schools' on the policy agenda of the 2010 coalition government in Britain.

The liberalisation, marketisation and de-professionalisation of compulsory state education means that *educational policy has become increasingly focussed on its economic function* (Beckman and Cooper, 2004, p. 3).

In fairness, perhaps this focus can be seen as simply being more honest about the main purpose of schools. It has long been argued that schooling for the masses is, and always has been, about disciplining and equipping most young people with the knowledge and skills for the workplace (see Chapter 3). The tensions in this situation result in an exhausted and stressed profession (ATL/Teacher Support Network, 2008) and pupils moulded into *uncritical thinkers, compliant to the needs of the market* (Beckman and Cooper, 2004). The current system of state schooling is seen by many as harmful to both professionals and children. Cooper (2004, p. 17) captures a situation in which they *have both become victims of a brutally uniform and authoritarian education system*.

## Anti-social schools?

The expanding body of literature on violence within schools suggests a global concern (see Harber, 2008), which has produced a situation whereby schools *have become even more enmeshed in rules and regulations about the expected behaviour of teachers, other staff and pupils* (Potts, 2006, p. 329). Within the United Kingdom this latter point is no more evident than in the use of anti-social behaviour measures to address school discipline and attendance problems (see Riley, 2007). Furthermore, the extent to which any such measures are making schools safer must be questioned for it is important to acknowledge Potts's addendum to his observations that regulatory measures are *not enough to reduce the dangers that schools can pose* (2006, p. 329). In both the literature and wider public discourse, too much attention focuses on the behaviour of young people, or their parents, as *the problem* (Brown and Munn, 2008), rather than acknowledging the *widespread evidence that schooling can be directly harmful and actively make society worse* (Harber, 2008, p. 459). Despite this growing body of evidence the focus has remained on the behaviour of pupils, and there is little recognition that the problem lies in the structure and provision of compulsory schooling itself, by the way in which it both creates and magnifies the problem through *normalised practices of power* (Bansel et al., 2009, p. 67). These practices serve to reproduce class-based and gendered inequalities (see Brown, 2007; Evans, 2007; Paterson and Iannelli, 2007; Smith, 2007) and reinforce wider classist and ageist discourses and practices against young people (Stephen, 2009).

These inequalities are fundamental to understanding the problem facing schools and there is much merit in Furedi's (2009) analysis of the current situation; he argues that education has lost its way in the pre-vailing belief that schools are expected to resolve the problems of the wider society. Yet, simultaneously, consumerist school policies reinforce class and racial divisions (Byrne, 2009) and further entrench disadvan-tage. Edwards (2008) examines the enduring nature of class difference in educational opportunities and outcomes and the waste of ability for those on the wrong side of this *educational apartheid* (p. 370). Those on the advantaged side of this divide are subjected to ever-increasing pressures to be successful with troubling consequences, for example, upon middle-class young women's sense of selfhood (Rich and Evans, 2009). Class and gender inequalities are shown to impact on subject choice (Davies et al., 2008) in a way that reproduces existing differences. Davies and colleagues highlight the influence of teachers' assumptions about their pupils, that have been raised in other works, as *positioning pupils within educational and occupational hierarchies* (Dunne and Gazeley, 2008, p. 451) that perpetuate extant disadvantage. These factors are dis-turbing when contextualised by evidence about children and young people's increased risk of social harms in the United Kingdom when compared to other European countries (Pantazis, 2010), alongside the erosion of rights and the precarious positioning of marginalised young people (Stephen, 2008, 2009). The connections between precariousness, marginalisation and the increased likelihood of offending behaviour is well documented. Furthermore, this is set against a backdrop of widen-ing and deepening institutionalised distrust of young people more gen-erally (Stephen and Squires, 2004; Squires and Stephen, 2005; Stephen, 2006). This is happening alongside fundamental societal changes, including the collapse of youth labour markets, lower collective efficacy and consumerism (see Margo et al., 2006), which exert harmful influ-ences upon children and young people's experiences and life chances.

The links between school disaffection and disengagement and crim-inality are well established (Stephenson, 2007), yet instead of 'nipping problems in the bud' through addressing young people's educational needs, anti-social behaviour and criminal justice measures are being made available to schools (see Riley, 2007). Such measures are likely to entrench problems for children, and for society. Solomon and Garside (2008) reveal the absurdity of recent years in that that there has been a significant deployment of social expenditure into youth justice budgets. As Solomon and Garside illustrate, the youth justice system has received the largest real-terms increase of all the main criminal justice agencies and almost two-thirds of the Youth Justice Board budget is spent pur-chasing custodial places. The vulnerability and complexity of needs of most young people caught up in the youth justice system is depicted by Solomon and Garside (2008, p. 11) in the following way:

> The overall picture is of a youth justice system that was designed with the best of intentions of providing multi-agency provision but that in practice is struggling to meet the needs of a group of vulnerable children and young people who require carefully coordinated specialist support. YOTs do not appear to be able to successfully meet the complex needs of children and young people. This raises questions about the significant investment in youth justice and whether resources should instead be directed to social support agencies outside the criminal justice arena.

The perceived irrelevance of schooling to the highly gendered self-conceptions, skills, needs and aspirations of working-class boys has given rise to what at times seems to be a moral panic, focusing on their underachievement at school, relative to girls (see Smith, J. 2007). Smith offers a refreshing challenge to the highly determinist gendered assumptions in both the literature and in extant approaches to 'the problem', but the undoubted strength of his article lies in his heuristic concept of teachers as 'cultural accomplices' in constructing hegemonic masculinities. This is a fruitful concept for it enables a broader understanding of teachers as 'cultural accomplices' within the 'total institution' (Foucault, 1977) of school in a state system founded on the perceived need to regulate and control the masses, in order to prepare the children of the 'dangerous classes' for the disciplined world of work (see Hendrick, 2006).

Morrison's work on encouraging men (in the Scottish Highlands and Islands) into higher education illuminates some of the deficits in men's past experience of compulsory schooling. The reasons the men had not engaged in further and higher education were identified as lying in four main categories: psychosocial, such as fear of failure, lack of confidence or negative past experience of school; informational, most notably the lack of adequate information or encouragement at school; lifestyle; and the need for a relevant curriculum design and style of delivery (Morrison, 2007; Cameron and Morrison, 2008; Morrison, 2008). For the men who participated in the various creative initiatives the success of the Engaging Men project lay in the non-threatening, confidence-building orientations of the courses, which they felt were relevant to their needs, lives and aspirations. It followed logically, therefore, that one recommendation in Morrison's report highlights the need to provide *a user-friendly, non-threatening atmosphere where men can feel relaxed and are never put in a situation where they are made to feel stupid* in order to counter *poor experiences from school and to whom the formal college class is a terrifying prospect* (Morrison, 2007, p. 62). In drawing upon these insights it is possible to appreciate that we will never tackle the roots of disaffection from school from many working-class young men until we understand the factors that contribute to making formal education such a terrifying prospect.

Although physical punishment is against the law in the United Kingdom, status degradation ceremonies (Garfinkel, 1956) have not been eradicated and institutional aggression in the form of various sanctions still prevail. At the most apparent level, the literature is peppered with accounts of teachers shouting at pupils (Evans, 2007; Horgan, 2007) as well as authoritarian means of surveillance and coercion being deployed (Harber, 2004). Teachers' frustrations and responses to their charges might be understood with reference to the broader collapse of adult authority (see Furedi, 2009). And, whilst some forms of institutionalised coercion may serve to develop resilience and may be argued to be 'character building' for working-class children, there are profound psychosocial considerations insofar as these forms of discipline are enacted upon the broader and deeper social and cultural restrictions and status degradations associated with their poverty. The Child Poverty Action Group's (CPAG) campaign 2 Skint 4 School highlights the impact of the inequitable nature of contemporary schooling upon the one in three UK children growing up in poverty:

> By 3 years old, poor children may be up to a year behind the wealthiest children in terms of cognitive development and school readiness.
>
> Wealthier pupils perform better at all stages of schooling than pupils eligible for free school meals, regardless of race or gender.
>
> By the time they move to secondary school poorer children are on average 2 years behind better-off children.
>
> (CPAG, 2009, paras 1–3)

The combined effects of poverty foster lasting harm to the children in terms of the reported anxieties and poor self-confidence found amongst disadvantaged children, who are already in a highly precarious position educationally, at school (Hirsch, 2007) (Wilkinson and Pickett, 2010). Horgan (2007, p. 57) explains how the pressures combine:

> The evidence...points towards the interaction of educational disad-
> vantage faced by children growing up in poverty, the difficulties faced
> by teachers in disadvantaged schools and gendered socialisation of
> children leading to boys particularly being failed by the education
> system. It seems that, for these children, school reflects – and repro-
> duces – disadvantage in society generally. The poorer they are, the
> more likely their experience of school is to be impacted by their place
> in society.

Horgan's study found signs of disenchantment with school in boys as young as 9. Disaffected children have been shown to feel *a lack of control over their learning, and to become reluctant recipients of the taught curriculum* (Hirsch, 2007, p. 1) despite the official discourse about the stated commitment that *every pupil will go to a school where they are taught in a way that meets their needs, where their progress is regularly checked and where additional needs are spotted early and quickly addressed* (DCSF, 2009b, p. 7). The renewed commitments outlined in this White Paper, Your Child, Your Schools, Our Future: Building a 21st Century Schools System are clearly necessary because needs are not being met and in recent years there has been an increasing readiness of the criminal justice system to respond where the education system has failed.

Poverty does not merely impact on the level of educational attain-ment, it markedly affects young people's social and cultural well-being at school:

> Key areas of concern identified by children are...visible signs of
> poverty and difference: a lack of the same material goods and clothes
> as their peers, and an inability to take part in the same social and
> leisure activities meant that children experienced bullying and were
> fearful of stigma and social isolation.
>
> (Ridge, 2009, p. 56)

Poverty is a factor that is directly implicated in children being bullied (Ridge, 2009), as is special educational needs (Harber, 2008) and other forms of 'difference' (Hall and Hayden, 2007). Being bullied has negative consequences on the child's ability to concentrate and learn (Boulton et al., 2008). Ridge's thorough review of the literature highlights the broader combined impact of poor neighbourhoods, inadequate housing, financial tensions within the home, a lack of essential items, such as food and bedding or a place to study, all of which limit children's ability to establish friendships, participate in social activities, have friends visit their homes and, of course, their ability to learn. This form of social exclusion relates to the anxieties children have about their parents' income, as well as their own participation in work in order to contribute to family finances. Ridge highlights the resourcefulness of many young people in the way that they contribute to the family income. These factors contrast with the cultural capital, material advantages and extra-school activities enjoyed by middle-class children (Horgan, 2007; Ridge, 2009), which are shown to boost social skills and self-confidence (Hirsch, 2007) and exert influences on achievement and aspirations (Cabinet Office, 2008). A focus on aspirations is essential to the debate about what state schooling is for (see Chapter 12).

## Education: a route out of poverty?

Education has been the traditional route out of poverty, and is also a well-known protective factor against offending. These are major reasons for any government to be interested in enhancing educational opportunity. The Equalities Review (2007) looked at the longer view in considering the pattern of changes in Britain since the welfare state was established in 1947. This review was wide-ranging and focused not only on the existing patterns of inequality and discrimination, but also on the challenges posed by demographic changes and globalised labour markets. This government-initiated review acknowledges that by the mid-1990s the United Kingdom was second only to the United States for income inequality, with the very richest people increasing their relative share to date:

> Today's top Chief Executives are paid 100 times as much as the average worker: ten years ago their earnings were only 40 times higher. These trends have been paralleled by a widening gap in wealth inequality.
>
> (p. 32)

The review argues that there is *a uniquely destructive class of equality gap* (p. 47); one of which relates to education:

> People with low levels of educational achievement can expect to be less employable, therefore poorer, therefore less healthy and probably

less likely to participate in civic activity. The kinds of people who are less likely to be employable are also more likely to be involved in crime, to have shorter life-spans and to have less fulfilling family lives.

(p. 48)

The review highlights the patterns already noted in Tables 4.1 and 4.2 in noting the different patterns of achievement in relation to ethnicity in the United Kingdom, concluding that:

Though class background is still the strongest indicator of educational attainment, ethnicity can have a substantial impact. That is to say, groups of pupils of different ethnicities may do better or worse even if they have the same economic status.

(p. 52)

This very brief overview of existing patterns of inequality presents a picture of a society that is highly unequal but one in which there is not just 'the problem with boys', there is the issue of some working-class boys from specific ethnic groups. Boys in the past had a different range of opportunities for continuing education, training and work (specifically skilled manual work). There is wide recognition of the need for more apprenticeships and a national apprenticeship service (see http://www.apprenticeships.org.uk/). However, much more needs to be done because the skilled trades' aspirations of the young men are often based on outmoded masculine ideals in a school system and post-industrial economy in which 'soft' skills and knowledge are privileged. The broader public discourse is often based on securing academic qualifications, or by taking a fast route to celebrity (see Young, 2007). In this context is it any wonder that some young men disengage from school when it appears to reject the skills they privilege, does not support or nurture their aspirations and prepares them for low-paid service sector jobs? Jobs that do not offer the status and rewards for which their gendered socialisation and contemporary consumerist society has prepared them. The current precarious youth labour market, especially for those with poor qualifications (OECD, 2008), alongside high youth unemployment, has the potential to produce a 'lost generation' (Seager, 2009) and offers meagre long-term prospects for those who cannot, or will not, engage with the current school system.

## Three new Rs: resilience, respect and resistance

Notwithstanding the barriers that have been made apparent throughout this chapter: One of the tasks of the progressive educator...is to unveil opportunities for hope, no matter what the obstacles may be. (Freire, 1994, p. 3). This chapter is written from a standpoint of full appreciation of the shared tensions and 'obstacles' facing all teachers and young people across the whole mass state educational system (Stephen et al., 2008), and from a position which acknowledges *that the relationship between social inequalities, education policy, school processes and professional practice is complex* (Dunne and Gazeley, 2008, p. 461). As it has acknowledged that both teachers and pupils are subject to the same iniquitous and stressed environment, this chapter should not be taken as a critique of teachers, rather it is written with the intention of encouraging teachers to consider how they might become stronger 'cultural accomplices' (Smith, 2007) in reducing the likelihood that some young men (and young women) will find their own illegal means of achievement as a result of school failure rooted in their wider social, cultural and economic marginalisation. As such, this concluding section begins by focusing on developing resilience, highlighted by Ridge (2009), and the means by which teachers might foster this. One of the most remarkable aspects of my own work with 'offending' and 'anti-social' young men has been their reflexive resilience in the face of apparently insurmountable structural constraints, especially the ways in which they are able to effect alternative transitions to adulthood in the absence of the usual legitimate transitional markers, such as schooling (Stephen and Squires, 2003; Squires and Stephen, 2005). Accordingly, the key to fostering a climate conducive to resilient engagement appears to lie in Morrison's (2007) recommendations for a 'non-threatening' educational experience to redress disadvantage, and in working with disaffected young people this is shown to be *most effective where it makes them feel more involved in their own futures* (Hirsch, 2007, p. 1).

As Hirsch (2007) argues, the imperative is to involve disaffected pupils in decision-making and in this regard it seems significant to support Whitty and Wisby's (2007, p. 317) conclusion that *teachers themselves need to take the initiative and play their part in helping pupil voice to develop in the context of collaborative rather than managerialist cultures* which are said to deny pupils the experience of citizenship (Covell et al., 2008). This collaboration needs to be built on a foundation of respect. It is with some irony that, within the Respect Action Plan (Home Office, 2006b), addressing behavioural problems in schools is regarded as one means of promoting a more respectful youth, yet, as a society, we seem unwilling to respect young people in return. In focusing on this important point, Gaskell (2008) shows the interrelationship between young people's street and school cultures, and the way in which what can be regarded as school behavioural problems are actually young people's attempts to *act out other routes to gaining respect through for example peer groupings, violent posturing and actual violence* (p. 235). This is an issue that teachers can address, if only by not propping up such behaviour in boys through the reinforcement of misplaced masculinity. The latter is shown in Smith's (2007) work and begins at the pre-school level (see Brown, 2007). Pre-school interventions in the form of 'caring, responsive environments' are also vital to beginning to redress the already extant educational disadvantage rooted in inequality (Wilkinson and Pickett, 2010, p. 110). Thus, the current focus on citizenship in school, despite notable criticism of this initiative (see, for example, Furedi, 2009), needs to take on board the more enlightened approaches to this issue:

> by recognising that children, including very young children, are rights-bearing citizens...when children become aware of this, and when their rights are respected in classrooms and schools, then they are much more likely to think and behave as rights-respecting citizens.
>
> (Covell et al., 2008, p. 337)

Teachers too can reinforce their citizenship rights more vociferously. The campaign against compulsory testing ('Sats' or Standard Attainment Targets) by teachers in 2010 (see, for example, NAHT, 2010) shows that, despite managerialist pressures, the profession can still exert a rebellious agency. More such resistance is to be welcomed, perhaps even by teachers' using their powerful position to work overtly with such agencies as the Child Poverty Action Group to campaign against educational disadvantage. Rights-based resistance can also be achieved at the level of the individual, as Freire (1994, p. 3) pointed out, and perhaps the most radical work teachers can do is to *unveil opportunities for hope*. The ability of teachers to do this is attested to in the exemplary work celebrated by the annual Teaching Awards (http://www.teachingawards.com/), in the noted increase in the numbers of disadvantaged young people succeeding educationally and in increased opportunities for higher education over the last decade (National Audit Office, 2008). There is a need, however, for more positive ways of working with disaffected young people who will not secure, nor even aspire to, further or higher education. It is here that teachers could perhaps show the greatest resistance, by drawing upon their expertise as educators to reveal the futility of current efforts to force those young people to remain within a school system that is harming them. It is important to be reminded that:

> It is education, not school, that is compulsory; a fact ignored by studies that appear overly concerned with getting the truanting child back into school, rather than back into suitable, efficient and appropriate education per se.
>
> (McIntyre-Bhatty, 2008, p. 381)

McIntyre-Bhatty shows the weaknesses in most attempts to re-engage disaffected young people and her study serves as a salutary wake-up call to the fact that we cannot continue to accept the failure of our current school system to engage boys and young men on the margins.

There are a range of initiatives that aim to extend the opportunities of young people who are not gaining from full-time schooling, such as part-time attendance in further educational colleges, where they can attend different courses. Other initiatives have focused on sport (for example, Sandford et al., 2008) as well as using the help of football clubs in work on numeracy and literacy (Sharp et al., 2003). Mentoring is well established and based on work with individual young people (see also Chapter 12). Various faith-based and charitable organisations also offer opportunities. For example, Skill Force (an educational charity) offers an alternative curriculum to help young people gain vocational qualifications and develop life skills. The organisation's own highly favourable assessment is supported in an academic evaluation (Hallam et al., 2007), which highlights the importance of the positive relationships fostered between staff and pupils and, most significantly, the building of the youngsters' self-esteem, confidence and emotional well-being. Instead of increasing recourse to anti-social behaviour or criminal justice measures to tackle behavioural problems in schools, let us press for more such creative and engaging education, which offers a curriculum that addresses the needs and aspirations of previously disaffected young people.

The 'opportunities for hope' (Freire, 1994) in the current system can feel difficult to locate, when even government departments make observations like this:

> Britain's school system today is, frankly, unfair. Too often, opportunity is denied in a lottery of education provision where geography or parental income determines outcomes rather than academic ability.
>
> (DfE, 2010d)

Concluding this chapter at a time of major public-sector spending cuts and debates about the extent to which these cuts will fall disproportionately on the poorest sectors of society make it difficult to feel optimistic about the extent to which contemporary state schooling can help to break the link between inequality and achievement. The problems are structural and without an administration truly committed to broader social justice we are faced with a retrenchment of any gains made under the 1997–2010 Labour governments. The proposed 'freedom' schools will have from state control, and the increased emphasis on parental 'choice', alongside reaffirming commitment to the disciplinary power of schools and teachers in relation to problem behaviour, is highly unlikely to address the inequalities outlined in this chapter. It is not a simple case of 'the problem with boys'. The problem lies in an education system that is contradictory in the aims espoused and the relatively limited opportunities available, particularly for some working-class boys. We should not forget, though, the limited opportunities that are also available for some working-class girls.

# 5
# Safety, School Connectedness and Problem Behaviour

*Carol Hayden*

## Schools and safety

Troublesome (and troubled) behaviour is a feature of all schools and some of the behaviour is simply part of growing up, testing the boundaries of adult authority, as well as the changes associated with adolescence. The difference between 'troublesome', 'anti-social' and 'criminal' is an ongoing debate within this volume. At the most basic level for children in schools it is about whether or not the behaviour they present or experience in and around school affects their achievements in school and general sense of well-being, including whether they feel safe. All this in turn can affect their participation in the life of the school and their sense of belonging or 'connectedness' to school. Feeling safe is a basic human need and young people are unlikely to achieve in a context where they do not feel safe. Troublesome behaviour in the school gets in the way of the well-being and potential achievements of the young people involved. Furthermore, some types of behaviour in school are either criminal in their own right, or are related to the later development of criminal behaviour and involvement.

Concerns about school safety have become more prominent in recent years partly because of the growing awareness of high-profile (and rare) events that have led to multiple deaths on the school site. Such school shootings have occurred worldwide and over some time, for example: 1964 Cologne, Germany (10 victims); 1974 Maalot, Israel (26 victims); 1989 Montreal, Canada (14 victims); 1996 Dunblane, Scotland (17 victims); 1999 Columbine, Colorado, USA (13 victims); 2001 Osaka, Japan (8 victims); 2004 Ruzhou, China (8 victims); 2007 Jokela, Finland (8 victims). However, as Debarbieux (2006) points out, most perpetrators of these multiple deaths in schools have been adults. It would be interesting for the reader to reflect for a moment about whether this last point accords with their perception of who the perpetrators (and victims) are likely to be in these kinds of event. Although schools have had to become more aware of the possibility of mass killings on the school site, most of the time their focus is on the more common and everyday 'micro-victimisations', particularly those between young people. Nevertheless, major events often act as a reference point and culmination of adult fears about safety, young people and schools. Of particular relevance to this chapter is the fact that analysis of the background of young people involved in school shootings has revealed that they themselves had sometimes been bullied and evidence that the young people involved did not feel connected with or included in school and the activities of their peer group.

This chapter focuses on the more common issues that relate to feeling safe and getting into trouble in school, as well as the connections between these issues and out-of-school behaviour. The chapter presents the findings from original research in the form of a survey of young people from mainstream secondary state schools in a provincial city in England. The survey was carried out during anti-bullying week in late 2007 and is used as a point of comparison with other research available.

## School connectedness and belonging

A sense of belonging and feeling connected to school (and other organisations or institutions) is important in helping to keep young people safe and out of trouble. The need to belong is argued to be a fundamental motivation that functions across a broad variety of settings and influences cognitive and behavioural patterns. Failure to fulfil this need is said to create long-lasting pathological consequences (Baumeister and Leary, 1995). Schools are an important opportunity to belong or feel connected. The broader role of school in enhancing protective factors against adverse social circumstances and outcomes is becoming more appreciated in the United Kingdom. There is more research on this theme in the United States, some of which has singled out the concept of 'school-connectedness' as the most important school-related variable that is protective against adverse outcomes, such as substance use, violence and early sexual activity (Resnick et al., 1997).

One measure of 'school connectedness' in research uses ratings for five main statements that include the following issues: the extent to which young people feel close to people at school, part of a school, happy to be at a school, fairly treated and safe. For example, one study of over 83,000 pupils in the United States found that four attributes explained a large part of the variance in school connectedness between schools (McNeely et al., 2002). These attributes included classroom management climate, school size, severity of discipline policies and rates of participation in after school activities. School connectedness was found to be lower in schools with difficult classroom management climates and where temporary exclusion was used for minor issues. Zero-tolerance policies (often using harsh punishments like exclusion from school) were associated with reports of pupils feeling less safe, compared to pupils in schools with more moderate policies. Pupils in smaller schools felt more 'connected' or attached to their schools than those in larger schools. Not surprisingly, students who participated in extracurricular activities reported feeling more connected to school; they also achieved higher grades (McNeely et al., 2002).

The study by McNeely and colleagues (2002) shows that:

> the average level of school connectedness in all schools is 3.64 on a scale of 1 to 5, indicating most students in most schools feel attached to school. The restricted range of mean connectedness across the 127 schools (from 3.1 to 4.4) indicates that at no school do the majority of students feel totally disconnected, and at no schools do all students feel enchanted with their school career.
>
> (p. 144)

Other research has used a more detailed 18-statement self-report measure known as the Psychological Sense of School Membership, PSSM (see Goodenow, 1993), that also uses a five-point Likert scale. Using this latter measure Australian researchers (McGraw et al., 2008) found a very similar mean measure of 3.61 to the research by McNeely and colleagues in the United States.

Comparative research on bullying and victimisation in Australian and Japanese schools found poor psychological health was related to a lack of a sense of belonging to school (Murray-Harvey and Slee, 2006). This research also reminds us of the need to understand different cultural interpretations of commonly used concepts, such as bullying. The study highlights the differences in western interpretations of bullying, which tend to be more direct and often physical, and the Japanese concept of *ijime*, which relates to psychological harm.

## Feeling safe

The nature of relationships between young people is a major issue that relates to whether pupils at school feel unsafe (Cowie and Oxtug, 2008). Feeling safe or unsafe is obviously a subjective experience but is likely to affect pupils' well-being, attendance and achievement at school. 'Staying Safe' is a cross-government strategy (in England and Wales) for improving the safety of children and young people and is part of the Every Child Matters agenda (DfES, 2003a). Worldwide there are initiatives that explicitly relate to making school safer: for example, Safer Schools Partnerships (SSPs) (see Chapter 9).

The Youth Justice Board (YJB) for England and Wales commissioned a series of surveys of young people from MORI between 2000 and 2008 (see summary for the five years MORI, 2006 and YJB, 2009a, b). The samples were, in each case, divided between mainstream pupils and excluded young people, with the latter group attending a variety of 'education projects' rather than schools. Questionnaires were filled in during class time in school, supervised by researchers (the same methodology adopted in the original research reported upon later in this chapter). It is clear from the MORI (2004) evidence in Table 5.1 that most young people feel relatively safe at their school or education project. It is interesting to note that excluded students attending education projects are proportionately more likely to feel 'very safe' compared with young people in mainstream schools.

Perceptions of safety from young people within their education setting reflect the levels (and locations) of victimisations reported. That is, young people feel safer where they are least victimised. In all types of victimisation in the MORI survey, a higher proportion is reported

*Table 5.1*   Perceptions of safety at school or education project

| Relative level of safety | Mainstream pupils ($N = 4{,}715$) | Excluded pupils attending education projects ($N = 687$) |
|---|---|---|
| Very safe | 27% | 51% |
| Fairly safe | 49% | 26% |
| A bit unsafe | 11% | 5% |
| Very unsafe | 3% | 3% |
| Don't know | 4% | 8% |
| Not stated (i.e. missing) | 5% | 8% |

*Note*: % don't add up to 100, due to rounding.
*Source*: MORI (2004, table 4.4, p. 56).

to occur in schools for mainstream pupils. For excluded young people attending education projects, victimisation was proportionately more likely to occur outside school in community settings.

## Worries about bullying and physical attack

'Worries' are likely to interrelate with feeling safe or unsafe and with school climate as reflected in school connectedness, as well as experiences of bullying and physical attack. Echoing the patterns to do with feeling safe in school, fewer excluded pupils report being worried about being bullied or physically attacked, in comparison with mainstream school pupils.

One finding of particular note in Table 5.2 is that proportionately more young people in the MORI survey reported being worried about being physically attacked at school than being bullied at school. Again, mainstream pupils are more likely to be worried about bullying or physical attack than those attending education projects for excluded pupils.

## Bullying

Bullying behaviour in school is of international concern, and substantial research evidence is available on this issue, as we have already noted in Chapter 2. The first large-scale school-based intervention campaign against bullying was launched in Norway in 1983 by Olweus (1993), who has since been particularly influential both in academic debate and in the development of interventions. Smith and Sharp (1994) were responsible for the first evaluated intervention programme in the United Kingdom. There is now research evidence about bullying available from most European countries, North America, Australia, New Zealand and

*Table 5.2* Whether worried about bullying and physical attack

|  | Mainstream pupils | Excluded pupils |
|---|---|---|
| Being bullied at school | 35% worried | 10% worried |
|  | 61% not worried | 79% not worried |
| Being physically attacked* | 47% worried | 26% worried |
|  | 46% not worried | 60% not worried |

* This proportion *doesn't specify where*; see Table 2.4 for more detailed analysis of those who report being bullied or physically attacked.
*Source*: MORI (2004, table 4.1a, p. 50).

Japan. Smith (2002a) is one of the well-known UK experts on bullying; he bases his definition on the work of Olweus:

> Bullying is usually seen as a subset of aggressive behaviours, characterised by repetition and power imbalance. The behaviour involved is generally thought of as being repetitive ie a victim is targeted a number of times.
>
> (p. 117)

The two key characteristics that are often said to mark out bullying from other types of aggressive behaviour are repeated victimisation and power imbalance. It is the relative defencelessness implied by the 'power imbalance' that leads to the argument that intervention is necessary. Bullying takes various forms – physical, verbal, social exclusion and indirect forms such as spreading rumours (Smith, 2002a, p. 118). Technology has increased the forms bullying can take, such as text messages, emails and through the use of social networking sites such as Facebook.

A considerable amount of research on bullying and young people has established that bullying is relatively common but decreases with age. Although much of the research has been school based some research includes other settings. Bullying surveys produce fairly wide-ranging estimates of prevalence, depending on the way questions are asked and the timescale involved (see Table 5.3). Overall, Smith and

*Table 5.3*   Bullying prevalence

| Authors | Area | Respondents | Prevalence (% bullied) |
|---|---|---|---|
| Morita (2002) | Comparative study: England, Holland, Japan, Norway **(same questionnaire, Olweus revised version)** | 10- to 14-year-olds in school | *During a school term:* England: 39.4%; Holland: 27.0% Japan: 13.9% Norway: 20.8% |
| MORI (2004) | England and Wales (4715 mainstream; 687 projects for excluded pupils) | 11- to 16-year-olds (mainstream) 11- to 17-year-olds (projects for excluded pupils) | *During the last 12 months:* Mainstream: 23% Excluded: 16% |

Myron-Wilson (1998) have estimated that: *around 1 in 5 children are involved in bully-victim problems* (p. 406) in the United Kingdom, with similar incidences reported in other countries. For example, it is estimated in the United States that 23 per cent of school students report being the victims of bullying (Green, 2008). The Department for Education and Skills (DfES) research in England has shown higher rates of bullying with 51 per cent of year five pupils (9- to 10-year-olds) and 28 per cent of year eight pupils (12- to 13-year-olds) reporting being bullied in a school term (Oliver and Candappa, 2003). Similarly, the comparative study reported by Morita (2002) shows a higher rate of bullying in England than has been shown in some studies. Morita (2000) has highlighted that certain aspects of bullying in Japan occur at a higher rate than the other three countries in his study: long-term victimisations and the frequency of victimisations.

A number of roles have been identified in the research on bullying: most obviously 'bully' and 'victim'. However, sometimes the person who is bullied also bullies others; these young people are often referred to as 'bully-victims'. It is thought that 'bully-victims' may come from particularly problematic families and circumstances. Other roles include defenders (those who help the victim) and bystanders (those who stay out of things). These roles are important in the development of some of the responses to bullying (see Smith, 2002b; Young Voice, 2008). Smith (2002b) has outlined a number of 'risk factors' associated with being bullied: these are varied but generally relate to individual and group differences such as disability and special educational needs, race and ethnicity and sexual orientation, as well as family/parenting issues (such as over-protective or enmeshed families) and the peer group (having few friends or friends that can be trusted).

## Gangs

As with research on bullying, there is a long history of international research into 'gangs' and 'gang culture', much of it relating to involvement in criminal behaviour. Research in this area is beset with arguments about terminology. Hallsworth and Young (2008) argue that caution should be exercised when entering into the discourse about 'gangs' and that applying the term carelessly can undermine our understanding of the realities of the situation. The YJB research prefers to use the term 'troublesome youth group', whilst Home Office research used the term 'delinquent youth group' (Sharp et al., 2006). One of the key international experts is Malcolm Klein (an American academic), who has researched gangs in the United States and in Europe (the latter as part of the 'Eurogang' project). The 'Eurogang' definition of street gangs is as follows:

> A street gang (or a troublesome youth group corresponding to a street gang elsewhere) is any durable, street orientated youth group whose identity includes involvement in illegal activity.
>
> (Klein et al., 2006, p. 418)

In identifying 'gang members' Klein and colleagues advise the use of self-definition plus the indicators (in the definition above) to differentiate between 'gangs' and other youth groups. Durability, street orientation and identity connected to illegal activity are key to differentiating 'gangs' from other youth groups. Being a member of a gang (as defined by Klein et al., 2006) is associated with proportionately more violent, aggressive and criminal behaviour than that of young people who are not members of a gang. Klein and colleagues (2006) argue that:

> Many European countries face such youth groups, which may be called street gangs although researchers and policy makers often hesitate to call them this because they compare their own groups to an America stereotype.......
>
> (p. 414)

Practitioners in England and Wales (interviewed as part of research funded by the YJB) were said to be concerned by what they saw as the indiscriminate use of the term 'gang'. Nevertheless, practitioners and young men involved in group offending did agree about the nature of 'real gangs' involved in more serious types of behaviour:

> real gangs were distinguished by transgressing certain norms... particularly regarding the use of unacceptable levels of violence.
>
> (YJB, 2007, p. 9)

The YJB (2007) research concluded that 'real gangs' are more likely to involve young adults than teenagers. Group offending by young people was thought to be a wider phenomenon, but did not necessitate being part of a gang.

*Table 5.4*  Prevalence – 'gangs' or 'delinquent youth groups'

| Authors | Area/sample size | Respondents | Prevalence |
| --- | --- | --- | --- |
| Weerman (2005) | Netherlands, 13- to 17-year-olds in several cities, including The Hague | 1830 school pupils | 6% |
| Klein et al. (2006) | United States, 13- to 15-year-olds in 11 cities | 5935 school pupils | 8% |
| Smith and Bradshaw (2005) | Scotland, 13-year-olds in Edinburgh | 4299 school pupils | 3.3% |
| Sharp et al. (2006). | England and Wales, 10- to 19-year-olds | 3827 young people from the OCJS survey of 2004 | 6% (10- to 19-year-olds)<br>9% (16- to 17-year-olds)<br>12% (14- to 15-year-olds) |

Home Office (Sharp et al., 2006, p. v) research characterises 'delinquent youth groups' in the following way:

- Young people who spend time in groups of three or more (including themselves)
- The group spend a lot of time in public places
- The group has existed for three months or more
- The group has engaged in delinquent or criminal behaviour together in the last 12 months
- The group has at least one structural feature (either a name, an area, a leader or rules)

The above markers are based on the 'Eurogang' definition. Sharp and colleagues (2006, p. v) found that being in a delinquent youth group is associated with having friends in trouble with the police, having run away from home, commitment to deviant peers, having been excluded from school and being drunk on a frequent basis. This research also illustrates the different rates of prevalence according to age group, with 14- to 15-year olds having the highest rate of prevalence for being part of a delinquent youth group.

Gordon (2000) presents a more useful distinction between various forms of youth group, youth movement, 'wanna-bes', street gangs and organised criminals. A 'street gang' is defined as:

Groups of young people, mainly young adults, who band together to form a semi-structured organisation, the primary purpose of which is to engage in planned and profitable criminal behaviour or organised violence against rival street gangs.

(p. 48)

'Wanna-be groups' are defined as:

> ... young people who band together in a loosely structured group to engage in spontaneous social activity and exciting, impulsive, criminal activity including collective violence against other groups of youths. A wanna-be group will be highly visible and its members will openly acknowledge their 'gang' involvement because they want to be seen by others as gang members.

(pp. 48–9)

In Gordon's research both of the above groups self-identified as being part of a 'gang'. Pitts (2008) concludes that in trying to agree the definition of a gang we need to take into account the particular locality and situation we are researching. Furthermore, he notes that *gangs range from the relatively innocuous to the highly dangerous* (p. 20) and that we need to be able to distinguish between these different kinds of gang. He also points to the lack of reference to 'conflict' as a central issue and situation that binds 'gangs' together. Protection from and responses to violence are central features of neighbourhoods where 'gangs' are likely to flourish.

## Carrying weapons

Weapons carrying is a highly topical and emotive subject, particularly in the school context. Furthermore, the weapons available and attitudes towards carrying items, such as knives or guns, vary across and within cultures. It is also difficult to get accurate and meaningful prevalence data because questions can be asked in very different (and sometimes misleading) ways. In contrast with research on 'bullying' and 'gangs' there are no internationally accepted research questions or instruments about 'weapons carrying', therefore we will concentrate on the varying estimates produced by research in England and Wales and consider why these estimates vary so much. Table 5.5 summarises a number of these estimates.

Some surveys examined what schools as a whole experienced (Gill and Hearnshaw, 1997), others questioned teachers about what they had witnessed (Neill, 2008), while still others asked young people/or 'school pupils' to self-report aspects of their behaviour in the last 12 months (or

*Table 5.5* Weapons carrying in school in England and Wales

| Authors | Area/sample size | Respondents | Prevalence |
|---|---|---|---|
| Gill and Hearnshaw (1997) | England: 3986 schools | Secondary school teachers in 3986 school | Weapons carried by pupils, on school site *in the last year* in **12.1%** of *schools* |
| CtC (2005) | Inner London schools: 11,400 pupils | Secondary school pupils aged 11–16 | **23%** of *pupils* had carried a weapon anywhere *(i.e. either in or outside school) in the last 12 months* |
| Neill (2008) | 13 local authorities in England and Wales: 1500 teachers | Schoolteachers | **22.5%** of *teachers* witnessed a pupil with an offensive weapon, *during the last year (of which 5.2% did so monthly or weekly)* |
| Rowe and Ashe (2008) | England and Wales: 5353 young people | Young people: 10- to 25-year-olds living in private households | In the last 12 months: **3%** of *young people* carried a knife (6% of 14- to 16-year-olds) <1% carried a gun |
| YJB (2009a, b) | England: Mainstream, 4750 Excluded, 914 | Pupils aged 11–16 | Weapons carried *by pupils, anywhere in the last 12 months: mainstream:* **31%** knife or gun, of which 17% penknife; 15% BB gun; 3% real/loaded pistol or firearm *excluded young people: 61%* knife or gun, of which 32% penknife; 34% BB gun; 7% real/loaded pistol or firearm |

a year). Some surveys have differentiated by type of pupil (mainstream or excluded) and whether weapons have been carried in school or out of school (or both). As with the research on bullying and gangs, surveys on weapons carrying in the United Kingdom have produced different prevalence rates; partly because of the way questions have been structured, as well as the populations surveyed. Available research in the United States generally shows higher rates of weapons carrying on school property, than the United Kingdom: for example, one study showed 3 per cent of middle school students had carried a gun and 14.1 per cent had carried a knife to school (DuRant et al., 1999). A large proportion of the fatalities from 'school shootings' worldwide have occurred in the United States.

The Offending, Crime and Justice Survey (OCJS) provides more complex data on weapons carrying – showing this to be very much a minority activity (Rowe and Ashe, 2008). Questions about frequency of weapons carrying are also asked in this survey; this shows that around half of those admitting to carrying a knife in the last 12 months, did so only once or twice. The YJB surveys (2009a, b) have refined their questions from earlier surveys (see, for example, MORI, 2004) but still show higher rates of weapons carrying for 11- to 16-year-olds than many other surveys. These surveys consistently show higher levels of offending and weapons carrying amongst excluded pupils. To some extent these higher rates of weapons carrying in the MORI surveys may be also related to the age group (as OCJS includes young people up to age 25).

Available data on weapons carrying by young people in Britain provide a confusing array of estimates of prevalence. So, whilst the Communities that Care (CtC) survey is focused upon communities already viewed as 'at risk', it shows lower levels of weapon carrying than the YJB surveys, as does the OCJS, alerting us to the need to look carefully at how and where these surveys are carried out, whether they are nationally representative and what specific questions are asked. However, whatever study we refer to there are no grounds for complacency. A minority of young people do admit to having carried a weapon on the school site. The evidence points to particular challenges for adults who are responsible for keeping young people safe in the circumstances of large institutions such as schools.

## Perceptions of 14- to 15-year-olds in a provincial city

This next section will present the findings from a survey of 14- to 15-year-olds in one provincial city in England. The city could be described as relatively deprived: it is in the top third of the deprivation indices for England and Wales and overall educational performance is below the national average. Violent crime is twice the national average. However, as with most cities, these latter generalisations mask massive differences in circumstances of individual schools across the city: for example (at the time of the survey) 5+ GCSE passes A*–C[1] ranged from 23 per cent to 83 per cent; absence from 5.6 per cent to 14.3 per cent and special educational needs (SEN) from 8.6 per cent to 59 per cent. This survey set out to investigate the prevalence and interconnections between the issues already outlined in this chapter.

The survey was conducted for a multi-agency group concerned particularly about safety, youth gangs and weapons carrying. It was carried out during Anti-Bullying Week in November 2007 in order to try and minimise concerns for young people, parents and schools by asking about these controversial issues at a time when they were already being talked about in schools. Schools were understandably very wary at first and took part on the understanding that their individual school results would be given to the head teacher alone, who would decide with whom the results could be shared. Schools were concerned about the likelihood that a league table of institutions would be created by such a survey, either by the local authority or through unhelpful and sensationalist reporting in the media. In the course of working with this multi-agency group it was interesting to observe that agencies outside schools did not always fully understand why image management is so important to schools. A large part of the fieldwork for the survey was undertaken with the help of youth workers from the city. The involvement of the youth workers meant that access to independent help could be offered to young people at the same time as the field research was done.

In all, the survey obtained the views and experiences of 1426 pupils from the 14 mainstream state secondary schools in the city. Eight schools were mixed sex, three were boys only and three were girls only. One each of the single-sex schools was a faith school. In seven schools it was possible to carry out some consultations and activities with the young people that have helped to add meaning to the survey data. Around 15 per cent of pupils were from black and minority ethnic backgrounds, the rest were 'White'.

## School connectedness

The survey used the five-item scale used by McNeely and colleagues (2002) and referred to earlier in the chapter. The mean responses for each of the five items are shown in Figure 5.1 below, as well as the overall mean of 3.42, which is lower than the means in the United States (3.64) and Australia (3.61) discussed earlier. The range for mean school connectedness across the 14 schools was from 3.00 to 3.8.

Feelings on individual items were strongest, and most positive, in relation to feeling close to people at school, and most negative in relation to perceptions of teacher fairness.

## Safety

The overall rating for the statement 'I feel safe in my school', used as one of the statements about school connectedness was 3.52, with 84.5 per cent of young people giving this statement a score of 3 or

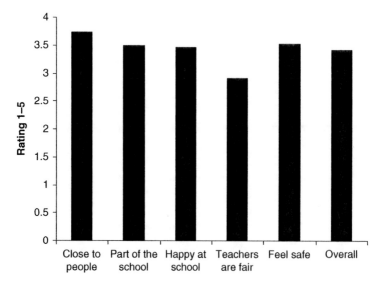

*Figure 5.1*   School connectedness

more (out of a possible 5). Our survey also asked about perceptions of safety in more than one context, rather than safety in general (see Figure 5.2). In many ways schools came out as the safest places for most young people. In particular, young people felt safest in the classroom.

Typical comments from students follow:

*I feel safe with friends but without them I feel less safer than normal...*

*At school I feel safe because of the teachers...*

*I'm kind of safe but there are lots of chavs and gangs...*

*I don't think we need any additional safety to the school! I think everyone's reasonably safe around the school.*

## Worries

Most (80–90 per cent) young people were not particularly worried about either physical attack or bullying (see Figure 5.3). Where young people were worried, this was focused proportionately more on physical attack and particularly on the way to school. Worries about bullying were more focused in school and on the way to school, rather than elsewhere out of school. This suggests that 'on the way to school' is a risky place (see Chapter 6) for some young people.

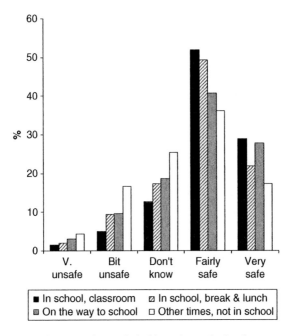

*Figure 5.2*  How safe or unsafe pupils feel *in and out* of school

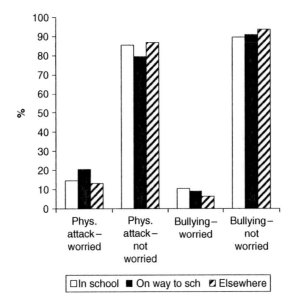

*Figure 5.3*  Worries about bullying and physical attack

## Bullying

The questions on bullying were based on those developed by the Anti-Bullying Alliance (ABA, 2007). The overall prevalence of bullying in schools in this survey is very similar to some other studies, with around a quarter (25.7 per cent) of young people experiencing bullying in school during the last year. We distinguished between being bullied 'a lot' (4.9 per cent) and 'a little' (20.8 per cent) in school; as well as out of school ('a lot', 2.6 per cent; 'a little' 11.6 per cent). The data show (in common with other research) that schools are places where bullying is more likely. Further analysis showed that overall, nearly a third (31.8 per cent) of the young people in this survey were bullied *either* inside *or* outside school.

Figure 5.4 illustrates how over three-quarters (78 per cent) of young people had witnessed or 'seen' bullying in school (22 per cent 'a lot'; 56 per cent 'a little').

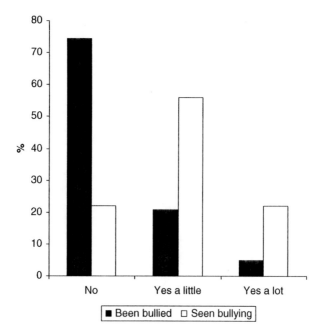

*Figure 5.4*  Percentage of pupils who have *been* bullied or *seen* bullying *in* school (over a 12-month period)

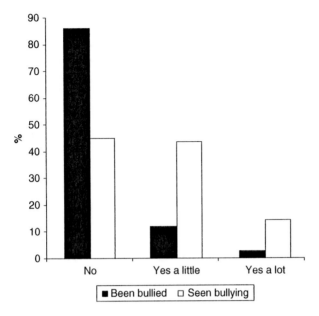

*Figure 5.5*  Percentage of pupils who have *been* bullied or *seen* bullying *outside* school (over a 12-month period)

Figure 5.5 shows that these young people experienced less bullying outside school; most (85.8 per cent) had not been bullied outside school and over half (56.3 per cent) had not seen any bullying. However, being bullied in school was highly significantly associated with being bullied outside school, particularly with the group who were bullied 'a lot' in each context.

In common with most surveys that include questions on bullying, those admitting to bullying are less numerous than those who report being victimised (see Figure 5.6). In the current survey 18 per cent of young people admitted to bullying somebody in school and 15.9 per cent admitted to bullying somebody out of school. This difference in prevalence might be explained either by one person bullying several people, unwillingness to admit to bullying or lack of awareness that the behaviour is bullying. However, given the prominence given to anti-bullying initiatives in schools in the United Kingdom, the last explanation seems unlikely. Indeed, when young people were asked to say what they understood by the word 'bullying' some young people gave

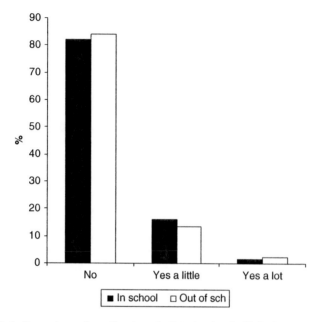

*Figure 5.6*   Percentage of pupils who admit to having *bullied others* in or out of school (over a 12-month period)

very detailed and accurate answers; the most comprehensive example follows:

> Name calling, physical violence, racial violence, racial discrimination, sexist discrimination, horrible looks, excluding someone from the group. Continuous picking on someone because of their difference. Internet abuse eg MSM, BeBo or Myspace. Mentally bullying.

Other young people gave shorter responses that showed they could distinguish between bullying and other forms of aggression:

> *Picking on someone (long term).*

Interestingly, some young people chose to write comments on the questionnaire too, for example:

> *I would never bully anyone.*
>
> *A heartless piece of action, people also don't think.*

## Gangs

The questions about gangs were informed primarily by the 'Eurogang' criteria (see Klein et al., 2006) with two funnelling-style questions, where a question is asked twice, first in a general way, then in a more specific way, at the start of this section (see White and Mason, 2006). We wanted to ask a question about whether young people were part of a gang that had a name, as there are some very well-known 'gangs' in this city. The local authority would not allow this question because they thought it could lead to conflict.

Overall, 23 per cent of young people in the survey saw themselves (self-nomination) as part of 'a gang' (see Figure 5.7), however, in most cases this related to being a group of friends who shared a number of things in common; they did not qualify for what constitutes a gang for criminologists. Young people were asked two 'self-nomination' questions and a further five statements relating to their 'gang'. These five statements were developed from criteria used by other researchers on gangs to differentiate youth groups from youth 'gangs' (or 'delinquent youth groups', as they are referred to in Home Office research, see Sharp et al., 2006). These additional five statements (or criteria) are as follows:

I have been part of a gang for 3 months or more. I think that doing things that are against the law is ok

I do things that are against the law, as part of a gang. We have our own territory/area of . . . . . . . . . . . .

We spend a lot of time together 'on the street'.

Using these additional five 'Eurogang' criteria, 55 individuals or 3.9 per cent of the young people in the survey can be viewed as a member of a youth gang or delinquent youth group that does things against the law, as part of a gang. Another 57 individuals, or 4.0 per cent, meet all but one of the criteria or self-definition questions ('near to Eurogang criteria' in Figure 5.7).

The range in the proportion of young people who meet all the 'Eurogang' criteria for being part of a gang across the 14 schools is: none in a small sample from a high-achieving and popular girls' school to 11.3 per cent in a mixed-sex school in a poorer area. Home Office research indicates higher levels of 'delinquent youth groups' within the 14–15-year-old age group, at 12 per cent. Comparison with the Home

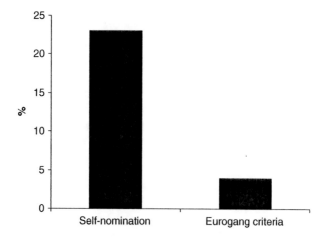

*Figure 5.7* Percentage of pupils who report being part of a 'gang'

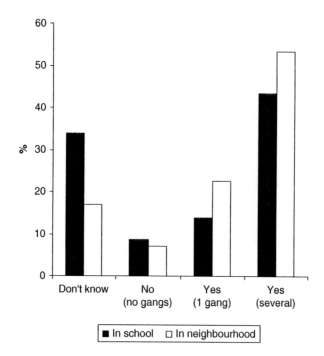

*Figure 5.8* Percentage of pupils who report 'gangs' in school or in their neighbourhood

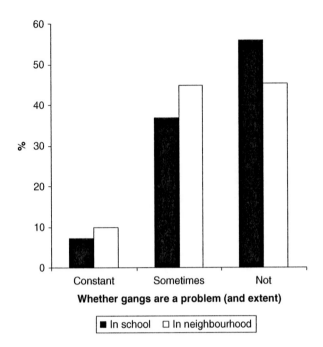

*Figure 5.9* Percentage of pupils who report that 'gangs' are a problem in their school or neighbourhood

Office survey shows a lower rate of 'gang' membership in our survey compared with this national data, especially when the age group in the current survey is compared with the same age group and higher rate (12 per cent) in the Home Office study.

It is clear that most young people (76 per cent) believed that there was one or more 'gang(s)' in their neighbourhood; with a lower proportion (57.3 per cent) believing the same thing about their school (see Figures 5.8 and 5.9). In interpreting this finding we should remember that for many young people 'youth groups' rather than 'gangs' may be what they are reporting.

Nevertheless, when asked 'what is a gang?' many young people connected the concept with breaking the law and carrying weapons:

*A gang is a group of people who hang around the street and go against the law.*

*A gang is where you are with loads of people hanging around the shops and walking the streets and breaking the law, fitting in with other people and carrying weapons.*

Other young people wanted to distinguish between 'gangs' and 'groups of young people' who were seen as a problem by adults:

> *A group of people who spend time together. Mostly innocent, spend time outside together because they have nowhere else to go. Are falsely accused.*

## Weapons

Many surveys (such as the MORI survey) ask young people about whether they have carried a weapon 'in the last 12 months'. The current survey also asked whether young people had carried a knife, gun or 'other weapon' in or out of school. We decided at this stage not to go into detail about types of weapon and frequency because the schools were not comfortable with more detailed questioning.

Figure 5.10 illustrates the proportion of young people in the survey who admitted to carrying some type of knife, gun or another item as a weapon at some point *in the last 12 months*. In all cases a much higher proportion of young people admitted having carried a weapon outside school, in comparison with in school. Overall, nearly one in five (268, 19.3 per cent) of the young people answering this question in the survey

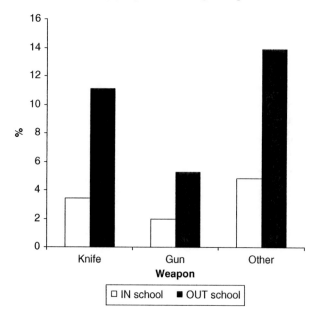

*Figure 5.10*   Percentage of pupils who report carrying a weapon either in or out of school (in the last 12 months)

admitted to carrying some form of item as a weapon either outside school or, in fewer cases, in school,[2] in the last 12 months. A small group of young people (35, 2.5 per cent) did not answer these questions.

Of the 268 young people (or 19.3 per cent of those answering this question) who admitted to carrying a weapon in the last 12 months, the breakdown of where they did this is as follows:

In school only: 14 young people, 1% of the survey
Both in and out of school: 71 young people, 5.1% of the survey
Out of school only: 182 young people, 13.2 % of the survey

'Weapons' carrying was the most emotive aspect of this survey for the steering group and schools involved. It was emphasised that any interpretation of these findings was measured, based on the question asked and informed by what other research has been done on this issue and with this age group. For example, evidence from the MORI (2004) survey shows that *most* 'knives' that are carried by school-age young people are penknives. Indeed, as one of the police officers involved with this research emphasised:

*Small folding penknives are not weapons per se and are often carried for lawful purposes.*

The reasons young people gave for carrying a weapon in the current survey most commonly related to self-defence or protection (as was also found in the CtC, 2005 and OCJS/Roe and Ashe, 2008 surveys): around six in ten (59.7 per cent) of all responses indicated this. 'Attack' was rarely given as a reason for carrying a weapon (20 of 248, 8 per cent). A variety of 'other reasons' for carrying a weapon were cited by about a third (80 of 248, 32.3 per cent) of those who responded to this question, many of which have nothing to do with either self-defence or attack. A comment made by a young person during the fieldwork makes the important point that:

*Anything can be a weapon if you want it to be.*

More young people knew about weapons carrying by others, especially outside school (see Figure 5.11). Young people are more likely to perceive that other young people carry a weapon for the purpose of attack (22.9 per cent report this, compared with 8.0 per cent when they are reporting about themselves).

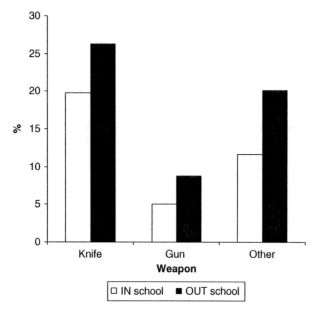

*Figure 5.11*   Percentage of pupils who report knowing of *another pupil* carrying a weapon either in or out of school (in the last 12 months)

## Conclusions

This chapter has explored a number of issues that present a picture of young people's experiences in and out of school in a relatively deprived provincial city. Although it shows schools to be a place where young people are more likely to feel safe, as opposed to outside school, it also shows a sizable minority who are victimised through bullying, as well as young people worried about being bullied or physically attacked. It confirms other research findings in the United Kingdom that although weapons carrying for the purposes of attack is concentrated within a minority, a bigger proportion of young people have carried weapons for the purpose of self-defence – perhaps because of the victimisations and worries already identified. 'Gang' membership (as defined by Klein et al., 2006) involves only a small proportion of the school population. Analysis of the associations and correlations in this survey shows how many of the issues explored are interconnected.

Potential associations between variables (such as bullying and worries, gender and weapons carrying and so on) were explored using the Chi-Square test to see if any of the observed differences in the survey were significant. Potential correlations between key variables at school level (such as the percentage of pupils who carry a weapon and those who would qualify as being a member of a 'gang') were also explored. All associations and correlations that are reported as *significant* are significant at the 0.01 (1 per cent) or 0.05 (5 per cent) level. In addition, correlation effects are reported (as 'small', 'medium' or 'large').

## School connectedness

At the school level, 'school connectedness' had a medium-sized effect in relation to school attendance: the higher the level of school attendance, the higher the level of school connectedness. Small effects were found in relation to the size of school, knife carrying and the carrying of 'other weapons'. Larger schools had a lower rate of connectedness. Lower rates of connectedness were also correlated with knife and other weapons carrying. However, *none* of these correlations were significant at the 1 per cent or 5 per cent level.

At the level of the individual pupil, school connectedness is strongly associated with many aspects of the survey. All associations reported were *highly significant*. The more connected young people felt to school the more they felt safe both in and out of school and the less worried they were about bullying in and out of school, or physical attack in/on the way to school. The more connected young people felt to school the less likely they were to be bullied in or out of school or to have been seen bullying in school. Lower levels of connectedness to school were strongly associated with 'gang' membership and weapons carrying. No associations were observed between school connectedness and ethnicity or gender.

## Bullying, worries and safety

The prevalence of bullying in this survey is similar to many other surveys. One in four young people reported being bullied in school *in the last 12 months* (20.8 per cent were bullied 'a little'; 4.9 per cent 'a lot'). The survey also asked about bullying outside school (16.5 per cent were bullied 'a little'; 2.8 per cent 'a lot'). The overlap between those bullied in and out of school means that in total around three in ten (30.8 per cent) young people in the survey had been bullied either in or out of school in the last 12 months. Being bullied in school is *highly significantly associated* with being bullied outside school. Young people who have been bullied are more likely to worry about being bullied. Young people who have been bullied feel less safe in school. Boys are more likely than girls to admit to bullying someone. Ethnicity only becomes significantly associated with being bullied at the 0.057 level (i.e. just outside the parameters set above) and only if all black and minority ethnic groups are in one category, compared with white students. A bigger proportion of young people are more worried about being physically attacked than bullied.

Overall, most young people feel safer in school than outside school (80.8 per cent feel 'fairly safe' or 'very safe' in the classroom; 71.2 per cent in school outside the classroom; 54.5 per cent when outside school). Perceptions of safety in school are not significantly related to whether the school is single or mixed sex. There are *no* significant differences in perceptions of safety in school by gender.

At school level there is a small to medium effect in relation to the percentage of young people who report being 'bullied a lot' and various forms of weapons carrying. That is, the higher the proportion of pupils who admit to weapons carrying, the higher the proportion of pupils reporting that they are bullied a lot. There is a medium effect on the proportion bullied a lot and the proportion of GCSE passes. That is, the higher the proportion of pupils achieving five A*–C GCSEs, the lower the proportion of pupils reporting that they are bullied a lot. There is a medium effect on the proportion bullied a lot and the proportion of children with SEN. That is, the higher the proportion of children with SEN, the higher the proportion of pupils reporting that they are bullied a lot.

## Weapons and gang membership

Overall, nearly one in five (19.3 per cent, 268) young people reported having carried an item as a weapon either in or out of school at some point in the previous 12 months. A minority of young people (2.5 per cent, 35) did not answer this question. Carrying an item as a weapon and gang membership are *highly significantly associated* at the level of the individual pupil and correlated also at the school level. The proportion of young people identified as being in a 'gang' is inversely correlated with the proportion of minority ethnic pupils: that is, the schools that were predominantly 'white' had the highest proportion of pupils identified as being part of a 'gang'. At the level of the individual young person, girls are significantly less likely to report carrying any kind of item as a weapon in or out of school, in comparison with boys. Boys make up 77 per cent (201) of those admitting to carrying any weapon, in or out of school in the last 12 months; girls make up 23 per cent (60) of this group (seven young people who admitted to carrying a weapon did not indicate their gender).

At the school level the prevalence of carrying any item as a weapon is lower in the 'girls only' schools (6.6 per cent, 23) in the survey. However, the overall prevalence was the same in the 'boys only' schools (23.5 per cent, 53) as the mixed-sex schools (23.5 per cent, 192). Boys were more likely (5.6 per cent, 38) to meet the full criteria for being a member of 'a gang' than girls (2.0 per cent, 14) (three young people did not indicate their gender). Interestingly, slightly more girls than boys reported that they considered their special group of friends to be 'a gang' (24 per cent compared with 22 per cent), and that they were a member of 'a gang' (24.8 per cent compared with 21.2 per cent). This latter difference is *not* statistically significant. *No* significant differences were found in relation to weapons carrying and 'gang' membership, when black and minority ethnic students are compared with white students. Young people reported that gangs were either a 'constant' problem or 'sometimes' a problem in their neighbourhood in areas where there were more 'gang' members identified by the survey.

The proportion of pupils with five A*–C GCSEs is correlated with all types of weapon carrying and the proportion of gang members in a school (medium effect). Carrying a knife is correlated with the proportion of young people with SEN in a school: *this correlation is statistically significant.* Schools in the research presented in this chapter illustrated the connections between poor socio-economic circumstances (specifically white working class), a lower level of academic achievement and greater challenges from bullying, weapons carrying and gangs. Bullying is clearly a problem that affects a lot of young people and it is important to note that for some bullying is happening both in and out of school. On the other hand, young people are more worried about physical attack than bullying. The connections between these issues present major difficulties to some schools, particularly those that already cater for children in poorer and more vulnerable circumstances. It is clear that the solutions to the issues covered in this chapter cannot be found in schools alone. Later chapters will explore the evidence about SSPs, the work of educationalists and others in addressing the issues discussed here.

## Notes

1. 5+ GCSEs A*–C is the key benchmark when comparing and evaluating the achievement of schools. It is from these results that newspapers, and others, have created 'league tables'.
2. Please note the percentages in Figure 5.10 do not add up to 19.3 per cent, as some young people admitted to carrying more than one type of weapon and some had carried a weapon both inside and outside school.

# 6

# 'Risky Places' – Young People's Experiences of Crime and Victimisation at School and in the Community

*Denise Martin, Caroline Chatwin and David Porteous*

## Schools, offending and victimisation

Schools have often been data-gathering sites for studies about victimisation. As we have seen in other chapters, bullying surveys have been around since the early 1990s (see Smith and Sharp, 1994) and a number of Home Office (Graham and Bowling, 1995; Roe and Ashe, 2008) and Youth Justice Board (YJB) surveys (see, for example, MORI, 2000; YJB, 2009a) have added information about offending behaviour and victimisation in this age group. Ongoing academic research on youth transitions and crime tracks a cohort of over 4000 secondary school children in one city (Edinburgh, Scotland) (Smith and McVie, 2003). However, some surveys have mixed up behaviours that are clearly against the law, with behaviours that may not be. Furthermore, some surveys do not always make clear where the offending behaviour took place. It is relatively rare to have research that provides us with a clear picture of offending behaviour on the school site.

Despite the lack of good quality evidence about any trends in highly problematic and criminal behaviour in and around the school site, it is common for teaching unions and the media to provide us with stories and anecdotes that fuel the perception of an increasing problem. These concerns (as we have argued elsewhere in this volume, for example Chapter 3) are part of the wider discourse about 'risk' and 'safety', and the anxieties adults project on to children and schools. The particular reference to 'schools' or 'pupils' within the latter discourse is sometimes a demographic description or grouping, rather than a factor within an environment that is adding to wider concerns about 'risk' and 'safety.' Furthermore, the focus on the school environment can fail to acknowledge places where children are more 'at risk' and feel less safe. Research reported in Chapter 5 illustrates (in common with other research) that young people tend to feel safer in school than in the community.

This chapter will begin by exploring the broader context of young people, offending and victimisation. It will go on to explore where this victimisation occurs, drawing on research completed by the authors in an inner London borough during late 2006 and early 2007. The chapter will conclude with a reflection on how young people as victims can be helped so that they feel safer.

## Young people, offending and victimisation

In popular discourse young people are more frequently considered in relation to their position as offenders (Brown, 2005). Although there is a growing concern over young people's safety in recent government policy (DfES, 2003a), their status as victims has often been secondary and much attention has focused on reducing their 'anti-social behaviour'. This is evident in the way that the victimisation of young people has been recorded. While the British Crime Survey was established in 1982 to explore adult victimisation rates, it was not until 1992 that the Home Office included those under the age of 16 (Aye Maung, 1995). Other studies of young people's victimisation, such as the YJB MORI survey, which began in 2000 (MORI, 2000), presents some data on the rates of victimisation among young people (aged 11–16/17 years) as well as their feelings about safety. However, the main focus of the MORI survey is offending rates among young people. The Offending, Crime and Justice Survey (OCJS) started in 2003 and similarly uses self-report data to explore young people's (aged 10–25 years) experiences of and views about offending. While victimisation is a consideration in the OCJS, the key focus of the study is a longitudinal survey on offending rates and anti-social behaviour (Home Office, 2008).

Ignoring or minimising the victimisation of young people is unhelpful, particularly when research (including the OCJS) has shown that offending and victimisation are clearly linked (Smith, 2004; Smith and Ecob, 2007; Roe and Ashe, 2008). Wilkstrom and Butterworth (2006, p. 41), in their exploration of adolescent crime, found that young people who were offenders were nearly twice as likely to be a victim of crime as non-offenders (69.2 per cent compared with 36.2 per cent). Furthermore, the mean rate of victimisation was particularly high for those with higher offender prevalence rates. In relation to specific types of offences, the strongest relationship was between those that committed and had also been a victim of a violent act. In the OCJS lower rates of victimisation of offenders were found – as compared to the Wilkstrom and Butterworth research – but the broad pattern was similar, with offenders more than twice as likely to be a victim of crime as non-offenders (50 per cent compared with 19 per cent) (Roe and Ashe, 2008).

Another major issue to consider, when thinking about rates of offending and victimisation experienced by young people, is that of accuracy. Findings from self-report studies are notoriously deceptive and can be accused of both underestimating and overestimating the scale and nature of a problem. Available evidence suggests that not many young people will report their victimisations to professionals, which means that many incidents of victimisation are likely to go unrecorded. For example, a Home Office study found that young people between the ages of 12 and 15 were more likely to report incidents of crime to either friends or parents, and that only 6 per cent of those sampled reported the incident to the police (Aye Maung, 1995). Although the police were actually told about 12 per cent of the crimes reported overall, these were more likely to be reported by parents or teachers. The MORI Youth Study (2004) also found that young people tended not to report crime to official sources, choosing instead to inform someone else. Over half (56 per cent) of young people in mainstream school (and 43 per cent of excluded pupils) reported their victimisation to parents or carers. Another common response was to tell a friend (43 per cent for mainstream school pupils and 38 per cent for excluded pupils) or to deal with the situation by themselves (26 per cent and 39 per cent respectively). This compares to only 13 per cent of mainstream pupils willing to report an incident to the police and 21 per cent of excluded pupils willing to do the same. This is a key issue as, in order to fully understand victimisation, we need to know more about the extent of it. This is an issue to which we will return. We will now explore existing evidence about the victimisation of young people and the types of offences they experience.

## Experiences of crime and victimisation

Although a focus on young people's offending is more common than studies of criminal victimisation in research and government policy, there is some good quality evidence about these victimisations and young people. Some of the key studies are outlined in Table 6.1. The

*Table 6.1*   Victimisation and young people – some key survey findings

| Authors | Area/sample size | Respondents | Key findings |
|---|---|---|---|
| Aye Maung (1995) | England and Wales 6–8 months in 1992, part of British Crime Survey | 1350 12- to 15-year-olds in school | 34% assaulted<br>23% had something stolen<br>20% harassed by someone their own age<br>19% harassed by someone over the age of 16<br>69% of victims had experienced more than one incident<br>High level of incidents occurring at school |
| Wilkstrom and Butterworth (2006) | Peterborough Youth Study, 13 state schools between 2000/1 | Nearly 2000 14- to 15-year-olds in school | Half had been a victim of crime<br>65% of those victimised experienced victimisation more than once<br>Theft, violence and vandalism were the most likely offences experienced |
| Wilson et al. (2006) | England and Wales: (third sweep, 2005) representative sample | 4890 (4164 from previous sweeps of survey) 10- to 25-year-olds; different age groups 10–15, 16–25 | 31% of young people between the ages of 10–15 had experienced personal victimisation (either theft or assault)<br>Males significantly more likely to experience crime than females |
| MORI/YJB Youth Survey (2009) | England and Wales in 2008 194 schools | 4750 pupils, 11- to 16-year-olds | 51% of young people in survey had been victimised (note – bullying is included, which isn't a crime)<br>69% of offences committed were committed by another young person under the age of 18<br>Most common offence experienced was theft<br>Boys more likely to be victims of crime |

*Note*: The findings selected here were common across a number of the studies and have therefore been used to highlight a few key issues identified across a range of surveys. These surveys provide a much more in-depth portrayal of young people's victimisation and should be viewed individually to get a fuller picture of young people's experiences.

study by Aye Maung (1995) claims to be one of the first to explore the criminal victimisation of young people in the United Kingdom. The research used self-completion questionnaires as an addition to the British Crime Survey. It explored a number of different types of crime including assaults, harassment, theft of unattended property, theft and attempted theft from the person, harassment by other young people and sexual harassment. The study found high levels of victimisation in relation to these forms of criminality among 12- to 15-year-olds. Other studies have shown similarly high rates of victimisation among young people. For example, the first MORI poll conducted for the YJB found that half of those surveyed had experienced some form of criminal victimisation. This level of victimisation has been replicated by other studies. The MORI 2008 survey (YJB, 2009a) showed a shift in the types of criminal victimisations that young people were likely to experience, with more young people experiencing physical assault and reporting having their mobile phone being stolen, as well as an increase in young people reporting being racially abused.

These surveys also illustrate that criminal victimisation often varies according to gender, with most indicating that boys are more likely to experience incidents of crime than girls. It should be noted, however, that some surveys (e.g. MORI surveys for the YJB) include bullying, which is not a category of crime (although bullying may include actions that are criminal). The gender patterns in relation to bullying are more complex (see Chapter 5). In Aye Maung's study, half the girls reported *no* criminal victimisation, compared with only a third of the boys. Wilson and colleagues (2006) found that males were significantly more likely to experience criminal victimisation than females (31 per cent compared with 22 per cent). Wilkstrom and Butterworth (2006, p. 34) also found that boys were victimised more than girls, particularly with regard to violence. Age can also be a determining factor in relation to types of offending and types of victimisations experienced. In general, victimisation reduces with increasing age.

For the first time, the British Crime Survey included a sample of 3661 children aged 10–15 years during 2009. This survey has taken a more nuanced approach to levels of victimisation (Millard and Flatley, 2010). The authors point out that Department of Children School and Families/Association of Chief Police Officers (2007a) guidance allows for incidents on school property, that are in law a crime, to remain within school disciplinary processes – unless the child or parent/guardian asks for the incident to be recorded as a crime or the crime is deemed more serious. Table 6.2 illustrates how the rate of victimisation varies

*Table 6.2*   Levels of victimisation from personal crime – different conceptions

| Different conceptions | % risk of being a victim | Number of crimes |
|---|---|---|
| 'All in law' | 23.8 | 2,153,000 |
| 'Norms-based' | 13.5 | 1,055,000 |
| 'All in law outside school' | 9.3 | 643,000 |
| 'Victim perceived' | 6.0 | 404,000 |

*Source*: Millard and Flatley (2010, pp. 16–17). Number of children aged 10–15 in England and Wales = 3,909,680.

according to the conception or definition of victimisation used. Interestingly, the lowest rate of victimisation (6.0 per cent) relates to whether the victim perceived the incident as a crime.

## Young people, schools and crime

Research about crime on the school site is limited. One important study does, however, give us some insight into offending in Cardiff city schools (in Wales). This self-report study of a sample of pupils from 20 state secondary schools (3103 respondents) found that a fifth (20.3 per cent) of all pupils reported involvement in one of five categories of offence on the school site during a one-year period as shown in Table 6.3 (Boxford, 2006).

Table 6.1 illustrates the differences in prevalence of offending behaviours between boys and girls. Interestingly, this study also reports varying levels of impact on offending behaviour in relation to individual and lifestyle factors, with the school context exercising a different level of relative protection in relation to these factors. The study confirms the

*Table 6.3*   Offending on the school site (over a one-year period)

| Offence | All (boys and girls) | Boys only | Girls only |
|---|---|---|---|
| Assault | 13.2% | 18.8% | 7.7% |
| Vandalism | 6.7% | 8.3% | 5.2% |
| Theft | 6.0% | 7.7% | 4.2% |
| Robbery | 0.7% | 1.1% | 0.4% |
| Break-in | 0.7% | 0.8% | 0.1% |
| *Any offence** | 20.3% | 26.9% | 13.6% |

* Some have committed > 1 type of offence.
*Source*: Adapted from Boxford (2006, p. 71).

importance of school climate (defined as encompassing school ethos, respect for authority and parental school interest) and adds to current understanding in the finding that pupil relations (defined as based on pupils' social capital and school disorder) also have significant associations with pupils' involvement in crime in schools. This sort of study is important in a number of ways: it illustrates the high level of offending that may be occurring in schools, it adds to the debate about the extent to which schools (in combination with other agencies) can address these issues and it reminds us that some of the acts dealt with as a within-school disciplinary issue could be treated as a criminal offence.

According to this research, much offending in school relates to what can be considered 'volume' crimes, including theft, minor assault, vandalism and robbery. This reflects the victimisation of young people more generally. There are also differences in experience depending on age group, status as a pupil (for example, whether the young person is currently excluded from school) and gender. Overall, excluded pupils and boys are more likely to report offending behaviour than pupils in mainstream schools and girls. Surveys that have been completed in relation to some forms of victimisation, such as bullying, have generally identified school as being a place where this more frequently occurs (see also Chapter 5). Aye Maung (1995) shows that a high proportion of offending took place at school; nearly half (46 per cent) of all incidents reported. In Maung's study, theft of personal property was the highest recorded offence in schools (76 per cent of all incidents), with assault being the second highest offence (62 per cent of all incidents), followed by the harassment by other young people (39 per cent of all incidents). A third of thefts were reported as also involving assault or harassment, suggesting a link between these categories. In contrast, Wilkstrom and Butterworth (2006) found a lower proportion (around a quarter) of the offences reported to them during their survey occurred in the school environment.

## Experiences of young people in an inner London borough

The research reported here took place in a London borough and was funded by the local authority who wanted to explore the level of young people's victimisation. The area experiences high levels of deprivation and also has a high level of resident minority ethnic groups. In comparison with the previous studies on young people's victimisation that have been outlined, the approach taken here was to explore the issue in more depth with a smaller group of young people. The study was focused on three secondary schools in the borough; these were selected by the local authority that requested the research. Interviews and focus groups were the main forms of data gathering in the research, although a website was also set up to encourage further pupil participation and comment. The website was advertised by posters and through the use of school assemblies. Assemblies also proved a useful tool to identify young people who were interested in participating in the research. The research team sought to include young people who had experienced victimisation and also to include a range of pupils in terms of age, gender and ethnicity. Overall, 70 young people were involved in the research, either in focus groups or interviews. The young people provided in-depth accounts of their levels of victimisation, but clearly their views cannot be generalised in relation to a wider population. In particular it is acknowledged that the young people who were willing to take part in this research were likely to be motivated by having had some experiences of victimisation, crime and anti-social behaviour.

## Crime and victimisations in school and in the community

It was apparent from the interviews and focus groups that many of the young people in our research had experienced or witnessed crimes and victimisations both within and outside school. These included robbery, 'hustling' (a terms frequently used by young people to refer to theft), emotional and physical bullying, 'gang' fights, assaults, criminal damage and theft (of belongings). Crimes of a sexual nature were also reported. Victimisations that occurred within the school environment tended to be reported more by younger pupils and often related to being bullied or theft of personal belongings. Fights between pupils were a frequent occurrence. The following quote illustrates common experiences and perceptions:

> This boy bullied me, but it was not a serious one. He was just calling me names and I don't know why he was doing it.
>
> (Year 7, Girl)

While many incidents that were reported did occur within the school environment there was a common theme from the focus groups and interviews that the real dangers were beyond the school gates and within their communities and were actually part and parcel of everyday life (Porteous et al., 2007). Typical comments included:

The area I live in is just based on crime.

(Year 11, Girl)

There is a lot of crime where I live [name of place], fights, thieving, smashing windows and things like that.

(Year 9, Girl)

Also, these incidents outside school appeared to be more serious and often involved the threat of or actual violence. For example, one year 9 boy described during an interview how he had been mugged twice on the way home from school. On one occasion he had a hammer held to his head. Two girls who were friends provided an account of being chased, threatened and then finally beaten up by a group of boys. The following story provides a typical account of the types of crime young people faced.

I was with my cousin, when he got his mobile phone stolen in the park… we were playing and we were going home and then some boys came and my cousin had his hand in his pocket so they said show me what you've got. He said nothing so they said 'don't lie to me' and they made him show them. So he pulled out his phone. And the boys took the phone off him and my other cousin and they told us to go out the park the other way.

(Year 9, Boy)

The most serious crimes reported to us involved a rape, attempted rape and sexual assault. The rape and attempted rape occurred outside of school. The rape victim knew her attackers as they were boys from her school whom she had known for some years. The attempted rape happened to a 14-year-old girl close to the vicinity of the school and a large supermarket. The girl was dragged into the bushes by the man, who then attempted to force himself on her; the girl managed to escape and report the incident to a security guard in the supermarket. Other incidents of sexual assault included a girl being sexually harassed (involving physical contact) by boys in her school.

## Risky places

When asked where crime most often took place, inside school was not identified as being the place that posed the most risk. The periphery of the school, however, was the first area identified as a 'risky place'.

For example, one pupil recounted the story of a young male pupil who was stabbed outside the gates of the school and had managed to get back into the school gates for safety. This is reflected in other findings, for example, a survey of youth victimisation by Catch 22 (2009) found that the area beyond the school gates was seen as one of the least safe places by young people. Surrounding streets, parks and areas tended to be named as dangerous and places to be avoided. Particular areas were mentioned as high risk because serious offences had occurred in these locations; frequently these offences included homicide and stabbings. The statements below provide an insight into the awareness of crime by these young people, and their associated anxiety.

> Someone was killed on my street a couple of years ago, another person was murdered at the pub where my dad used to drink about a month ago.
>
> (Year 7, Boy)

> There's a pub where junkies hang out, [name of road], at night, they shout and ask for money.
>
> (Year 8, Boy)

> There's a corner with a lot of people hanging around there at night. Sometimes, last month, there was a bonfire night and they were throwing them [fireworks] around in the streets and no-one came out to stop it because they were scared they might get fireworks thrown at them.
>
> (Year 9, Boy)

When asked whether she felt safe in her local area one girl said:

> Not really down my street but there has been a lot of crime there in the last few years like people having guns. I remember last year there was a person with a gun and they blocked the whole street and I could not go to school or anything. And there have been a few murders in my area. It does not really make you feel safe in my area anymore but I have lived there my whole life so you just get used to it.
>
> (Year 10, Girl)

High levels of insecurity were frequent among young people in our research. Both in the school environment and externally it was apparent that young people had developed strategies to keep themselves safe (Porteous et al., 2007). These strategies included sticking together in groups in areas where young people feel safer in a collective rather than on their own (see also Chapter 5). As acknowledged by a male participant in one of the focus groups:

> you need to be smart and stay in groups of two (any larger and there is the potential for conflict) and stay in areas where you are sure who is around.
>
> (Year 11, Boy)

Others in the research had become more aware of crime and taken other precautions to try and protect themselves. For example, a 14-year-old boy reported that, following an attack, he had become more cautious:

> ever since then, I've been looking around and keeping track of the situation. I go home early. If you see people who you know will cause trouble, you take a safer way.
>
> (Year 10, Boy)

Young people became more conscious about their actions and surroundings to address safety concerns, and they also practised techniques such as the avoidance of both people and places that they felt might pose a potential threat to them. Schools or teachers had also used strategies to try and help pupils, for example, for those who were being bullied, they might move pupils to another class or try to ensure that young people would let them know about the incidents and if they continued. Young people also tried to avoid bringing in goods that were likely to be stolen, although some just accepted that this was likely to happen and, despite having property stolen, such as mobile phones, continued to bring these items to school. On a more serious note, one of the boys' focus groups highlighted how victimisation could lead to weapons carrying as a means of protection.

## Consequences of victimisation

While many of the studies described earlier in this chapter have explored levels of anxiety about crime, they have often failed to explore the impact that crime has had on young people individually. Being the victim of crime can have severe consequences for young people both physically and psychologically. Both incidents of bullying and violence had led to injuries for young people. For example, one year 9 boy reported having a fractured ankle after it was jumped on by two boys. The rape victim had nightmares a year after the incident. Another female victim experienced panic attacks. There was a sense of their feelings of vulnerability in many of the young people's stories, particularly when they felt that their victimisation was unexpected. This was reflected in the story of the victim of sexual assault in school; when asked how she felt after the incident the victim replied:

> It makes me feel like a little child because I cannot go out on my own but I feel a lot safer going out with a big gang of mates or just my family and that. Also if I go out with my mates they always drop me home because they know what happened to me.
>
> (Year 10, Girl)

Feelings of 'being unsafe' were relatively common among the victims of crime in our study. These were a direct result of the victimisation and meant that young people either felt fearful of being by themselves in case they experienced another incident or were scared of being in certain environments, which included the school, within their local community, on public transport and even within the London borough in general.

Repeat victimisation was a common concern, being mugged more than once, or the continuation of bullying despite reporting it to someone. The girl who experienced sexual assault in school described how she had to face the boys who committed the offence at school and they were still calling her names. Despite thinking of changing school, a teacher persuaded her that this would not be the most sensible solution.

Parents were also reported as likely to feel more vulnerable when their child had been the victim of crime. Young people said that their parents had reacted by, for example, preventing them from leaving the house in fear that they may be exposed to crime again. Following an incident where two girls were chased and attacked by a gang of boys, one girl's parents *were scared and stopped me going out for a couple of months.*

## Guns and 'gangs'

There was a concern amongst young people that 'gangs' were becoming a more prominent feature in their area. The use of the word 'gang' here was the term that young people used, although this often referred to fights involving groups of young people. In the time period in which the research was conducted there was growing concern about the levels of violence in inner city London, particularly among young people, with media reports of frequent shootings and stabbings. Various interpretations were offered to describe gangs. As also noted in the research literature outlined in Chapter 5, our research acknowledged that interpretations of 'gang' behaviour can vary and are subjective. At times the definition applied by young people related to large groups of other young people that simply hung about together both in and out of school. Others applied the definition of gangs to groups of older youth or young adults who were associated with serious criminal activity such as drugs. Gangs were also seen as being organised along ethnic lines and specific groups were mentioned that were believed to be engaged in criminal activity, for example, the Triads and Eastern European groups.

There was support for the view that knives and weapons were becoming an increasing problem despite the fact that, as already discussed in Chapter 5, the research on this issue shows a varied picture. Many of the young people mentioned the use of weapons in their discussions in relation to crime, sometimes as a direct experience or as an insight into the current situation. The use of weapons was reported in a couple of cases, the girls chased by a gang of boys mention a knife being used, a hammer was mentioned as a threat used in a mugging. There was a perception that knives were increasingly being carried as protection and that gangs were becoming a part of everyday life in high crime and deprived areas (as in the area where the research was conducted).

> there are loads of places where there is too much crime, around here you see a bit of a copy of the south in America where there is lots of gangs and crime. Around here there is a lot of that because wherever I go, there seems to be someone carrying a knife. That is what mostly happens you see people carrying knives.
>
> (Year 7, Boy)

## Reporting incidents

Most young people in our study did inform an adult in authority when an incident occurred within the school environment. Young people frequently stated that they had reported incidents to their teachers or head of year. In one school a counsellor was mentioned, although this individual was no longer employed by the school as a result of funding cuts. Also, as shown by the surveys outlined earlier in this chapter, young people said that they were most likely to report incidents to their friends, rather than adults.

While some young people reported any incident they experienced to parents, others were reluctant to do so. Young men in one of the focus groups discussed their reluctance to tell parents about their experiences or anything that happened at school, for example, fights, because of their parents' fears about crime and the direct impact that such fear had on their independence. A consequence of telling adults could be restrictions on freedom. Some of the boys in the groups discussed how they had had curfews placed on them and they were not allowed to go out after a certain time at night. Some of the younger girls also mentioned their parents not letting them out after dark, particularly in the winter, due to the threat of what might happen to them.

As with research mentioned earlier, young people in our study were also more reluctant to report their victimisation to the police. Some comments suggested that this was based on a distrust of the police and those in authority, sometimes due to previous experiences. Young people reported getting moved on by the police or not being taken seriously, or treated with consideration. In the case of an attempted rape, the victim, who went to a nearby supermarket chain to report the incident, was left alone by a security guard until the police arrived an hour later. In the case of the girls who were beaten up by a gang of boys, the incident was reported to the police, but they did not turn up to speak to the victims until five days later. These findings reflect previous findings which suggest crimes reported by young people are often taken less seriously by the police, particularly when young people are viewed themselves as posing a risk or seen as a potential offender (Loader, 1996). Pain (2003), in her research of young people's experiences of fear of crime identified that young people, especially those already excluded (she included young homeless people and those excluded from school), experience a form of secondary victimisation by authorities who fail to treat them adequately as victims. As Hudson (2003) argues, once you are identified as 'a group that poses a risk', your rights as a victim diminish.

It was not just the police that were seen as ignoring young people's victimisation; some of the young people in our research reflected on how their victimisation had also been ignored by other adults. This is illustrated by the case of the 13-year-old who had had his mobile phone stolen in the park. He told us that there was a lady watching us *but she didn't do anything, just watching us*. A 14-year-old attacked on the bus was also let down by onlookers:

> I was amazed because there were people on the bus and they didn't do anything. I looked at them and they were silent, they didn't do

anything and they were adults. I was quite shocked. . . . I wish that the people downstairs would have stopped it. . . . I was thinking while it was happening why didn't they do anything, why were they just staring. I was amazed I felt like lashing out at them. I don't know them but its part of the cycle to help out I think.

(Year 10, Boy)

## 'At risk' or 'risky'?

As discussed in the introduction and above, attention is more often paid to the risks posed by young people, rather than the risks they face. Kelly (2003) argues that while adult concern about young people's behaviour is nothing new (and neither is youthful delinquency) we have arrived at a new era of 'anxiousness' that drives systematic responses aimed at targeting young people to reduce the risk they are perceived to pose. Kelly (2003, p. 167) suggests that: *institutionalized 'relationships of mistrust', can have a range of often negative consequences (intended or otherwise) for individuals and populations of young people.* In the external environment, fear of crime has come to affect the way that public spaces, where young people do 'hang out', are controlled and regulated (Pain, 2003, p. 154). Young people in the focus groups discussed how young people were seen as anti-social just because they hung about in groups. As highlighted above, a strategy in relation to keeping safe was for the young people to be with others in their peer group. According to the YJB (2009a), most (82 per cent) young people report being part of 'a group'. However, recent legislation actively prohibits groups of young people hanging out together in parks and the street. Dispersal orders introduced under the Anti-Social Behaviour Act 2003 allow the police and local authority to designate areas of concern as dispersal order zones. In these zones, groups of more than two young people can be dispersed if it is believed that the group could potentially cause distress or alarm to others.

Another issue was young people's relationships with organisations such as the police when they were in public space within their local community. The situation was described by one 15-year-old male from our research:

The only way that we can feel safer is to get young people involved with the police. At the moment when the police come it doesn't make any difference. At the moment if school kids are walking past another school they won't help each other. Down here if you look at someone you could get attacked. That's how it is. A few police have a bad attitude. They say something to us and if we say what they have said no-one will believe us. The police need to take a step forward to us.

(Year 11, Boy)

This finding is not uncommon across other research that has identified an adversarial relationship between young people and police. McAra and McVie (2005, p. 14), who explored the relationship between young people and the police, found that just under two-fifths of 12-year-olds had experienced some form of adversarial contact with the police; by the time they reached age 15 this proportion had risen to half. The most prevalent type of contact was being told off or told to move on. This is not to suggest that young people's engagement with street life is entirely unproblematic. As mentioned above, many young people are both offenders and victims; the problem arises when these positions are treated as separate entities. Seeing young people simply as offenders and designing policies around this belief ignores the close relationship between offending and victimisation already highlighted. Smith (2004, p. 14) argues that:

To a large extent they are twin aspects of the same social setting, social interactions, behaviour patterns and personal characteristics. There are probably casual chains running from one to the other in both directions.

In particular, Smith found that the most important factors explaining the link between victimisation and offending were getting involved in risky activities and situations and having a group of friends who also engaged in delinquent activity. Yet it is young people's status as offenders that is the first consideration when implementing strategies to deal with problems of crime and anti-social behaviour.

In addition, it is argued that risk has been defined too neatly in relation to spatial boundaries. In thinking about the risks faced by young people it is common to make a distinction between the public and private spheres. Home is often conceptualised as a safe place, whereas public spaces are seen as more dangerous. As Pain (2003) notes in her research, home is not necessarily a safe place, particularly for those young people who are homeless, as often the reason that they leave home was because of the victimisation they faced there. Furthermore, research about the abuse and murder of young people illustrates that parents and other significant adults – rather than strangers – are more frequently the offender (Cawson, 2002; Povey, 2009).

## Increasing safety at school and in the community

Much has already been done to try and increase security and safety in the school environment (as these are discussed extensively in Chapters 3, 9 and 12 they will not be repeated here). Safer Schools Partnerships (SSPs) (introduced in 2002) are now seen as possible for all schools and are widespread. Other initiatives and strategies to address bullying and other problem behaviours have been around for some time. All of these initiatives and strategies seek to improve safety within schools and, more broadly, the safety of those attending that school, though the effectiveness and underlying principles of some of these strategies has been questioned (see also Chapters 3 and 12; Simon, 2007; Hirschfield, 2008). 'Staying safe', as we have noted elsewhere in this volume, is one of the key themes of the Every Child Matters agenda and this is a continuing theme in subsequent government policy. The National Children's Plan (DCSF, 2007a) acknowledged the need to recognise the safety of children and young people with the explicit aim of making it everyone's priority. The subsequent Youth Crime Action Plan (HM Government, 2008) also highlighted young people's victimisation as a key issue to address, proposing to implement improved services for young victims. Other proposals in the action plan included providing young people with greater information about potential risks that they may face, including young people in decisions that affect them in relation to crime and trying to improve the relationship between the police and young people. The Metropolitan Police and other forces have attempted to do this recently, and have introduced strategies aiming to increase the level of youth engagement in deciding on the priorities for their local area. Various initiatives, such as the introduction of restorative justice approaches in schools (see Chapter 11), are common and, as Chapter 12 illustrates, there is a wide range of other approaches and initiatives designed to improve the behaviour, social adjustment and safety of children and young people.

There has been a flurry of relatively recent activity about supporting young people as victims and improving their safety, yet underlying contradictions remain. As the anecdote at the beginning of Chapter 2 reminds us, police in schools are still often there to deal with behavioural and discipline issues that would traditionally have come under the role of the teacher. This police role risks jeopardising the development of trust required to improve the relationships between the police and young people. At the time of writing, the coalition government in Britain emphasises improving 'discipline' in schools, which seems likely to increase punitive rather than the restorative approaches. The desire of many adults to try and control young people's behaviour is often underpinned by negative attitudes to young people in general (see Joseph Rowntree Foundation study on *Contemporary Social Evils*, 2009). A better understanding and appreciation of the links between offending and victimisation is necessary both for the individual young people affected, as well as for part of a strategy for crime reduction, reducing fear of crime and increasing feelings of safety.

# 7
## Teachers' Experiences of Violence in Secondary Schools

*Denise Martin, Nicola Mackenzie and Jane Healy*

### Is violence in schools a growing problem?

Earlier chapters have already noted the widely held popular perception that the behaviour of young people has somehow got worse and that media representations help contribute to this perception. We know that adult concerns about the behaviour of children and young people have been common throughout history and that it is difficult to verify these perceptions because of a lack of meaningful longitudinal data, as well as changing behavioural norms (Hayden, 2007). Teachers are not immune to this wider discourse and indeed are at the forefront of everyday experience and in contact with large groups of young people, so we need to take notice of their accounts. In Chapter 10, Visser presents the perspective of an educationalist. It is interesting to note that the word 'violence' is hardly used in this chapter. Educational researchers in the United Kingdom have been much more cautious about using the word 'violence' in relation to the behaviour of young people in school, in comparison with their European counterparts and other disciplines, such as criminology. As discussed in Chapter 1, some of this is to do with language and meaning – violence is more frequently seen as having a physical impact in the English language, whereas it is used as a more generic term in some languages, such as French (Hayden, 2009). It is also important to consider the terminology used in the context of debates about the criminalisation of social policy (see also Chapter 3) in which young people's behaviour is constructed as more serious by the label of violence. Once a playground 'fight' is labelled as 'an assault', it also becomes 'violent' and the response may be more severe.

There is a relative lack of independent academic research on teacher experiences of violence in the school context in the United Kingdom. Many of the existing surveys of teacher perception and experience are conducted with (or for) teaching unions. This needs to be considered in relation to how this might affect the sample. Furthermore, response rates are often low, which is likely to mean that only the more motivated (or victimised?) staff may have responded. That said, the events reported are worthy of our interest; they may not be representative, but they nevertheless provide frontline experience. The current chapter reports on a study of teachers in North London, Hertfordshire and Essex.

Violence in schools is increasingly recognised as a social problem (Debarbieux, 2006). In particular, 'violent' pupil behaviour targeted at teachers is seen as having a negative impact on the profession. Zeira and colleagues (2004, p. 150) stress that the way that teachers experience, feel and perceive this violence may impact upon their teaching performance, on their relationships with their students and on the school's overall social climate. Steffgen and Ewen (2007) report how violence can also impact upon teachers' emotional and physical well-being.

In the United States, for example, the Indicators of School Crime and Safety (see for example Dinkes et al., 2009) has been published in annual reports since 1998. Included in this is a staff survey that gathers national data on teachers' experience of victimisation. This shows that (in 2007/08): 7 per cent of teachers were threatened with injury; a similar level to 2003/4 when the previous survey was undertaken. This figure demonstrates a decrease from the mid-1990s, when this level was 12 per cent. The proportion of teachers physically attacked in 2007/08 was 4 per cent. This figure has remained relatively stable since the first data were available in 1998. In addition, this survey also reports that teachers in urban areas are more likely to experience criminal behaviour than teachers in rural areas. Teachers in secondary schools are more likely to experience higher rates of violence than others (Dinkes et al., 2009, p. 18). Gottfredson (2001), repeating earlier academic research from the 1980s in the United States, found that contrary to popular belief, victimisation in school generally involved minor incidents, but that it was the frequency and volume of these incidents that caused concern. The latter pattern of minor but frequent incidents was found in government enquiries into pupil behaviour in England (such as the Elton Report, DES/WO, 1989 and the Steer Committee, DCSF, 2009a).

While the United States collects annual statistics about the issue of violence against teachers this is not commonplace in all European countries (Smith, 2003), not least because of the lack of agreement that 'violence' is the appropriate term in relation to the behaviour of children. Nevertheless, some research in European countries has explored teachers' experiences of violence. For example, a survey of a representative sample of 399 teachers in Luxembourg in 2007 (Steffgen and Ewen, 2007) found that nearly a quarter (23.9 per cent) of teachers reported some form of verbal abuse several times a year. They also found a similar proportion of teachers in Luxembourg experienced some form of physical assault, as they did in the United States. Studies in Germany have also found similar rates of physical assault among teachers (Greszik, 1995; Varbelow, 2003 cited in Steffgen, 2009). While Blaya's (2006, p. 657) research did not look directly at victimisation, teachers' perceptions of violence were measured in England and France. English teachers were less likely to see violence as a problem in their school, compared with French teachers (12.8 per cent and 36.8 per cent of teachers, respectively). Other research on violence against teachers has also taken place in other parts of Europe (see Smith, 2003).

## 'Violence' in schools: the UK context

Over the years there have been a number of government enquiries that have included investigations of teachers' perceptions and experience of young people's behaviour in school. The Elton Report (DES/WO, 1989) and, more recently, the Steer Committee (2009) have responded to and reported on these issues, concluding that in general schools are orderly places and that the biggest issue for teachers is low-level disruption (see also Chapter 3). Nevertheless, certain things have changed, and in relation to the focus of this chapter (and as noted by Steer), the tendency of parents to challenge the decisions of teachers and schools and the use of mobile phones and computers to intimidate and communicate means that teachers are likely to feel more vulnerable in relation to how they respond to pupil behaviour. Furthermore, teachers and schools are undoubtedly under more pressure to maximise pupil achievement, a context that can amplify anxiety for both teachers and pupils.

There is no central register of violent incidents that occur in schools in the United Kingdom, making it difficult to examine the number of incidents, type of incidents, the frequency of these and where in the country they occur. There are a number of individual studies that have sought to investigate the levels of violence experienced by teachers in schools. In the United Kingdom, the National Association of Schoolmasters/ Union of Women Teachers (NASUWT) (2001, cited in Wright and Keetley 2003, p. 16) interviewed a total of 1007 full-time or part-time teachers in England and Wales. Of these, 27 per cent quoted disruptive or violent pupils and indiscipline as a major concern. The Teacher Support Network (2005) found that 84 per cent of teachers answering a questionnaire had been verbally abused by pupils, 29 per cent had been physically assaulted by pupils, 12 per cent had been abused or assaulted by parents and 22 per cent reported that incidents occurred daily. Furthermore, 63 per cent of teachers had considered leaving the profession or changing schools because of pupil behaviour. The terminology used in these latter studies shows that the focus of surveys within the educational service is usually on different forms of problematic behaviour in the school setting, rather than on violence.

Gill and Hearnshaw (1997) provide a picture of what a random sample of 3986 schools experienced in one school year. This latter study was undertaken by criminologists and is one of the earliest examples of the use of the word 'violence' in relation to the behaviour of school pupils. Selected findings from this research are presented in Table 7.1, which illustrates how physical violence is more prevalent between pupils, rather than between pupils and staff.

One example of research that begins to answer questions about trends in the behaviour experienced by teachers in schools is the two national surveys conducted for the National Union of Teachers (NUT) by Neill in 2001 and 2008. Interestingly, in terms of his use of terminology (as an educational researcher), the first survey referred to 'unacceptable behaviour', the second survey referred to 'disruptive behaviour'. Neill (2008) concluded that the overall pattern of behaviour was similar, although he reports that some serious behaviours did show an increase, such as pushing and touching teachers and teachers witnessing a pupil in possession of a weapon in school.

Furthermore, the tendency was for experiences of these sorts of behaviours to have polarised between 2001 and 2008, with some teachers experiencing more severe problems in 2008. Table 7.2 shows

*Table 7.1*   Violence in schools (at school level)

| Type of incident | % Schools reporting *in the last school year* |
|---|---|
| **Physical violence** – pupil to staff | 18.7% – member of staff – hit, punched or kicked<br>2.9% – member of staff – hit with weapon or other object, stabbed or slashed |
| **Physical violence** – pupil to pupil | 50.7% – pupil – hit, punched or kicked<br>6.9% – pupil – hit with weapon or other object, stabbed or slashed |
| Theft with threats **or actual violence** | 1.9% of schools |

*Source*: Adapted from Gill and Hearnshaw (1997, pp. 1–2), in Hayden (2009).

*Table 7.2* 'Unacceptable' and 'Disruptive' behaviour in schools (reported by teachers in 2001 and 2008)

| Behaviour (frequency experienced by TEACHERS) | Year | |
|---|---|---|
| | 2001 | 2008 |
| **Disruption to lesson** | % | % |
| Yearly | 3.1 | 5.2 |
| Termly | 5.2 | 6.2 |
| Monthly | 12.5 | 8.5 |
| **Weekly** | **68.9** | **68.5** |
| *Behaviour not reported* | *10.3* | *11.6* |
| **Offensive language** | % | % |
| Yearly | 4.0 | 5.2 |
| Termly | 6.7 | 6.4 |
| Monthly | 13.8 | 10.4 |
| **Weekly** | **60.3** | **59.8** |
| *Behaviour not reported* | *15.1* | *18.2* |
| **Pushing/touching of the teacher/other unwanted contact** | % | % |
| Yearly | 10.9 | 8.8 |
| Termly | 8.2 | 6.3 |
| Monthly | 8.9 | 6.6 |
| **Weekly** | **8.9** | **11.6** |
| *Behaviour not reported* | *63.1* | *66.7* |

*Source*: Adapted from Neill (2008, Appendix 2, pp. 13–17), in Hayden (2009).

that disruption to lessons and offensive language are frequent experiences for teachers, with over 60 per cent experiencing this form of behaviour weekly. On the other hand, pushing, touching and other unwanted physical contact was *not* experienced by two-thirds of teachers within a year, although 11.6 per cent (in 2008) experienced this weekly.

Research that has explored teachers' experiences over time has been conducted in Scotland. Munn and colleagues (2007, 2009) have examined a range of types of behaviours from general disruption and talking out of turn to aggression, since 1990. These are national surveys. Between 1990 and 2004 they found that an increasing proportion of teachers and head teachers reported an increase in serious indiscipline in their schools (Munn et al., 2007, p. 64). By 2009 the picture appeared to have changed for the better, although the exact wording of questions in the 2006 and 2009 surveys are not directly comparable. Table 7.3 presents the 2009 data.

*Table 7.3*   Staff perceptions of the overall impact of serious indiscipline/pupil violence (Scotland, 2009)

| Seriousness of impact Five-point scale | Secondary School Teachers (%) ($N = 1,427$) | Secondary School Heads (%) ($N = 237$) | Secondary Support Staff (%) ($N = 633$) |
|---|---|---|---|
| Very serious | | | |
| 1 | 8 | 1 | 9 |
| 2 | 16 | 5 | 15 |
| 3 | 25 | 16 | 33 |
| 4 | 30 | 45 | 24 |
| Not at all serious | | | |
| 5 | 21 | 32 | 19 |

[Question asked: How serious is the impact which serious indiscipline/pupil violence has on the running of the school?]
*Source*: Adapted from Munn and colleagues (2009, p. 59).

Table 7.3 illustrates that only a small minority of staff rated the impact of serious indiscipline/pupil violence on the running of their school as 'very serious' (teachers: 8 per cent, head teachers: 1 per cent and support staff: 9 per cent). Many staff rated the impact of these behaviours as 'not at all serious' (teachers: 21 per cent, head teachers: 32 per cent and support staff: 19 per cent). However, we should not lose sight of the majority of staff who indicate through their responses that these behaviours do have some impact in most schools. We can also see from this survey that head teachers tended to be more positive than teaching and support staff. It is also important to bear in mind the differences between individual schools. Teachers' experiences in the research reported in the next sections varied according to where they worked.

## Researching teachers' experiences

The next part of this chapter will use findings from an empirical study that was conducted in 2008. The aims of this research were to examine the nature and extent of violence experienced by secondary school teachers, to identify teachers' concerns about risks associated with their profession and the effect this has on their working lives and to examine teachers' perceptions of current government policies on violence in schools.

The study used a mixed-methods approach, collecting both quantitative and qualitative data. Firstly, a postal questionnaire was distributed to 2100 secondary school teachers who were members of the NUT in North London, Hertfordshire and Essex. This survey yielded a 13 per cent response rate (a total of 275 completed questionnaires). However, the demographics of the respondents were comparable to that of the NUT's membership at large. Following analysis of the questionnaire survey, 24 semi-structured interviews were held with 20 teachers and four senior managers in four schools. In addition, four focus groups involving 17 teachers took place in two of these schools. Informal discussions with members of the NUT and other educational personnel helped to inform the research and add to the data analysed.

## Defining violence

Standing and Nicolini (1997) highlight the importance of ensuring that any definition of violence should be relevant to the context in which research is being conducted. For example, the National Association of Head Teachers (NAHT, 2000) refers to violence as:

> Any incident in which an employee is abused, threatened, or assaulted by a student, pupil, or member of the public in circumstances arising out of the course of his or her employment.

This definition certainly moves beyond violence as merely a physical act and incorporates threatening behaviour; it also incorporates actions not only from pupils but also from parents or members of the public. It ignores, however, the potential for violence between colleagues.

A pilot study conducted by the authors in 2005, with university staff, indicated that a range of behaviours were considered to be violent by participants; these ranged from verbal abuse to more aggressive physical assault. Taking the results of this study and the NAHT (2000) definition we decided upon the following working definition:

> Any incident, in which a person is abused, threatened or assaulted in circumstances relating to their work as a secondary school teacher that was perpetrated by pupils, colleagues or members of the public.

This definition was provided to teachers at the beginning of the questionnaire, and in the interviews and focus groups participants were asked about their thought on the definition. Within this definition, the term violence covered incidents such as: verbal abuse; threats made to or against the individual or others; threats to damage property; non-verbal intimidation; physical assaults, for example pushing, shoving, punching, kicking; and sexual assaults.

The extent to which teachers agreed with this definition varied greatly. In the interviews teachers were asked to comment on what they felt about the definition applied in our research. In some interviews there was agreement that violence did mean more than just physical acts and should include aggressive and threatening behaviour. For example:

> Yes. I do. I like the, the idea behind abuse, and threats, as being part of violence. A lot of violent attitudes come through that without actually any physical altercations between two people, teachers-students, students, one on one, so I think that encompasses all of that, which is good.
>
> (Male, 11 years' teaching experience, aged 30-39)

This kind of comment corresponds with other research (Garland et al., 2007) in that behaviour commonly defined as 'unacceptable' is sometimes reported and experienced by some teachers as a form of violence. The cumulative effect of continual and minor infractions can lead to teachers feeling insecure about the environment in which they work. As argued by Debarbieux (2006, p. 31) *what counts is not a minor victimisation but its repetition, associated with other incidents of micro-violence; this repetition can have serious consequences on the victims, or even on the social corps.* As will be outlined below, our study also showed that it is the frequency, rather than the level of violence, of incidents that can have more impact on teachers' feelings of insecurity and of being under threat.

Conversely, some teachers were reluctant to attach the label of 'violence' to some actions and referred to violence as actions that were physical. Some participants were concerned about the use of the word 'violence' in an educational context and expressed apprehension about the term being applied to school settings. Teachers often said that the experience of an act as 'violent' depended on personal subjectivity. There were concerns that young people were already labelled negatively outside the school environment and that by applying or doing research into 'violence' in schools negative stereotypes could be sustained. This view is exemplified by the following quote from a senior manager:

> The great problem with all these definitions is...when you're talking about something which is relatively subjective, erm, as soon

as you............ see that incident as abusive to me, whereas somebody else would say well that's not abusive, it's just about managing a young teenager in a particular circumstance... there's always this sense of what is reasonable – so there's kind of a sort of greyish definition of what is reasonable and I think the sense of any incidence in which a reasonable person considers they've been abused or threatened or assaulted, then I could live with that.

(Male, 27 years' teaching experience, Senior
Management Team, aged 50+)

Despite the difficulties and discussions surrounding agreement about a definition of violence, when asked to provide experiences of violence teachers did provide examples of a wide range of behaviours suggesting that they did consider a wide range of behaviours as violent to them. Most of the incidents recounted did not include serious physical injury. The extent and type of violence experienced will now be discussed.

## The extent and type of violence experienced by teachers

Nearly three-quarters (73.4 per cent) of the teachers who responded to our survey had experienced some form of violence in the past 12 months, and over 90 per cent said that they had experienced some form of violence during their career as a teacher (see Table 7.4). In order to try and gain a broader picture of the extent of violence teachers were also asked to provide information about their colleagues' experiences of violence. Again, a very high proportion of teachers reported that colleagues in their school had also experienced violence.

Teachers detailed the number of incidents of violence that they had experienced in their careers. There was a great variation in the number of incidents reported, from those experiencing one incident (7 per cent) to those experiencing more than 20 (5 per cent) or 'numerous' (14 per cent) incidents (see Table 7.5). A third of respondents reported between two and five incidents of violence, with a further 12 per cent stating

*Table 7.4* Whether teachers had experienced violence in school

| Whether teacher had experienced 'violence' | In last 12 months (%) | In their career (%) |
|---|---|---|
| Yes | 73.4 | 90.5 |
| No | 26.6 | 9.5 |

*Table 7.5*    Violent incidents experienced in the last 12 months

| Number of incidents | Number of participants | Percentage of participants |
|---|---|---|
| 1 incident | 15 | 7 |
| 2–5 incidents | 66 | 33 |
| 6–10 incidents | 24 | 12 |
| 11–20 incidents | 12 | 6 |
| 21–50 incidents | 5 | 2.5 |
| More than 50 | 5 | 2.5 |
| Numerous | 28 | 14 |
| Not specified | 47 | 23 |

they had experienced between 11 and 20 incidents. Qualitative data in the response to the questionnaires also showed that the words 'often', 'too many to count', 'numerous' were used to describe the number of incidents that had occurred in teachers' schools. Many of the incidents reported involved minor, rather than serious, violence.

Table 7.6 outlines the forms of violence reported to us in the questionnaires. The majority of teachers who responded to the questionnaire stated that they had experienced verbal abuse. Teachers were asked to describe their experiences in an open-ended question. From a content analysis of these responses the types of verbal abuse and other forms of violence were further analysed. In relation to verbal abuse, out of those incidents detailed (204) roughly two-thirds (68 per cent) were non-specific – not directly aimed at the teacher – and involved some form of swearing and bad language. Less frequent forms of verbal abuse involved personalised insults towards the teachers, only a very small number of which were racially or sexually orientated.

While verbal abuse was the most common type of behaviour mentioned by teachers, physical assault also featured highly, with just over

*Table 7.6*    Types of incidents experienced by teachers

| Types of incident | Teachers' own experiences (%) | Colleagues' experiences (%) |
|---|---|---|
| Verbal abuse | 92 | 87.7 |
| Threats against them | 58.2 | 53.7 |
| Threats against property | 29.4 | 40.5 |
| Non-verbal intimidation | 59 | 47.1 |
| Physical assault | 68.3 | 77.5 |
| Sexual assault | 2 | 8.8 |
| Other violence | 14.1 | 8.8 |

*Table 7.7* Types of physical attack reported

| Type of attack | Number of incidents | % of all incidents |
|---|---|---|
| Pushed/shoved/tripped | 98 | 31.1 |
| Punched/hit | 57 | 18.1 |
| Object: object thrown at them | 48 | 15.2 |
| General/not specified | 37 | 11.7 |
| Grabbed | 18 | 5.7 |
| Kicked | 17 | 5.4 |
| Door is slammed/pushed on teacher | 14 | 4.4 |
| Spat on | 10 | 3.2 |
| Perpetrator blocks teacher's way | 9 | 2.9 |
| Scratched/bitten/stabbed | 7 | 2.2 |
| Total incidents | 315 | 100.0 |

68 per cent of teachers stressing that they had experienced some form of physical assault. Again, the types of incidents reported were analysed and broken down into different types of physical assault.

Table 7.7 analyses 315 incidents of physical attack reported by teachers in their open responses in the survey. These incidents were classified into different forms of violence. Nearly half (49.2 per cent) the incidents involved teachers being pushed, shoved or tripped, punched or hit. Having objects thrown at them was the next most common type of incident; this ranged from something small like a pen, to larger objects such as a chair.

Incidents of violence where physical actions were involved were a relatively high proportion of incidents reported by our respondents, but these incidents had to be analysed further to get a clearer picture of what was involved. For example, teachers' experiences were not always as a result of an incident aimed at them personally. Teachers recounted experiences where they had been injured in the process of trying to break up a fight or in order to protect one pupil from another. That is, they were often 'caught in the crossfire' in an incident between pupils. When all the incidents reported to us in the questionnaire were analysed, they were broken down into incidents which were *direct* (this included incidents where they were aimed specifically at an individual teacher) or those that were *indirect* (an incident where teachers were indirectly caught up, say, in a dispute between pupils): 58.9 per cent of teachers experienced direct violence only, 11.6 per cent of teachers experienced indirect only and 29.5 per cent experienced both types of violence. Some teachers had experienced both of these forms of incidents and certainly the point remains that a high number of incidents reported did involve quite serious actions by pupils. Although it is difficult to provide a typical experience the following open responses provide examples of what teachers told us:

> I have witnessed two fights in my school where students were attacking each other on the first occasion and were in a group on the second. I tried to stop the fights and on both occasions was shoved, hit, pushed. This also happened to a number of other members of staff. Students have also verbally abused me telling me to F*** off or to go F*** myself. As I am head of year part of my role is to assist when there are problems in lessons – students are very angry and can swear, make threats or damage school property. This has happened on a number of occasions.
>
> (Female, 7 years' teaching experience, aged 20–29)

> Kids fighting – trying to break up fights get punched, kicked. Pushed in corridor, kids not moving out of way. Threatened with violence, swearing when disciplining students.
>
> (Male, 3 years' teaching experience, aged 40–49)

> Apart from being rude and not following any instructions, the most common experiences are – pushing, shoving – verbal abuse – threats to 'sort us out' outside school – using 'F' word.
>
> (Male, 5 years' teaching experience, aged 30–38)

## Emotions and feelings

One of the other key considerations that should be taken into account is how experiences of violence have impacted upon teachers. Teachers were asked to provide an account of how incidents they had faced had made them feel.

Again, there was a variety of emotions expressed by teachers (see Table 7.8). These ranged through feeling angry (15.4 per cent of responses), being shocked by their experiences (13.6 per cent of responses) and feeling upset (10.3 per cent).

Teachers often experienced more than one of these emotions, as these comments from the questionnaires demonstrate:

> Shaken, frightened, concerned for the other students in the classroom/playground. Worried about how this would later impact on me and my status as a teacher.
>
> (Male, 1 years' teaching experience, aged 20–29)

Shaken and threatened. Still concerned, student said may damage my property. I still have to teach him which is not easy.

(Female, 4 years' teaching experience, aged 30–39)

Teachers' emotions could also change depending on the extent and frequency of the incidents they experienced. Recurrent comments in both the questionnaires and interviews related to feelings of insecurity and vulnerability, however, it was not always easy for teachers to articulate the way they felt about a particular incident. The need to present a professional stance often meant that teachers would try to conceal their feelings in front of pupils. It was apparent, particularly in the interviews, that some of the teachers were deeply affected by what had happened to them on an individual basis. Some teachers reported having to take time off work or feeling apprehensive about having to face the perpetrator of the act immediately following the act or the next day. There was a realisation though that they had to just 'get on with the job', while others resigned themselves to the belief that these acts were just 'part and parcel of the job'; a viewpoint which could lead to teachers' feeling demoralised. This discussion about emotions associated with

*Table 7.8* Emotions and feelings expressed by teachers in response to violence

| Emotions and feelings | Number of participants | Percentage of participants |
| --- | --- | --- |
| Abuse | 9 | 1.6 |
| Anger | 85 | 15.4 |
| Concern | 23 | 4.2 |
| Demoralised | 16 | 2.9 |
| Embarrassed | 20 | 3.6 |
| Fear | 53 | 9.6 |
| Frustrated | 29 | 5.3 |
| Leave | 4 | 0.7 |
| Little effect | 15 | 2.7 |
| Physical response | 11 | 2.0 |
| Sad | 32 | 5.8 |
| Self-doubt | 27 | 4.9 |
| Shock | 75 | 13.6 |
| Stress | 13 | 2.4 |
| Supported | 11 | 2.0 |
| Tired | 7 | 1.3 |
| Unsupported | 64 | 11.6 |
| Upset | 57 | 10.3 |
| TOTAL | 551* | 100 |

* Some teachers expressed more than one emotion.

teachers' experiences is an important one. It demonstrated that teachers' perceptions can differ greatly and that understanding these variations may be important in understanding how to deal with such issues.

## Variation in teacher experiences

Trying to establish the impact of gender, ethnicity and age was difficult in this research. There were a number of reasons for this. Firstly, due to the relatively small sample size, and, secondly, because participants were asked to classify their own ethnicity. There were some suggestions from the accounts provided that teachers did experience racism, although the number of cases was small. In relation to gender, little differentiation in experiences was found in the SPSS analysis. The only associations found were that men were significantly more likely to have threats made against them than women ($\chi^2 = 13.292$, $df = 1$, $p = 0.000$) and they were also more likely to have threats made against their property than women ($\chi^2 = 4.110$, $df = 1$, $p = 0.031$).

Future research could explore the variety of teacher experiences (by age, length of teaching experience, gender, ethnicity and so on) of violence in more detail. Research in other settings (for example, the probation service) has shown the importance of gender in relation to responses to violence (O'Beirne et al., 2004). This research identified that female probation officers were more likely than men to apply the terms 'anxiousness', 'vulnerability' and 'worry' as alternative words when discussing fear in relation to violence at work. Male probation officers tended to use word such as 'wariness' and 'concern', demonstrating a different experience and impact, compared with women. The difference in the discourse of violence applied could relate to male victims trying not to show their insecurities.

In the open responses in our research there was some evidence that gender could impact on how teachers responded to incidents. For example, male teachers expressed concern about dealing with female pupils and the need to ensure that any actions were not misinterpreted. Also some male teachers felt that gender was an issue in being able to control the behaviour of female pupils.

> Yes. I mean, erm, a girl fight I thinks [is] a lot more vicious, and they're a lot more determined, and you know, from my point of view, from a male teacher, they're that bit harder to separate. Because you can't go to, you know, you've got to be very careful where you touch

them and stuff like that you know. For example there's a colleague of mine in a school, and, erm, he separated a student by coming up behind her grabbing her round the waist and just twisting her and throwing her out of the way, and the parents made a complaint about that, of a sexual nature you know, so I find that if they're small enough, just get them under the armpits, and just lift them, physically lift them, and just drop them out of the way, you know.

(Male, 13 years' experience, 50+)

Some female teachers expressed concern about the physical form of some male pupils and that they could be intimidated by the sheer size and demeanour of older male pupils. One factor that was mentioned many times was experience. Teachers believed that level of experience was a determining factor both in reactions to violence and in the ability to deal with it. Many believed that teachers who were at the start of their career were more likely to feel anxious about their experiences and feel more threatened by things like verbal abuse or minor forms of disruptive behaviour. More experienced teachers felt that, in a sense, being able to manage challenging behaviour and 'have a few knocks' was a rite of passage to becoming a fully fledged teacher. Experience also meant getting to know pupils and understanding why they could sometimes 'act out', and then in turn having strategies for responding to their behaviour.

## Who were the perpetrators?

Most (79 per cent) of the violence reported to us referred to incidents between pupils and teachers. Many teachers said that young people often did not always think issues through logically and this was partly due to the fact that many adolescents are experiencing many stresses and strains, which could be difficult to cope with. So, in a sense, there was an expectation that at times young people could be irrational and act first then think later. Parents' attitudes towards staff was an area of increasing concern, and a number of teachers indicated that it was in fact a parent who had been violent towards them (parents accounted for 15 per cent of the violent incidents in our survey). This concern about parents is reflected in the following quote:

......some parents who are very, initially anyway, very aggressive, and I think if you are dealing with parents, you need to have either formally or informally, a number of strategies up your sleeve to diffuse situations with parents. Some parents will come in all guns blazing, and they are very aggressive. Now that usually takes the form of being abusive, but sometimes it's threatening, and, erm, certainly I have been in situations personally, where I have felt the behaviour of parents has been highly threatening.

(Male, 29 years' experience, Senior Management Team, 50+)

Teachers felt that often parents were blinded to the behaviour of their children and were not willing to accept their own active participation in the disruptive or challenging behaviour their child presented at school. Some parents felt that there was a need to personally challenge the teacher about their reaction to the child's behaviour.

## Teachers' narratives of violence

Watkins and colleagues (2007) warn against seeing organisational differences as the only way to identify levels of school violence. They argue that another key aspect of understanding violence is exploring the discourses of violence. As Watkins and colleagues (2007, p. 69) emphasise, narratives of violence as provided by individuals can be explored to *identify wider patterns in their content and style.* Our research identified that there were varying ways that teachers interpreted their experiences of violence. This included teachers' own professional identity, both external and individual interpretations of risks, and wider social and economic influences.

Waddington and colleagues (2006, p. 150) suggest that workers' perceptions of violence will vary according to the moral contact between professionals and their clientele. Their research established that Accident and Emergency staff who felt threatened or challenged in the course of their work were the most aggrieved, as their role is to help the patient. A negative reaction from the patient is therefore not expected and taken as a challenge to their professional status as a carer. In contrast, police officers were much more nonchalant about their experiences. Part of the reason for this was the expectation that during the course of their work they would at some time face aggression. Teachers often interpreted their experiences in relation to how they viewed themselves as belonging to a profession that incorporates a set of core responsibilities. One of the key roles for teachers was a 'duty of care' and the responsibility that they had to the young people under their supervision.

I mean the school is very good about establishing our relationships with each other and we all really regard ourselves as a family. But I have to say that as a teacher, you have to be willing to look at these kids from the right perspective, and you have to remember sometimes their background, you have to remember their personal situations, you have to remember that they're kids, you can't take things personally. All of those contribute to, I believe, whether or not you consistently then have these violent situations upon your doorstep, or if you've had maybe minute experiences with it.

(Female, 4 years' teaching experience, aged 20–29)

As well as a duty of care, teachers also described a need to protect pupils from harm. As illustrated earlier, teachers were frequently exposed to 'indirect' violence where they were injured as a result of getting in the middle of a fight or dispute between pupils. Although some teachers clearly felt that they had an obligation to get involved, despite a sense of duty, there were some who obviously balanced this against their own personal safety. This focus on safety could also be altered according to previous experiences. A teacher who may have experienced some form of violence may be reluctant to get involved in any subsequent disagreement between pupils. Certainly, teachers were conscious that in the process of intervening they themselves were potentially exposed to the risk of getting hurt. For some this risk was seen as too great, for others it simply formed part of the job. This relatively negative finding – that verbal abuse and minor acts of disruptive behaviour were incorporated into the daily routine – was quite commonly stated in open questions and in the interviews.

## The outside coming in

Violence in schools is not equally distributed, and studies have sought to identify whether those schools that face other social inequalities are more prone to violence. For example, Lindstrom (2001) found that schools in deprived urban areas were twice as likely to report violence than schools in privileged suburban areas. Teachers' accounts of violence often related to the wider context of societal and other external influences on young people. Teachers accepted that students' actions were not always as a direct consequence of anything related to the school environment but in fact could be influenced by the students' home life or external experiences that were out of the control of the school. During a discussion of experiences of how behaviour can vary across schools, one teacher pointed out that these variations can be determined by outside influences:

> We're not, like some little unit on our own, we don't exist outside of society in a kind of another dimension, I know some people think we do, but we don't, we're part of society, and we, we just have to work the coal face, that's all it is for us, everything that's going on out there comes in.
>
> (Female, 15 years' experience, 30–39).

This was reflected in a number of the experiences teachers had then had with violence. Incidents sometimes involved students who had been excluded from previous schools and had a history of problematic behaviour. Teachers also acknowledged that many of the young people that proved to have difficult behaviour were experiencing problems at home.

While there was acknowledgement of the difficulties that young people can sometimes face in school, there was a general feeling from some of the teachers that pupil behaviour had worsened over time. There was a perception that this worsening of behaviour was partly influenced by a general culture of disrespect among young people. In particular, teachers mentioned the fact that levels of what was acceptable had altered. An illustration provided was the use of swearing or derogatory language.

Other teachers were keen to emphasise that negative assumptions about young people were inaccurate and that the current media portrayal of young people was not representative of the majority of young people that they worked with. The following quotes illustrate the view that the extent of violence in schools can be exaggerated:

> There is *huge* media hype and a moral panic – about young people, about violence and about crime. Of course, if you work in an inner city school, you will experience/see some violent or potentially violent behaviour – but it can be overstated. This doesn't mean we don't have to deal properly with something that happens.
>
> (Female, 22 years' teaching experience, aged 40–49)

> Students are being demonised – many of the appalling pressures of being a teacher are causing teachers to behave less humanely towards students and to be less tolerant. I am *very* concerned that students are being blamed for poor management, low staff morale and huge pressures upon schools to be competitive rather than inclusive.
>
> (Female, 15 years' teaching experience, aged 40–49)

As highlighted in Chapter 1, the negative portrayal of young people in the media is an issue that can lead to harmful consequences for them where they are perceived to be a threat. Many teachers felt that wider problems within the education system were also critical to understanding why some schools experienced violence. A key aspect to reducing the threat of violence to teachers was felt to be a focus on making teachers feel safe and protected.

## Organisational responses to violence

One of the main aims of this research was to explore the reporting mechanisms in place and to examine the response to violence in schools. Strong leadership that treats staff with respect and acknowledges their professionalism is seen as key to creating a positive atmosphere in schools (DES/WO, 1989). Teachers who felt that they were being supported by senior management and that any claims of violence were taken seriously were much less likely to have a negative view of their experiences. The majority (86 per cent) of teachers reported the violent incident they had experienced to someone ranging from the head of year to the senior management team. Reporting to external agencies including the police was rare and only occurred in the most extreme cases. Other forms of support included fellow colleagues, friends and family and teacher unions, including the NUT. While teachers stressed that they did receive support, the quality of this support varied. Some staff felt that they were well supported and that the incident was dealt with appropriately or in the correct manner. Other staff felt that the support given fell short of what they expected. There were a number of reasons for this, often focusing on the belief that the behaviour would be repeated. For example, feeling that pupils had not been given an appropriate sanction so were therefore likely to repeat the behaviour in the near future or dealing with the incident but not the culture creating the behaviour, again making a repeat of the behaviour likely.

Teachers were also asked whether their schools had clear official reporting mechanisms. From the participants that responded to this question around 55 per cent said that they had, 40 per cent said that they did not and 5 per cent said they did not know whether such systems existed. All of the schools visited, and where face-to-face interviews with staff took place, certainly had behaviour policies in place and any action that was considered against these policies should have been reported. However, the complexities perceived in reporting incidents meant that not all incidents were reported. Bureaucracy surrounding the process meant that teachers felt that they could not report every incident that they actually experienced. In addition, some felt that the school management would not always respond to some of the minor incidents that they reported, as these were viewed as either 'part of the job' or as a result of the teacher's inability to cope with pupils' behaviour.

Chapter 3 discusses the issue of increased surveillance and security measures in and around schools, and Chapter 8 looks at Safer School Partnerships (SSPs), so we will not cover the background here. One of the schools included in our research had a 'lock down policy' where certain areas, such as the reception, were locked and, after a certain time in the day, sliding doors between corridors were also locked and only accessible with a swipe card held by members of staff. The school also had a security guard stationed at the front door and a police community support officer permanently attached to the school. Aspects of these measures were found in other schools, although having all these measures is not as common in the United Kingdom as it is in the United States. Scanners to detect knives and other weapons within school buildings have been suggested in recent years and taken up in some schools (Townsend and Revill, 2008), and teachers have increased powers to search pupils under the Violent Crime Act 2006. While powers to search pupils are not new, teachers now do not have to have the consent of pupils and the focus is on the potential threat of weapons.

Teachers in our research were asked how they felt about having these powers over pupils. Teachers' opinions were varied about the extent to which they felt that these powers were necessary and whether they wanted to use them. Some teachers felt that having the ability to search pupils would mean that it would reduce the likelihood of weapons entering the school environment and therefore felt safer in having the ability to search pupils. Others did not want to make use of this power and thought that it could damage trust relationships between pupils and teachers. Some teachers were concerned that the use of these powers were not appropriate for teachers, as illustrated by the following quote:

> Oh I mean you see for me, schools are places of education, you know, and I think, it seems to me that schools are I think, perhaps I'm biased here, but probably for some students the only part of their life where they have like a little oasis, and they, you know, they don't bring their street culture as much into school as they would outside, so I think if we then try to police that I think we've got to be careful that we don't mix the roles up so that, I already feel that teachers sometimes are

social workers, and carers, and educationalists, and parents, I feel like I've done all of those roles, you know, and now we're law enforcers.

(Female, 20 years' teaching experience, aged 40–49)

Some teachers felt comfortable about searching pupils' bags and did not think that this was problematic. Certain teachers also believed that, although not necessary at their own place of work which they considered relatively safe, increased security was inevitable in some schools. Furthermore, teachers were conscious of the impact that increased security could have on the teaching profession and did not feel that these powers to search pupils encouraged positive relationships. The power to use 'reasonable force' was not viewed positively:

'Reasonable force' will not reduce violence, but more focussed effort on improving behaviour, and a promotion of the importance of the teacher and education, valuing teachers and respecting them would be more effective.

(Male, 5 years' teaching experience, aged 20–29)

## Conclusions

This chapter began outlining what is often perceived to be an increasing problem of violence in school as experienced by teachers. While our research certainly demonstrated that teachers have experienced violence in the context of their work, the picture is both a varied and patchy one. The number of very serious incidents where teachers were injured or had to take time off work were few. Some teachers did experience serious acts of violence: being kicked, punched, pushed, having objects deliberately thrown at them and so on. While many of these acts did not result in injuries, they could still cause distress to those that experienced them, particularly if they occurred more than once. On the other hand, a number of the acts reported as 'violence' by teachers were verbal abuse or incidents that were not directed at them individually. This leads us to the view that there needs to be much clearer distinctions made about the nature and intent of 'violent' incidents experienced by teachers. Verbal abuse or other minor forms of problem behaviour can have an impact on teachers, especially if this is a frequent experience. It is important to recognise this in any development of an agreed way of classifying and recording problem behaviour in schools. While not necessarily experienced as 'violent', it is still important that management record or keep track of these *incivilities*. As Waddington and colleagues (2006, p. 171) argue,

> 'dismissing incidents that distress and disturb staff as just "part of the job" proclaims loud and clear that "nobody cares" '.

The reactions within a school to violence are critical, failure to acknowledge 'violence' as an issue means that staff can feel unsupported, leading them to leave the profession.

Teachers' experiences also varied according to their own personal narratives of violence. How they interpreted acts of violence was determined by a number of factors, including the school ethos, but also through teachers' professional identity and role in the school. External influences about wider societal and cultural shifts could shape teachers' perceptions of whether violence as an issue in schools had worsened over time. Variations in the school climate contributed to whether teachers felt that school violence was problematic in their institution.

There is a need to acknowledge that most schools do operate successfully without the levels of violence portrayed by the media. According to Astor and colleagues (2010), greater understanding of the school context in which violence occurs is needed, taking into consideration both family and community relations as well as social-organisational factors such as teacher–student relationships, class size, teacher turnover and teacher training needs. However, the difficulty remains that schools that do need support may fail to speak up if they can be judged on their ability to 'control' pupils behaviour. In addition, the thirst for more 'security' and general risk aversion may dominate responses, ignoring the promise of other strategies, such as restorative approaches, that focus on conflict resolution (see Chapters 11 and 12).

# 8

# From *Troublesome* to *Criminal*: School Exclusion as the 'tipping point' in Parents' Narratives of Youth Offending

*Amanda Holt*

## Exclusion from school and offending behaviour

Much research has explored the links between school exclusion and offending behaviour in young people (Graham and Bowling, 1995; Hayden and Martin, 1998; Ball and Connelly, 2000; Berridge et al., 2001), as well as truancy and offending behaviour (Smith et al., 2001; McCormack, 2005), and indeed the links between truancy and school exclusion (Hodgson and Webb, 2005).[1] However, as Hayward and colleagues (2004) suggest, it would appear that it is the *lack of school participation*, rather than the particular reason for this (including exclusion or truancy), that appears to be the key issue in relation to offending behaviour. Research on 'school connectedness' (see Chapter 5) supports this argument. Furthermore, evidence about the links between (the lack of) school participation or exclusion and offending behaviour suggests that the links are complex and are not the product of a simple causal relationship.

Berridge and colleagues (2001) examined police data on 263 young people across six local authorities and found a complex relationship between permanent exclusion and subsequent offending. A third of young people had no official record of offending either before or after a permanent exclusion, although more than four in ten did have a record of offending after exclusion, when they had no record before. Moreover, where official records of offending followed permanent exclusion, there was often a significant time lag, which was as much as one year or more for half the sample. Berridge and colleagues (2001, p. 59) conclude that this made it difficult to posit a causal relationship between permanent exclusion and the official records of offending. However, follow-up interviews with some of this sample suggested that school exclusion may have been the catalyst that instigated a host of other psychosocial changes, which are likely to have led to subsequent offending. These changes included significant shifts in identity, family relationships, structuring routines and peer interaction, with a loss of pro-social peers and an increase in time spent with other excluded young people. Smaller scale research by Hodgson and Webb (2005), involving interviews with 56 young people who had been permanently excluded from school, found much higher rates (90 per cent) of offending *prior* to the date of their permanent exclusion. The MORI self-report pupil surveys, conducted for the Youth Justice Board (YJB), use two samples – mainstream pupils and pupils in educational facilities for excluded pupils – and have routinely found much higher levels of self-reported offending in the excluded sample. For example, in 2008, 23 per cent of pupils in mainstream schools admitted to committing a criminal offence, compared to 64 per cent of excluded pupils (YJB, 2009a, b).

These latter surveys tell us a lot about the prevalence of offending behaviour and associations between other aspects of young people's lives, but they do not give any insight into the lived experiences of young offenders.

Research suggests that parents might play a role in mediating what happens to a young person following exclusion from school. Hodgson and Webb (2005) found that parental practices were a key mediator in this process, with many young people reporting that they were *less likely* to offend following exclusion because their parents had 'grounded' them as a response; those young people whose parents did not take action were likely to increase their offending following exclusion. This mediating role of parents was also identified in an earlier study, which reported that almost half of non-truanting pupils claimed that it was the fear of their parents finding out which prevented them from truanting (O'Keefe, 1993). However, while there is much research which identifies a lack of parental supervision as a key 'risk factor' in young people's trajectory into offending (Graham and Bowling, 1995; Farrington and Welsh, 2007), it is again too simplistic to suggest this as a causal model. Much research looking at school exclusion has found high levels of social and economic disadvantage amongst pupils who experience school exclusion (Hayden, 2000, 2007; McAra, 2004; Hodgson and Webb, 2005; McCrystal et al., 2007). Indeed, government-monitoring data on exclusion illustrate the connection between exclusion from school and disadvantage – in relation to the over-representation of children on free school meals, those with special educational needs and particular minority ethnic groups (see Chapter 3). Research also indicates that these same disadvantages shape the ways in which parents are able to supervise and 'parent' their children (Drakeford and McCarthy, 2000; Ghate and Hazell, 2002). Thus, without taking account of the wider structural and institutional landscape of school exclusion, offending behaviour and parenting practices, we risk limiting our analytical lens to only the parent–child dynamic, which can quickly enable the blaming of individuals. As Blyth and Milner (1994) noted some time ago, 'blaming the victim' has certainly been a common feature of discourses of school exclusion, and continues to be so.

## The legal responsibilities of schools and parents

Chapter 3 explains the different types of exclusion available and highlights some of the complexities surrounding the rights and responsibilities for school attendance that may face parents who have children excluded from school. Of relevance here is a child's *right* to education (as set out in Article 28 of the United Nations Convention on the Rights of the Child (UNCRC), 1992) and the disjuncture between parents' and schools' *responsibilities* in enabling this. The Education Act (1996) lays down the responsibilities of the parent in relation to their child's schooling, requiring that parents ensure that their child attends school on time each day unless the child is being educated at home (in way that has been approved by the local authority) or has been provided with alternative provision (such as a home tutor or a place at a pupil referral unit, PRU). The school attendance order and the education supervision order are available to local authorities to enforce this parental responsibility, after which, under Section 444 of the Education Act (1996), prosecution and a £2500 fine and/or imprisonment can follow. Other measures made available through the criminal justice legislature include penalty notices, parenting contracts and parenting orders (see also Chapter 2); the latter threaten parents with further summary prosecution and/or a fine of up to £2000 if their parental responsibilities in relation to school attendance are not met. Home-School Agreements (see Chapter 3), while not legally binding, have arguably served to further reinforce a relationship between parent and school that is less collaborative and more adversarial (Hood, 1999). Like parenting contracts and orders, Home-School Agreements operate under the assumption that parents have influence over their child's behaviour in school (Hayden, 2007). Ensuring Children's Right to Education (DCSF, 2008a) is the policy document that sets out these parental responsibility measures; its title is perhaps a telling indication of the way in which children's rights are increasingly set up *in opposition to* parent's responsibilities in government policy, the possible consequences of which are discussed later in this chapter.

In parallel, schools and local education authorities have a number of responsibilities towards the pupils who they exclude, particularly in light of the Every Child Matters (DfES, 2003a) agenda and the Common Assessment Framework (CAF), which aims to ensure a consistency of response across local authorities and agencies working with children and young people. Head teachers must inform parents in writing of the length and reasons for exclusion, together with the procedures for appeal against the decision and the contact details of a specialist advisor. By the sixth day of exclusion, either the education department within the local authority (for permanent exclusions) or the school (for fixed-term exclusions) should provide the pupil with alternative educational provision (such as setting and marking work). In the case of a permanent exclusion, this may take the form of an alternative school, home tuition or a PRU, with the recommendation that excluded pupils receive approximately five hours of supervised education or another activity a day (DCSF, 2008a). However, in relation to schools and local authorities meeting these responsibilities, research that has investigated the long-term prospects of young people who are excluded from school paints a bleak picture. In a study looking at excluded young people from ten local education authorities, Daniels and colleagues (2003) reported that only 28 per cent of the sample passed one GCSE, and that 50 per cent were not in education, training or employment (NEET) two years after their exclusion. Furthermore, Daniels and colleagues reported that post-exclusion provision tended to be patchy, and was primarily determined by what local resources were available, rather than by the needs of the child or young person.

To reiterate, while there are clearly links between exclusion and offending, evidence suggests that this relationship is in no way linear, and a number of mediating factors – not least structural disadvantage – complicate this. Furthermore, while parenting constitutes one such mediating factor, this should not be understood within a linear causal model as structural disadvantage shapes the ability to parent effectively. Nevertheless, the dominance of such neat causal discourses, within policy and politics, raise interesting questions as to how parents might understand and account for their child's offending behaviour when school exclusion has featured in their children's lives, as does the question of how such parents navigate the contradictory terrain upon which the responsibilities of schools and parents play out. The remainder of this chapter explores these questions.

## Researching parents' narrative accounts of their child's involvement in offending

The findings discussed in this chapter come from a larger study, which examined parents' experiences of their child's alleged involvement in offending and their subsequent involvement in the youth justice system (see Holt, 2009a). The study also sought to explore parents' experiences of receiving a parenting order as a result of this, with a particular focus on the implications for parents' identity as a moral subject within wider cultural discourses of parental blame (see Holt, 2010a, b). Seventeen parents (15 mothers and two fathers) were recruited from four youth offending teams (YOTs) across England and were asked by the local parenting practitioners if they would be willing to participate in the research, after which the researcher contacted them. Participants had been issued with at least one parenting order during the previous two years and had attended, or were currently attending, a YOT-based parenting support programme as a condition of the order. The children in question (15 were sons, two were daughters) had been convicted of at least one offence at the time of the interview, and these offences included theft, assault, burglary and criminal damage. The young people had also received a court order as part of their sentence, ranging from anti-social behaviour orders (ASBOs) to detention and training orders (DTOs). The young people were aged between 12 and 15 years at the time of their offence(s).

## Using narrative in social research

To explore experiences of parenting a young person who is involved in offending, taking a narrative approach was considered to be a particularly appropriate method for both the production and analysis of data. Such experiences in their entirety will have taken course over a number of years and will constitute episodes that lack contours in both space and time. Thus, by enabling participants to assemble a *story* out of these episodes, both participant and researcher can 'impose order on the flow of experience' (Reissman, 1993, p. 2). Using a narrative approach means that significant information is unlikely to be omitted from participant accounts and that forms of causal thinking – that is, those which identify categories of information (such as *protagonist*, *situation*, *outcome*) and relationships among them – are foregrounded (Robinson and Hawpe, 1986). Thus, narrative data were produced by asking participants 'what happened?' regarding both their own involvement in the youth justice system and that of their son or daughter. This enabled participants to produce detailed stories of their lives, which might otherwise be curtailed using more structured interviewing methods (Reissman, 1993).

Analysis involved subjecting the data to discourse analysis (see Willig, 2008) to examine both the ways in which experiences were constructed in talk and the wider cultural discourses that were drawn upon to enable this. To maintain the narrative integrity of the data, which can be lost (along with the subject) during the discourse analytic process, the findings are presented within a temporal framework. This serves to emphasise the key chronological junctures that were identified by parents as being particularly significant in shaping their accounts of what happened, as well as enabling readers to follow the thread of a particular parent's story as the wider narrative of the chapter unfolds. Thus, the findings below should not be read off in terms of *the truth* of what *actually* happened, in any realist sense, but in terms of how such experiences are constructed by the parents whose own discourses and practices are integral to the shaping of events.[2]

## Before exclusion: narratives of troublesome behaviour

In tracing their child's trajectory into offending behaviour, *all* of the parents made their child's school experience a touchstone in their narratives. Indeed, school was such a significant aspect of their narratives that even parents' constructions of their child tended to be in relation to their child's identity as a school learner. Thus, when describing their child, parents would reflect on their child's intelligence and would often start with a disclaimer in relation to their child's educational aptitude:

> He's not a stupid boy...he's an average erm, standard you know, educationally he's average.
>
> (Barbara)

> Craig's a really bright kid, he's not stupid...he just acts stupid sometimes...I mean he's quite clever and he could do well at school...
>
> (Judy)

> She's even brighter than me and her dad. I think what a waste.
>
> (Kim)

Such disclaimers may constitute an act of resistance in response to having repeatedly been told that it is their child's *lack* of ability or competence that is the problem, a practice identified consistently in the research literature (Blyth and Milner, 1994; Gilmore and Boulton-Lewis, 2009) and which is evidenced in Suzy's extract below:

> All through primary school, 'cos he's in Year 9 now, all through primary school, they said to me he was the laziest, naughtiest, disruptive child they'd ever had to teach. Cos his behaviour, he'd throw things, lie on the floor acting like a baby, crawling under tables, singing, flicking things. Some of this he still does at High School.
>
> (Suzy)

However, while a couple of parents, including Suzy, traced their child's problematic behaviour back to primary school, the majority of parents pinpointed their child's move to secondary school – when the child was 11 – as the key juncture when their child became *troublesome*:

> The first three months were fine, in fact he was very good for the first three months and it deteriorated rapidly to such an extent that the headmaster asked me to walk Simon [her son] to school, to pick him up at lunchtime so that he couldn't associate with other children in the school, and to pick him up from school at the end of the day so that he couldn't associate and cause a nuisance on the way home. He was sort of disruptive in the classroom, out of the class, I don't know. I think one day he had a water bottle and he was sort of shaking it at the cars and shouting abuse at the cars and parents were coming in and out of the school and things like that. Er, generally not a very pleasant lad I'm very sad to say.
>
> (Keeley)

> But when they started going to secondary school...then it changed. Lee [his son] just basically got in with the wrong people...and then started smoking and drinking and, yeah, basically just doing what they [his friends] wanted him to do.
>
> (Peter)

> He went to secondary school, Grange Gate, and they were a really really good school, you know, they helped him out a lot and for the first month he was okay, going to school. But then after that it sort of all went downhill. His behaviour changed and he was hanging round with the older children and, you know, just getting into trouble,

not going to school, refusing to get up in the mornings to go to
school....

(Samantha)

From the extracts above, and the other parents' narratives more generally, it is clear that what is meant by 'going downhill' constituted a
wide range of behaviours, such as throwing furniture, shouting at teachers, refusing to work or follow instructions and arguing or hitting other
pupils. Such behaviours were generally described by parents as 'disruptive', 'naughty', 'unpleasant', and constitute what, in recent years, is
likely to be termed 'anti-social', although parents only used this phrase
when describing their child's behaviour *outside* of school. However, perhaps the biggest problem behaviour identified by the parents, in terms
of both frequency and seriousness, was the child's refusal to attend
school,[3] which all but one of the parents described as a key concern:

He hated school with a vengeance, made no secret about it and I
deceived myself into thinking he would never truant because he's an
only child he seeks other children's company but he did start truanting which just basically meant he was hanging out with other kids
who were truanting which weren't a particularly good influence and
it was just harder and harder to get him into school.

(Barbara)

It is worth considering some of these narratives in detail, given the
weight attributed by parents to the move to secondary school as the
catalyst for the significant change in their son or daughter's behaviour.
The move to secondary school is generally acknowledged as a time of
anxiety for both young person (Lucey and Reay, 2000) and parent(s)
(Roker et al., 2007). However, while parents located the time point of
the behavioural change to their child moving from primary to secondary school,[4] it is significant that parents did not necessarily locate
the *cause* of these changes to this disruption per se. Neither did they
relate it to institutional factors that were intrinsic to the new school,
such as poor discipline or a lack of monitoring. Rather than drawing
on wider structural and institutional factors, parents instead drew on
normative psychological discourses of development, locating the cause
of the behavioural change as coming from within the child him/herself
as a result of a biological and psychological change – that is, 'adolescence' – which coincides with the age when the majority of young
people move to secondary school. This is perhaps best exemplified in

Mary's extract below; she explained her son's misbehaviour in terms of pubertal changes:

> He hit puberty bad. He's rude, he's obnoxious, or was, he's not so bad now... silly little things, walking out of school smoking, being lairy with the teachers, I mean, the school he went to, Orange Grove, I don't actually rate that highly, they tend to, instead of dealing with the kids like Eric, who are sort of challenging, they just tend to turn their back on them and throw them out.
>
> (Mary)

Thus, a child's *age*, in conjunction with the age of her/his peers, was an important discursive concept in enabling parents to explain why their child was misbehaving. Although institutional factors were often drawn on (as in Mary's extract above), this was only in relation to *responses to* the already challenging child. Many parents constructed the teenage years as a time when young people are bored and seek illicit excitement, and this, to some degree, explained their child's misbehaviour, while other parents referred to their child having *not yet developed* the appropriate skills to manage their emotions, particularly anger. This *discourse of developmentalism* (Morss, 1996) enabled parents to construct their child's misbehaviour as temporary, as a 'teenage phase' – the implication being that they will *grow out of it*. However, the consequence of using this discursive strategy is that the assumptions that underpin it are left uncontested: the notion that the 'teenage years' is a stage of psychological and biological (and, consequently, behavioural) disruption is so dominant in popular discourse that it has become *naturalised* (Gillis, 1974). This results in the disenabling of any wider analysis of structural and institutional factors that may shape a child's particular set of behavioural problems.

## After exclusion: narratives of offending behaviour

In 12 out of the 17 cases, the young people had been excluded from school for some time, from between three months to three years. The specific incidents that led to exclusion included the theft of a school laptop computer, fighting with other pupils, criminal damage to school property and being intoxicated on school premises. However, despite a number of different incidents and reasons being cited for these exclusions, for all of these parents, the date of the exclusion was pinpointed as a significant juncture that demarcated the shift from 'misbehaviour' in school to 'offending behaviour' outside of school. Keeley and Jenny's accounts of what happened after their sons' exclusions were typical:

> As he's been excluded from school, he's got in with other kids that are also excluded from school. A lot of them are older than him. I'm not saying he's been led astray by older children, but he's certainly with older kids and that obviously hasn't helped at all. And obviously some of them have been into stealing and all the rest of it and Simon has gone down that road obviously of stealing, you know, the bottle of pop and the packet of crisps and maybe one or two other things that he's got away with, I don't know.
>
> (Keeley)

> David [Jenny's son] is actually special needs so he has got an anger problem anyway, but that was only sorted when they actually got him into a special school two weeks before the summer holidays, this year.... But he'd been off school for a year and I think it just took it out of him. He got in with the wrong crowd and they was causing trouble so he just joined in. He's quite easily led, sort of thing.

> Interviewer: And how did he come to not be in school for a year?

> Because the school wouldn't take him on, because they couldn't cope with him so he literally like just roamed the streets in the day, with the other kids that had been excluded or expelled or whatever.
>
> (Jenny)

As in the extracts above, a key factor for many of the parents was that exclusion from school meant that their child was now spending time with other excluded children, with a corresponding absence of non-excluded children who may have provided a counter-influence on their child. Both Keeley and Jenny's extracts implicitly allude to the classic sub-cultural theories of Albert Cohen (1955), which described young people developing their own routines and value systems out-side of mainstream (in this case educational) values and practices and who, in the words of Jenny, *just roamed the streets in the day, with the other kids that had been excluded or expelled or whatever* .... This particu-lar explanatory framework has produced its own 'folk devil' (see Stanley Cohen, 1972) in the form of 'feral kids', a construction that has increas-ingly been drawn on in the popular press over recent years in relation to concerns about young people and anti-social behaviour.[5]

However, direct references to sociological factors such as lack of opportunity were absent. Again, many parents instead drew on a naturalised developmental discourse in their references to the teenage years being a time when young people are *vulnerable* to the influence of others, making them inherently susceptible to going '*down that road*' and getting *in with the wrong crowd*. Other parents drew on a more psychoanalytically informed discourse of development in their reflections on their child's unsatisfied need for stimulation, which school once satiated; as Mary explained, ... *once he got out of the educational system that's when he started offending because apart from anything else he's bored, you know?* This was also apparent in Barbara's narrative when explaining her son's offending behaviour after he had been excluded from school:

> I just, I think for Bobby [her son], it was an element of excitement, something to take him out of his boring life, 'cos everyday for the last year, on and off, is the same for Bobby. There's no weekends, there's no Sunday early nights because of school or work, every day is the same.
>
> (Barbara)

Clearly, institutional practices of exclusion have contributed to this situation where, in many cases, no alternative provision is made (see Daniels et al., 2003, discussed earlier). According to Berridge and colleagues (2001), the result is increased disorientation and depression, and a lack of opportunity for young people who have already experienced pervasive social and economic disadvantage (Berridge et al., 2001). This was clearly the case in the present study, where the families were experiencing a number of social and economic stressors[6], and where parents spoke of their children being out of education for *months*, if not *years*:

> Even at 15, where he got put on tag, they told me to pull him out of school, right, and they'd send someone round to help him look for work, and to do home tuition with him. I never seen no-one. So he didn't even do the whole last year of school.
>
> (Ruth)

> So I talked to the school and said look he's scared [her son was being bullied], can we get him some kind of home tutor or put him in another school, but they said, because it's the only school around for kids like him, you know? Because he left a main school and went to that school, he can't go back to a normal school now. Which is wrong, I think. ... They should at least be allowed to try at

another school, you know? But no, they haven't really done nothing, I just don't know what to do about it actually.... I'm waiting for an education woman to come back off holiday and talk to me.

(Judy)

Like Ruth and Judy, many parents spoke of time spent *waiting for* the local authorities to organise alternative educational provision for their child once the initial exclusion had been processed. At a discursive level, there is little sign of parental agency in such accounts, but this apparent 'fatalism' may be a product of the ways in which social class shapes parent subjectivities and practices in particular ways. For example, in their studies of parents' interactions with school authorities, both Crozier (1997, 1999) and Reay and Ball (1997) identified similar intimations of 'fatalism' in working-class parents' accounts, something which might be interpreted as passivity when looked at in relation to the normative ideal of middle-class parents' apparent 'active' engagement. However, in the current research, the parents described a number of material consequences leading from the local authorities' failure to provide alternative educational provision – for example, one outcome was an increased pressure on parent–child relationships as parents struggled to cope with an additional child at home, often in cramped conditions, during the day, given existing childcare and work pressures that meant they were able to offer little to their teenage child. Seen within this context, the parents' attitudes look less like passivity and more like a means of managing a range of pressing demands in the face of multiple disadvantages.

While a minority of the young people remained out of school at the time of the interviews, most who had been excluded were now attending a non-mainstream school, and parents' appraisals of the alternative provision were mixed. A minority of parents, such as Mary and Samantha, were positive or at least hopeful that the additional resources within the school might equip it to respond more effectively to the challenges presented by their child. Other parents were less positive, having already identified problems with the new school. Below are extracts from Barbara and Lianne's narratives concerning their sons' move to non-mainstream schools following exclusion:

He was excluded and at that point he was not having any form of education for nearly three months because we were sorting out another school, which was a school for, if you like, wayward children which was more like a holiday camp. So Mondays and Fridays were leisure days, there was no school uniform policy, lunch was provided. Although it was a non-smoking school, they could have a cigarette if they were a bit stressed, a taxi picked him up and took him to school... but meanwhile he wasn't having any of that either.

(Barabara)

He's not in mainstream, it's called Mayflower House, he does a couple of hours a day. That's another thing 'cos he wasn't very good at following the discipline in school so they put him into this Mayflower Centre where I thought the staff would've been trained for, I'd call them difficult kids, you know, falling off the rails kids difficult. I mean, his first lesson, like on a Monday morning would be snooker and I'm thinking to myself, hold on a minute, 'cos it works out you spend about two maybe three hours a day... and like maybe two lessons in the morning two in the afternoon, that's it. I mean, start from six. Six till six.

(Lianne)

The lack of discipline, relaxed timetable and lack of pedagogical content is clearly a concern for Barbara and Lianne, and their concerns about educational provision in non-mainstream schools were typical of the parents' accounts. In particular, concerns over a lack of *authority* in schools to ensure discipline and concerns over whether schools were taking sufficient *responsibility* for their child's behaviour in school were key threads that weaved in and out of the parents' narratives. It is these two specific themes – and the tensions upon which they pivot – to which this chapter now turns.

## Responsibility and authority: sites of tension between parent and school

### Who has responsibility?

The question of who (or what) is responsible for the child's behaviour in school was continually grappled with in the parents' narratives, and the crux of the tension is perhaps best exemplified by an extract from Mary. Here she describes one of her son's first offences, which involved the police:

Eric, one of his offences, trespassing on school property, you know, he's gone to meet his friends and, you know, 'you shouldn't be at this school, you've been thrown out' and so it goes to court. I'M

SORRY! You know, when I was a kid, that would have been dealt with by the school, you know when you're in a school uniform, if anything happened between home and school then the school would take responsibility for that, and now its kind of like 'its outside the gates that's nothing to do with us', that whole sort of mentality. And I think that's kind of a shame because it's not working with the parents.

(Mary)

Mary's extract describes how the geographical parameters of a school's responsibility have reduced over time, so that incidents which would have been dealt with *informally* by the school a generation ago are now dealt with *formally* by the police (see also Chapter 2). Such generational changes have been traced by Furlong and Cartmel (1997), who suggest that social changes in late modernity have produced a shift from collective provision to a highly individualised response in dealing with young people 'at risk' from offending. This has resulted in an increased net-widening of youth justice agencies, with more and more 'everyday teenage behaviour' being criminalised, resulting in a significant increase in the number of young people drawn into the youth justice system (Squires and Stephen, 2005; Squires, 2008).

The notion of an increasing abdication of school responsibility was continually drawn upon by parents. A particular site of frustration centred on the schools' policy of contacting parents during school hours to make parents take responsibility for their child's behaviour in school. The parents' frustration at this practice is evident in Samantha's extract:

Sometimes when I've got him in there and they're phoning me up and I think well he is in school and he is your responsibility now because you are a special needs school; and you are quick to deal with his behaviour and ringing me up and asking me to come and collect him every five minutes is not really on you know, you should be able to sit down and talk to him and you know work it out but its hard enough getting him in there let alone once he's in there them ringing me up every five minutes.

(Samantha)

Furthermore, such frustration was compounded by the threat of legal action against parents for an apparent lack of parental responsibility; the inherent unfairness of this was articulated by Barbara:

When Bobby was truanting, I physically took him to school, he would go into registration, and then he would bunk off. How can I be held responsible? I have done everything within my power to get that child to school and when he did disappear, in second period, and they'd call me at work, and I just couldn't physically do any more, but I could have been punished, because Bobby refused to go, or stay, in school. He would go, but he just wouldn't stay in school. So, again it comes back to, you know, you can't be punished for something that is out of your control.

(Barbara)

For Pam, this threat was carried out by the local authority, which prosecuted her:

The problem was just that he didn't like school full stop. But then the education board kept on taking us to court and that, and then they gave up, because he was just so uncontrollable in school, the schools didn't want him. And then, in the last year of schooling, they decided to prosecute us, and that's how the first Parenting Order ever come about.

(Pam)

As discussed earlier in this chapter, both local education authorities and parents have legal responsibilities towards ensuring a child's *right* to an education, and both appear to have recourse to legal action if the other fails to meet these responsibilities. However, in terms of parental responsibilities, there appears to be a slippage from their ensuring that their child can *access* educational provision (by ensuring they *attend* school) to ensuring that the child behaves in a way which *enables that access once they are in school*, and it is difficult to see how parents can be made legally responsible for this – particularly given the limited economic and social resources available to such parents. Furthermore, although education welfare officers and other services that focus on ensuring children can access alternative education are well established, the particular problems they are dealing with are often complex and can be highly resistant to their interventions. This can lead to the perception that the only 'resource' available to either schools or parents is the threat of legal action. It may be that it is the continual presence of this threat that shapes the parent–school relationship into one where schools are positioned as adversaries (at least from the parents' perspectives), thus preventing any potential for schools and parents to work together collaboratively.

## Who has authority?

While parents talked about the school's responsibility for their child's behaviour, there was a tension here since many parents also drew on a *discourse of children's rights* to suggest that neither schools nor parents any longer have the authority to carry out their responsibilities. The notion of children's rights is enshrined in statutes such as the Children Act (1989) and the UNCRC (1992), and the argument that children's rights now supersedes adults' rights is increasingly invoked in discussions that seek to explain 'the trouble with kids today'. Such an argument was drawn on in Barbara's extract below:

> Schools have no control, I mean, when I was called in, 'cos he was being naughty, I would say 'Well, you know what you need to do, make them pick up litter.'
>
> 'They can't do that, that's blah blah of rights.'
>
> 'OK, well get him up in assembly, stand him up in front of everybody, and tell everybody what he has done.'
>
> 'No, you can't do that... Oh well we believe, you know, Bobby didn't have his school shoes on, erm, he had trainers on.'
>
> 'Well, Bobby's school shoes were in his bag, why didn't you take them out of his...'
>
> 'No, we're not allowed to touch his bag, not allowed to do that.' I mean, I even told them that I would get a solicitor's letter written to say that they could cane him...
>
> 'No, can't do that.'
>
> (Barbara)

For Barbara, 'children's rights' have become so dominant that they now provide young people with a buffer against adult authority, a problem that she saw extending not only to schools but also to the police, who she felt '*can no longer touch them* [i.e. young people]'. Indeed, for many parents, the dominance of children's rights resulted in an impotence that extended to the parents themselves:

... they've [successive governments] decided to give the children so many rights, parents haven't got any. I mean, I can't go to the police and say ... my son is mentally abusing me ... by not doing as he's told, cos you'll just get told well you're a bad parent. But if a child goes to the police and says 'my mother, my father, my brother or sister is mentally abusing me', then these big cogs get into play and this poor child has got to be looked after, do you know what I mean?

(Carole)

Implicit in this extract is the assumption that, when children's rights are prioritised (a priority which the Every Child Matters policy agenda has formalised), parents' rights are lost. This assumption is understandable given the way that children's rights are constructed in opposition to parental responsibilities in government policy (see earlier). The implications for parents drawing on this discourse is its prohibitive effect on agency – if parents no longer feel able to exercise authority over their children, because of the rights and freedoms guaranteed under UK and UNCRC statutes, then they will no longer do so. Similarly, if parents also feel, as the present study suggests, that children and young people now have the licence to challenge other adults' authority (such as schoolteachers and the police), then parents also lose faith in the power of state institutions to support them in tackling behavioural difficulties. As the above extracts show, such loss of faith appears to be already underway.

## (In)Conclusions

This chapter examined parents' narrative accounts of their child's trajectories into offending behaviour, for which they had all received at least one parenting order via the youth justice system. What was striking within these narratives was the role of 'school milestones' – specifically the child's *move to secondary school* and the child's *exclusion from school* – which were utilised to demarcate the junctures at which young people began 'misbehaving' and then began 'offending'.

As Hodgson and Webb (2005) suggest, the defining characteristic of these families is not 'school exclusion' per se but high levels of poverty and social and familial dislocation. Indeed, Hodgson and Webb make the point that any supposed links between school exclusion and youth offending comprise 'a set of ethno-sociological and commonsense assumptions about what is going on in the lives of young people' (p. 13). It may well be that the current lack of robust empirical evidence and detailed theoretical analysis of the complexities of youth offending has enabled simplistic causal models to dominate the dialogue, with *school exclusion* and *poor parenting* taking centre stage in such debates.

It is therefore unsurprising that, given this limited discursive context from which to anchor their accounts, parents' narratives of their children's (mis)behaviour appear to draw primarily from a *discourse of developmentalism*. Such a discourse functions to *psychologise* the perceived problems of young people and contain such 'problems' within a biological–psychological dynamic, which, for a large part, ignores their structural and institutional context. Indeed, the cultural dominance of this discourse almost certainly enables schools to position parents and their children as 'problems' as opposed to potential 'collaborators' with the school – a positioning that is supported by educational research in schools (see, for example, Hood, 1999; Roffey, 2004; Smith et al., 2008). The totality of this discourse is illustrated in the ways that the parents themselves draw on it (and thus maintain its dominance) to explain their own child's (mis)behaviour. When coupled with a *discourse of children's rights*, it renders parents unable to exercise agency in two specific ways. Firstly, in demanding the institutional and social changes that are needed to overcome structural disadvantage and, secondly, in working with and collaborating with their child to effect positive change. Moreover, the formalisation of parental responsibilities through the criminal justice system, coupled with the perception that schools and local authorities are not meeting their own responsibilities towards their child, is further hindering any possibility of a collaborative relationship between parent, school and child.

Furthermore, where institutional factors do feature in parents' narratives, they are played out through two very specific and related tensions. The first concerns the issue of *responsibility* and the question of *whose responsibility it is to resolve these difficulties*. The second concerns the issue of *authority* and the question of *who has the authority over young people to enable them to deal with these difficulties*. It may be that the lack of any resolution to these tensions is producing a particularly adversarial relationship between parent and school which, at least on the part of the parents, is characterised by resentment and a sense of impotence. Throughout all of the extracts discussed above (and in many other narratives besides), there is little evidence of parents *not caring* about their child's schooling, or of them *not engaging* with the schools to help resolve the difficulties. On the contrary, many parents made suggestions as to how their school and local authority might help to support their child: Barbara talked of how she had requested psychoanalysis for her son to help him deal with what she saw as his 'anger problems', other parents such as Judy requested home tutoring and others asked for boarding school, boot camp, or for social services to temporarily put their child into care. However, such requests were seemingly ignored, possibly for appearing too outlandish or unrealistic. Consequently, for parents who lack the social capital to request 'appropriate' forms of support, their ability to demand their child's right to an education is severely curtailed.

## Notes

1. However, with official records forming the basis for much of our evidence (and the inherent problems therein – see Vulliamy and Webb, 2000), there is still a gap in our understanding of young people who are not attending school, but who have not been officially excluded.
2. All names and places are pseudonyms to protect the participants' and their families' identities.
3. While some parents did use the term 'truancy', the majority of parents referred to their child's 'refusal to attend', a term that acknowledges the active and *agentic* element to this practice and that, in turn, perhaps acknowledges the parents' own impotence in countering this refusal.
4. Even for those parents, such as Suzy and Pam, who did trace their child's behavioural problems back to primary school, they nevertheless marked the child's move to secondary school as a juncture when their child's behaviour significantly deteriorated, as Pam explained: ... *then it came to like normal school, and he kicked right off.*
5. Encapsulated by headlines such as '*Feral kids should watch out, I've had enough*' in *The Times* (Morrison, 2009) and *Lame Justice for feral kids keeps us in fear* in the *Mirror* (Phillips, 2008).
6. Such stressors included poverty, unemployment, poor housing, mental health problems, disability and violence in the home (which, in some cases, was perpetuated by the child in question: see Holt, 2009b).

# 9
# Safer Schools Partnerships

*Andy Briers and Ellyn Dickmann*

## Origins of Safer School Partnerships

Safer School Partnerships (SSPs) in the United Kingdom came about as part of a Street Crime Initiative launched in 2002, around schools located within one of the Home Office's ten crime 'hot spots' (Bhabra et al., 2004). It should be said at the outset that the different jurisdictions within the United Kingdom mean that some of the work and evidence about how these SSPs work varies both between and within countries in the United Kingdom. A further complication is that from the start SSPs varied in the way they worked; some had a full-time police officer and support staff, others a lone police officer, whilst some officers worked with a group of schools. SSPs illustrate most clearly the more explicit end of the focus of this volume: they started in high crime areas because of concerns about young people's behaviour in and around schools, but have since evolved towards a broader remit, as this chapter will detail. Comparison will be made with similar established programmes in the United States, which influenced developments in the United Kingdom.

In the United Kingdom, at the time that SSPs were launched, there was evidence of a rise in the number of street robberies, with offences doubling over a four-year period (HMICA, 2003, p. 8). There was also concern about the number of robberies committed by 11- to 15-year-olds; data from the Metropolitan Police demonstrated that between 1993 and 2001 the number of 11- to 15-year-olds charged with the offence of robbery increased five-fold (Simmons et al., 2002, p. 54). Responding to this, the prime minister (at the time) called for a 'high intensity' drive on street crime, with £66 million being made available in March 2002, as part of the national strategy to reduce street crime (NAS/UWT, 2004, p. 7).

One of the key original aims of SSPs was the prevention and diversion of young people from offending. At this time there was a growing concern about problem behaviour and schools, and increasing evidence about the connections between truancy, exclusion from school and increased opportunities for offending. Parallel to the police interest in reducing crime was an interest from schools that needed additional support in managing pupil behaviour. Initiatives were also coming from the Department for Education and Skills (DfES) which actively encouraged schools to work with other agencies in order to address 'indiscipline and truancy' (NAS/UWT, 2004, p. 5). Initiatives such as the Behaviour Improvement Programme (which ran from 2002 to 2005) aimed to develop better responses to behaviour and reduce truancy and crime. As part of this programme multi-agency Behaviour and Education Support Teams (BESTs) were established around schools that were seen as having high levels of truancy and problem behaviour. The SSPs were linked to these BESTs; with attached police officers having a role in helping to create a safer school community, provide a support structure for victims of crime and anti-social behaviour and also work with those who had committed offences.

While having police officers in school in the United Kingdom is not a new phenomenon, the SSPs altered their existing role to one in which the police became responsible for assisting in the reduction and management of problem behaviour that was not necessarily criminal, as well as behaviour that was criminal (in a sense blurring the boundaries between problem, anti-social and criminal behaviour, as we argue in Chapter 1). This development is not unique to the United Kingdom, with law enforcement forming part of a whole school approach to crime reduction in the United States for a number of years.

Since the 1960s police have been working in varying capacities in schools across the United Kingdom. Traditionally officers have visited schools on an ad hoc basis as part of their community beat, providing a measure of reassurance and a familiar face to both teachers and young people. With the exception of the occasional presentation on the dangers of crossing the road and taking sweets from strangers, there was very little focused purpose within the interaction between schools and the police. Until the 1990s police visits to schools were primarily focused on their educational value, with officers preparing and delivering schemes of work, based mainly on issues to do with citizenship and the law (O'Connor, 2001; Avon et al., 2002). During this era, schools were considered to be private places and although the police were invited in to perform educational duties there was no real sense that they worked in 'partnership' in relation to a crime prevention role.

A number of dramatic events (or 'signal crimes') since the early 1990s in the United Kingdom (with new events unfolding at regular intervals) have been influential in relation to developing public opinion as well as responses to safety in and around schools. The Dunblane 'massacre' (1995) in Scotland involved the deaths of 15 primary school children and their teacher. A local man was responsible for the shootings. The following year saw the fatal stabbing of London head teacher, Philip Lawrence, (1996) at the end of the school day, at the gates, by a 15-year-old from another school. Lawrence was trying to protect the potential victim. These events followed a period of protracted debate after the abduction (during the school day in a shopping mall near Liverpool) and murder of 2-year-old Jamie Bulger (1992), by two 10-year-old boys. One of the sub-themes to the Bulger murder was that the two boys (Thompson and Venables) were truanting from school that day. These were clearly very different kinds of events to the norm; they required different types of response and had threats coming as much from the outside as within schools. But taken together they provided a persuasive backdrop to the argument for greater control and surveillance in and around school sites. Events such as these paved the way for an enhanced role for the police in and around schools, widespread use of CCTV and other safety and crime prevention initiatives in schools.

Alongside these high-profile events there were growing concerns amongst teachers that incidents of violence and aggression in and around schools were becoming more frequent. Ironically, in a television interview in 1994, just a year before his murder, Philip Lawrence had stated that he had increased security around his school by locking some of the gates and installing a video camera in an effort to better protect his staff and students (BBC, 8 December 1995). Following Lawrence's death, a Working Group on School Security (WGSS) was formed. This made a number of recommendations in relation to improving the security of school premises and encouraged schools to have an appropriate security strategy (DfEE, 1996). The WGSS looked at the relationship between the law and schools, acknowledging that the law did apply to schools and that the police should be contacted in the event of criminal behaviour (DfES, 1997). The recommendations of the WGSS were the start of encouraging greater cooperation between schools and the police. While schools continued to invite police officers to visit in the educational capacities already outlined, officers began to be deployed in a policing role, especially after the school day, to disperse large groups of children, many of whom were simply making their way home from school, who were now being targeted by local police as potential sources of conflict. There was no real evidence or intelligence to support the need for this action. There were no protocols in place and certainly no real engagement with the schools by the local police that went any way towards engaging the school community. The school site remained a closed place and to many police officers it was a 'no go area'.

By contrast, since the late 1960s in many regions of the United States, police officers started to visit schools, but had a limited formal school role. By the 1980s they were not only visiting schools on a regular basis but were frequently stationed in schools. The police had their own offices within schools and were consequently regarded by the parents, pupils and staff as being part of the school community because of their daily presence and the involvement and interaction they had with the school (Goggins et al., 1994). In essence, they were considered to be an integral part of the school's structure and operations and they were involved in key issues such as pupils' exclusion from school, assisting with the development of safety policies and devising critical incident plans (U.S. Department of Justice, 2001; Lambert and McGinty, 2002)).

In 1998 the Office of Community Orientated Policing provided financial support to law departments to place officers in schools on a permanent basis, this became known as the COPS in Schools programme, and in recent years there has been continued support in terms of resources and training for what are known as school resource officers (SROs). It should be noted that many of the SROs who attend schools in the United States are not police officers, but security guards, although police officers are placed on school sites as part of their duties and some officers do this work for additional pay.

The United States has had a number of very high-profile events in schools in the form of 'school shootings' (see also Chapter 5). Events such as those in Columbine High School (in 1999) are well known and suggest a different order of event and safety need in the United States, compared with the United Kingdom, as easier access to firearms in the United States can mean that pupils are able to perpetrate mass murders on the school site. Whilst these are extremely rare events, such murders have clearly influenced the development of heightened security measures in the United States, as well as elsewhere in the world.

In 2001, the Metropolitan Police Service replicated the policing programme approach utilised by the United States and placed a full-time police officer in a North London school. This was the first school-based police officer in the United Kingdom and through the officer's experiences both at the school and through a Fulbright Police Research Fellowship Award to the United States (see Briers, 2003; Briers and Dickman, 2009) he was able to assist in the development of the SSP Guidance, in conjunction with the Department for Children, Schools and Families (DCSF), the Association of Chief Police Officers (ACPO), the Youth

Justice Board (YJB) and the Confederation of Head Teachers (see DCSF, 2009d). Much of what SSP officers do today in UK schools has been influenced by the work of their counterparts in the United States.

## Police in schools – roles, responsibilities and relationships

In the United States, typically, school districts in collaboration with law enforcement jurisdictions have set aims and objectives for their school-based programmes and their officers have clear roles and responsibilities. Similar roles and responsibilities have been adopted by the police in the United Kingdom and include applying the law, education, an advisory role, working in partnership with other organisations and ensuring safety and security in the school environment. In addition, the police officer can act as a role model for children and encourage positive relationships between the police and young people.

In the United Kingdom the way that the aims of SSPs are presented varies in emphasis in relation to the agency or organisation outlining the aims, as well as the country within the United Kingdom. Figure 9.1 outlines the key aims of SSPs as presented to teachers (in England) at the time of writing.

One of the original key goals of the first SSPs was to reduce crime and victimisation as well as problem behaviour, truanting and exclusion, which were seen as having a negative impact on schools and on pupil achievement (DES, 2001). The contemporary focus, as presented to

---

All Safer School Partnerships (SSPs) aim to ensure:

- the **safety** of pupils, staff and the school site and surrounding area
- **help for young people** to deal with situations that may put them at risk of becoming victims of crime, bullying or intimidation, and to **provide support** to those who do
- **focused enforcement** to demonstrate that those who do offend cannot do so without **facing consequences**
- **early identification, support** and, where necessary, **challenge** of pupils involved in or at risk of offending
- improved standards of **pupil behaviour and attendance**, and less need for exclusions
- **more positive relations** between young people and the police and between young people and the wider community
- effective approaches to **issues beyond the school site** that negatively impact on pupil safety and behaviour.

---

*Figure 9.1*  Aims of Safer School Partnerships (England)
*Source*: Teachernet (2010).

teachers (shown in Figure 9.1) emphasises 'safety' first, then 'help and support'. Enforcement and behavioural issues are further down the list. The original focus (DES, 2001) had extended previous ideas about the use of the police to enforce the law in schools outlined by the WGSS (Bowles et al., 2005). In this early focus we can see the obvious connection to the high-profile incidents (such as the murder of Philip Lawrence) already mentioned. The original guidance about enforcing the law within schools in England was that it should be done in conjunction with the head teacher and that police should very much use their discretion when considering what laws to apply. Key areas of consideration include police 'stop and search' powers, making an arrest on school premises and the confiscation of weapons and drugs. Searching for weapons in the United Kingdom has become especially pertinent in light of the Violent Crime Reduction Act 2006, which sees teachers being given the legal right to search pupils who are suspected of carrying a weapon. Other areas where police and school concerns overlap include the use of an Acceptable Behaviour Contract, the widespread use of truancy powers (section 16, Crime and Disorder Act 1998) and understanding trespass, and laws contained in section 547 of the Education Act 1996. Additional issues include reporting crimes, information sharing and identification procedures. A key issue is that schools in the United Kingdom are still private premises and so police officers can only search people on the school site in certain circumstances and using specific powers. For instance, whilst there is provision to search for drugs and offensive weapons in private places such as a school, as yet there is no such provision to search for stolen articles unless the suspect is arrested and then subsequently searched.

As we have already noted in Chapter 6, recent guidance makes it clear that incidents on school property, which are in law a crime, should remain within school disciplinary processes – unless the child or parent/guardian asks for the incident to be recorded as a crime or the crime is deemed more serious (Millard and Flatley, 2010). Police officers in schools retain their primary role and have a responsibility to enforce the law; schools are not exempt from the Criminal Law (DfES, 1997). This primary role of the police (and its attendant strains in the school environment) has been a source of contention for teachers and police officers alike. Interviews with teachers have revealed that they dislike the freedom that police have to talk with pupils, which in their opinion often borders on interviewing them as a suspect (as depicted in the opening anecdote of Chapter 2). In the United States, concerns have been raised by students about the increase in power that the police have due to their greater presence in the school environment (Berger, 2002). Berger (2002) argues that the use of security measures and the number of police officers in schools in the United States are not actually supported by the levels of crime that occur. This is summed up by Robinson (2002, cited by Berger, p. 121) who states:

> There are more than 51 million students and approximately 3 million teachers in American schools. In 1996, there was approximately 380,000 violent victimisations at school against these roughly 54 million people. This means that the rate of violent victimisation at U.S schools is about 704 per 100,000 people. Stated differently, about 0.7% of people can expect to become victims of serious violent crimes at school.

Other reasons why schools can be wary of police officers on site include officers turning up at a school unannounced to arrest pupils who they have identified as suspects; instances where there has been interrogation of members of school staff to find out the current addresses of pupils and information about their home life, without being able to justify their reasons; the unauthorised use of school photographs to pick out friends and associates and map intelligence and a general expectation that school staff supply and pass on information about young peoples' activities, with no thought about the teacher's role (including any need for protection) or the needs of the child concerned.

There is evidence to suggest that some officers do feel uncomfortable with the crime management aspect of their role. A recent survey of Scottish school-based police officers found that they did not see detecting crime as a primary role, but still believed that if they felt a crime was committed they had to take action (MORI, 2010). Although discretion can be applied in many circumstances where the incident is minor, each school is likely to have different rules or thresholds about what is tolerable pupil behaviour. Such rules matter, because some police officers provide support to more than one school in an area. The bottom line is that what one person views as a 'serious matter' may be viewed as 'a minor incident' by another; an issue that is well documented in relation to the responses of schools and teachers to pupil behaviour in the United Kingdom (Hayden, 2007). This makes it particularly difficult for officers and can often lead to school staff not disclosing incidents and illegal activity within the school community for fear that the police may arrest pupils on each occasion and ultimately create an appearance that the school is a dangerous place. On the other hand, officers feel they are legally bound to investigate such matters and do not want to leave themselves open to criticism that they may have neglected their duty or ignored illegal behaviours.

Another pressure on officers is what has been characterised as the culture of sanctions and detections in the UK police. Police officers' ability to use their own discretion has become limited in the United Kingdom due to this culture and associated police performance targets (see Loveday,1999; Martin, 2003). Performance management has emphasised the number of arrests, detections and stop and searches. This reactive approach can have a negative impact on the relationship between the school and the police, especially where it is not carried out with the consent of all parties and without the best interests of all parties in mind (Hyman and Perone, 1998). In these circumstances an image of 'targeting youth' can be developed easily , often referred to as 'criminalising' young people (Crawford, 1997; Rodger, 2008), 'net-widening' (Cohen, 1985) or picking off the 'low hanging fruit' (Morgan, 2007).

The work that police in schools undertake cannot be easily measured by the number of stop and searches or arrests that they undertake; on the contrary, this can become counterproductive to the nature and responsibilities of their position. Rather, consideration should be given to the roles they perform that achieve the key aims of the programme, and the subsequent outcomes related to the unique nature of this primarily preventative role. Schools, in turn, are primarily learning environments, so that when they are working with other agencies they want to know how such partnerships will enhance this role.

## Enhancing the learning environment

As we have already seen, traditionally a key role for police in schools is as part of the education process. The crime prevention and disciplinary role has to be carefully managed in this context. In both the United States and the United Kingdom police officers continue to be involved in a range of activities that are clearly educational and also relate in part to improving relationships between the police and young people. In the United States, officers help to run alternative programmes such as vehicle driving classes or junior detective programmes. In England, there are junior citizenship programmes, which consists of activities designed to educate Year 6 (aged 10–11 years) pupils on issues of safety and awareness, road safety, personal safety, safety around water, railway safety and safety around and near the home. Many police officers now assist with the coordination of transition phase work for those pupils going from Year 6 (end of primary school) to Year 7 (first year of secondary school), focusing mainly on safety and support as pupils arrive at their new school and how they can tackle such issues as bullying and harassment. This strong emphasis on 'safety' can be seen in the title of SSPs, but is also clearly connected to the Every Child Matters agenda (DfES, 2003a), where 'safety' is one of the five key outcomes. Some officers assist with extended schools by running school clubs such as football, basketball and breakfast clubs for students who might otherwise be unsupervised before school. Police officers also educate pupils about safer routes to and from school, as it is well known that the majority of crime against young people occurs after school between 3 p.m. and 6 p.m. and is usually concentrated around transport hubs, such as bus terminals or shops. Pupils are made aware of these potential dangers and how to avoid being victimised (see victimisations described by young people in Chapter 6). A consequence of this is that some schools in the United Kingdom now have regular school officers (or PCSOs, police community safety officers) patrolling in and around schools and on the routes home.

The advisory role of police officers in the United Kingdom is often used in problem-solving and involves the school community and the police coming together to resolve key areas of concern. This may include environmental scans around the school looking at critical areas where safety can be improved, or places to avoid. This often involves working with other agencies such as the local authority, with the aim of designing-out crime through such modifications as improved lighting, removal of graffiti and the pruning of overgrown shrubbery. Crime prevention officers are regularly used to survey the schools and provide comprehensive advice around the security of the school and how to minimise the risks, such as intruders, fires and theft of property.

The 'role model' aspect of having police officers on the school site is often overlooked and includes the effect that the presence of a uniformed officer may have on the overall school community. In particular, it relates to how officers help build relationships with young people. For example, in the Metropolitan Police Service (London) an online survey was set up to enable young people to provide feedback to the police about the key issues that concern them and how they would like the police to address the issue(s). It is police-based activities such as this that are likely to enable and create more positive and meaningful interactions and allow young people to take an active interest in their school community. Establishing these types of activity within SSPs is critical to the success of the relationship between the police and the school.

There is also a general need for officers to liaise with other agencies within youth support services that can provide advice on drugs, housing placement, anti-bullying and sexual health. The need to develop good working relationships with social housing agencies is necessary when young people report being threatened and physically assaulted by other young people, often over issues of territory or misunderstandings about their relationships. Many of these young people are so scared that they cannot attend school or venture out into their neighbourhood for fear of reprisals. School-based police officers have been called upon to help provide a level of care for them, and in some cases assist them in being rehoused to an area where the child and family are able to live without harassment.

## Partnership protocols

Previous research by the authors (Briers and Dickmann, 2009), established that developing a good relationship between police officers and schools is fundamental to the ongoing success of SSPs. In the United States the majority of officers are interviewed for their post by the school principal and a senior police officer, who agree to the protocols, roles and responsibilities of the officer for the specific assignment or school. Often, a team of individuals from the law enforcement agency and school (or school district) are involved in the school police officer selection. However, this does not always happen, as illustrated in our own research where one officer explained how he was 'interviewed' for his post in a school. He was told, immediately after completing his night shift (and despite telling his superior that he did not want to work in a school) that he had to attend an interview and accept the post in a school, which he duly did. That said, agreements about roles are formalised once an officer is in post. Each person and their organisation are considered to be a key stakeholder in the partnership, and the protocol is used to clearly define both the officers' and the schools' expectations. This is referred to as a memorandum of understanding and formal documents clearly outline and detail areas such as line management, hours of duty, dress code, programme funding, leave and absence policies and communication expectations.

Evidence suggests that when school–police partnerships fail to develop a protocol, expectations are often unmet and partnerships become dysfunctional and ultimately unworkable. Basically, relationships between both parties become strained and the officer often feels isolated and lacking in support as they are pulled between (and lack guidance) from both the policing jurisdiction and the school (Dickmann, 1999; Lambert and McGinty, 2002). A good example of this can be seen in an interview with a school officer in the United States:

> I had one little boy pull a knife on another little girl and threatened her with it because he wanted her backpack. To me, that's a weapon and he's committing a crime. Now I heard about this second-hand the next day so I went to the principal and I said I'm filing charges on this kid as soon as I go find him. And they were in class, and I make it a practice not to take the kids out of class. I'll wait for them to get out of class and then I'll call them in while they're doing a transfer to their next class. The principal came into my office and said I don't want you filing charges.
>
> (Interview: US School Resource Officer)

In the above case, the school principal and the officer were not following a protocol regarding how they dealt with these types of incidents. The officer was bound by law to investigate the situation, but the principal was focused on the welfare of the student. This type of conflict results when protocols are not cooperatively written and put in place or when protocols are ignored by one of the partners. Similar problems have been reported in England. For example, in one London school an officer had arrived at the school for a full-time placement, without any of the staff outside of the senior management team having been consulted, or even having any prior knowledge of his appointment. This apparently led to bitter resentment from many of the teaching staff and concern amongst the pupils and parents, who found themselves with a full-time uniformed officer present in their school (Fitzgerald and O'Connor, 2005).

A crucial question in all this relates to the support provided for children and young people in trouble. If conflict and tension is displayed between the police and the school, then young people will pick up on this and the issue quickly becomes one of a power struggle between the main parties; the issue of the child's welfare and those of the children around them may become lost. Offences involving children are subject to strict guidelines of investigation and ensuring that the needs of the child are met, physically, psychologically, spiritually and so on. They are entitled to legal advice and should have their parents or an appropriate adult with them if they are questioned. However, when partnerships do not operate effectively then many of the key issues around child welfare are overlooked or compromised.

As the programmes in both the United States and the United Kingdom have developed, many of these initial problems have been overcome through joint training and more effective partnership development. In the United States the National Association of School Resources Officers (NASRO) holds annual conferences inviting school personnel and police to share their experiences and best practice from across the country.

## Evidence from formal evaluations

In general, formal evaluation of school policing programmes around the world is limited (Shaw, 2004). In the United States, although no formal national study of school policing effectiveness has been conducted, many school districts and police jurisdictions have conducted local evaluations related to meeting programme aims and objectives. For example, in Virginia the Department of Criminal Justice highlighted the roles of the school resource officer (SRO) and perceptions about the extent of their impact upon the school community:

> SRO's successfully perform as law enforcers, instructors of law related educational classes, crime prevention specialists, and community liaisons. They participated in schools security assessments, applied Crime Prevention through Environmental Design (CPTED), principles to reduce the probability of crime, developed or improved school crime prevention policies, intervened in conflicts before they escalated into reportable incidents and engaged students and staff in crime prevention activities.
>
> (Johnson, 1999)

The recognition and status levels of these officers is slowly changing as police organisations, senior police officers and school management staff have started to realise the contributions that schools' officers are making in communities and more specifically in the lives of young people.

The initial pilot of SSPs in England and Wales was evaluated by both Bhabra and colleagues (2004) for the YJB and DfES and Bowles and colleagues (2005) for the YJB. There were problems with both these evaluations, partly because it was difficult to measure how effective they were due to some of the criteria set up by the evaluations themselves. In common with many evaluations at the time in the United Kingdom, the time period in which change was expected to take place was very short (six months in the case of the Bhabra and colleagues evaluation). A summary of the outcomes of this research is provided below:

> Quantitative data showed an improvement in young people's perceptions of the quality of the school environment within SSP

schools. They thought the problems of bullying and substance mis-use had improved. They also felt that adult intervention at school to stop bullying had increased, and there was a rise in the proportion of young people expecting a police officer, in particular, to inter-vene. Rates of being bullied or victimised in other ways did not decrease however; and young people were not less worried about bullying by the end of our evaluation period. Problem behaviour, such as drinking, use of drugs, bullying others, truanting and anti-social behaviour, had also not decreased, according to young people's own reports. Although attitudes to the police remained broadly pos-itive, they cooled slightly over time, suggesting that young people's initially very positive expectations of the scheme had not entirely been fulfilled. Qualitative data did, however, suggest that, for certain young people and in certain groups, the scheme was perceived to have a positive effect.

(Bhabra et al., 2004, p. 6)

Bowles and colleagues (2005) had problems with obtaining reliable data on offending before and after SSPs were established, an issue that is highly problematic in schools, as we note in Chapter 6. However, tru-ancy rates did fall in SSP schools and pupils felt safer in these SSP schools, in comparison with schools in the study that were not part of an SSP. Qualitative data were mostly very positive in this latter study:

The comments of staff tended to cluster around some common themes on the advantages of the programme:

- more activities and pastoral work for pupils
- a quicker response to behaviour problems
- more engagement with the local community
- better attitudes and ethos in the school, with greater emphasis on mutual respect and inclusion
- the presence of SSP staff was supporting, challenging and engaging pupils

Pupils, parents and staff became accustomed to having a police officer in the school and were normally prepared to trust the police more as a result, provided that the officer demonstrated commitment to the school.

(p. 4)

However, Bowles and colleagues highlighted the fact that some school staff felt uncomfortable about the idea of a police presence in school and were unclear about their role. This is unsurprising as there were very few protocols in place that provided clear guidance around the clarity of roles. Officers voiced opinions about poor supervision and support from senior colleagues, and both teachers and officers felt that there was a distinct lack of training on how to work with each other in these 'partnerships'. Many of these concerns were also voiced in another report conducted at around the same time, which centred on schools within the jurisdiction of the Metropolitan Police Service. This echoes our comments earlier in this chapter by emphasising that policies and protocols should be agreed before commencing the programme and that not all schools actually warranted a police officer full time (KPMG, 2004). In 2005, research conducted by Fitzgerald and O'Connor (2005) highlighted a lack of training for school officers and a generally held belief by many officers that this was not a good career move in the United Kingdom, with very few prospects for future development. With the onset of training manuals and books dedicated to the subject (Briers, 2004) as well as an accredited Masters course in School Community Policing, officers and teachers in the United Kingdom now have access to an array of resources and online training to help develop SSPs.

## The development and future of Safer School Partnerships

Although this chapter is primarily limited to the discussion of key themes that relate to school policing in the United Kingdom (with much of the evidence relating primarily to England) and the United States, it is important to conclude with a brief discussion related to school policing programmes in other parts of the world (see, for example, Council of Europe, 2002). There are many differences in the way in which this work has developed worldwide. Differences can be found in the areas of objectives and organisation, philosophies and types of intervention approaches. Shaw (2004) detailed, through a study of school policing programmes around the world, that school policing programmes reflect the considerations in Figure 9.2. This illustrates that 'partnership' is not a feature of some programmes.

In comparison with the United States, it is not usual to have police placed within schools across Europe (Lou, 2008). In many cases, police work in schools is limited to that of a less intrusive educational role only (Shaw, 2004; Brown, 2006). However, Shaw's report (2004) indicates that there is a long history of police–school liaison in Norway, Finland,

- **Proactive or reactive** – in reactive mode, the police respond to incidents and requests from schools when an event has occurred, and take the appropriate measures. A proactive approach requires them to intervene to prevent situations or behaviours conducive to offending, violence, drug abuse or other problems.
- The police role may be primarily **deterrent or preventive**. Examples of a deterrent approach include the presence of uniformed officers for surveillance purposes, or the use of undercover police officers. A preventive approach may involve drug prevention education or close liaison work with 'at risk' children.
- Interventions may be **general or targeted** – directed to the whole school population, or targeted to specific children such as truants or to schools in more disadvantaged neighbourhoods.
- Programme goals may be **broad or specific** – to develop good relations with young people and break down mistrust, or focused on a specific issue such as preventing gang recruitment or drug and alcohol use.
- The way police perform their tasks in schools can be **formal or informal** – a uniformed presence and an emphasis on police knowledge and functions, or in civilian clothes and informal contact with the students or families, playing sports or developing closer ties as adult mentors.
- The intended outcomes of programmes may be **short term**, such as locating drug traffickers or gang members, or **medium or long term**, to change attitudes and behaviours and reduce the likelihood of future offending.
- Finally, they may work in a **bilateral or multi-lateral partnership** way – liaising just with the school or on a more multi-partnership basis with a range of other local services and organisations.

*Figure 9.2* Types of school policing programmes
*Source*: Adapted from Shaw (2004, p. 3).

Sweden and Denmark (Danish Crime Prevention Council, 1998), as well as in the Netherlands, Australia (Sutton, 2002) and Germany. Programmes can also be found in South Africa (Harber, 2001; Roper, 2002) and Canada (Ryan, 1994; Ministère de la Sécurité publique, 2002). More importantly, worldwide there is limited systematic, relevant and rigorous research and comprehensive evaluations of these programmes. Thus, there is a large gap regarding 'what works' in police work with schools and specifically what are the appropriate measures of success in such partnerships. Research needs to continue in the area of school policing programmes and specifically SSPs; furthermore, evaluated evidence could help play a part in creating safer schools.

In terms of the future for police in schools in the United Kingdom, the Youth Crime Action Plan (Home Office, 2008) encourages the development of more SSPs and sees the role of such officers as an integral part of its neighbourhood policing plan. This is based on the performance of the key roles of prevention, enforcement and support for young people in all areas – not just those which are highlighted as high crime areas. SSPs in the United Kingdom have progressed quickly since the original pilot in 2002. In May 2009 the secretary of state for children, schools and families announced the SSPs Guidance. This guidance was jointly developed with ACPO, the YJB and the Home Office (DCSF, 2009d). In announcing this guidance, the secretary of state advised all schools to consider establishing an SSP:

> In the Youth Crime Action Plan published in July last year, we said that we wanted to encourage the foundation of more Safer School Partnerships (SSPs), so that they become the norm rather than the exception. SSPs, an important part of neighbourhood policing, have a central role to play in supporting the triple track approach of enforcement, prevention and support on which the action plan is based. Taking early action to ensure pupil safety and to prevent young people from being drawn into crime or antisocial behaviour is important for all pupils and for all schools. And every school – not just those in high crime areas or which have serious issues of antisocial behaviour or offending among its pupils – should consider establishing an SSP.
>
> (Balls, 2009, para. 8)

The ACPO for England and Wales estimate that there are over 5000 schools that are part of the SSPs, or some 20 per cent of primary schools and 45 per cent of secondary schools (DCSF, 2009d).

Several years ago the introduction of police in schools in the United Kingdom was viewed as an unnecessary intrusion into school life, which sparked controversy and led to debates around human rights and the potential criminalisation of young people, as well as issues around freedom of information. The tension is ongoing in academic debate, although popular debate is much less critical. A major issue at the time of writing in the United Kingdom is public expenditure cuts and the extent to which they will affect SSPs.

# 10
# Affecting the Behaviour of Young People in Schools

*John Visser*

## Behaviour in schools – an educationalist's perspective

This chapter is written from the perspective of an educationalist with some 40 years' experience of working with children and young people who have been ascribed a variety of terms, all of which describe behaviours and emotions that adults working in a professional capacity deem inappropriate in the context in which they occur. Few behaviours are universally deemed inappropriate in all contexts or cultures. Fortunately, not only are these a relatively narrow band of behaviours, usually involving extremes of violence leading to physical harm of the person or others, they are for the most part rare, particularly within a school context. Nonetheless there is a perception, particularly in westernised societies, that the behaviour of children and young people has been on a downward trend. This perception is often portrayed in the media, which in the United Kingdom not infrequently describes schools as places where 'violent' behaviour pervades the everyday experiences of teachers and pupils alike. Other chapters within this volume detail some of the research that contributes to that perception as well as alternative views of that data. Visser (2006) showed that there is a tendency for the media and educationalists to get behaviour trends out of perspective. As Hayden (2007) argues, it is not so much that behaviours are getting 'worse' in schools and society as that they change and evolve. Buckley and Maxwell (2007), in discussing the problematic nature of violence in schools, quote the commissioner for children in New Zealand as saying:

> we simply do not know if there is more violence within schools, more violence within our communities and families or if we are tolerating less violence than before and responding differently to this violence.
>
> (p. 2)

What has been shown by reports on behaviour in schools over the past 50+ years (Underwood Report, 1955; Elton Report, 1989; Daniels et al., 1998; Visser, 2003; Ofsted, 2005; Steer, 2009) is that most behaviours that cause concern within schools and classrooms are 'low-level irritating' behaviours frequently displayed by pupils, which interrupt the 'free flow' of teaching and learning. These behaviours range from the absence of the right equipment for particular lessons, through talking 'out of turn', to swearing and verbal abuse. Whilst these types of behaviours can be challenging for teachers, they can also be viewed as part of the spectrum of behaviour that will be displayed by most young people at some time.

## The pursuit of an agreed label

Between the 'rare' and the frequent but 'low level' lie another range of behaviours that have a qualitatively different 'feel' to them. They are often intense, unpredictable, constant and difficult to ignore. Moreover, still other behaviours, equally intense and constant, are overlooked because the behaviour doesn't impact on the teacher's perception of control of the classroom. Educationalists over time have used a variety of terms to label these behaviours and more latterly have increased the range, incorporating some of the more controversial ones in their repertoire, such as ADHD or attention deficit hyperactivity disorder (Visser and Zenib, 2009). Educationalists do not have one term used consistently to describe the behaviours or the children or young people whose behaviour they deem to be inappropriate (Visser, 2003).

The ascription of labels by teachers and other professional groups in education is determined by prevailing fashions and 'routes' to intervention (Visser, 2003). Many writers have also discussed the problematic nature of moving from the 'label' to defining the behaviours appropriate to that label (see, for example, Cooper, 1996, 2001; Cole et al., 1998; Thomas and Glenny, 2000; Cooper et al., 2009). The terminology used by educationalists to describe behaviours within schools is thus idiosyncratic to education, with the possible exception of terms such as ADHD, which are of medical origin. Whilst educationalists may use terms such as 'antisocial' and 'criminal' behaviour these will largely be ascribed to behaviours occurring *outside* of the school day.

Within the education service in England there is the concept of some children and young people having special educational needs (SEN), and within that group sits those whose primary SEN lies within social, emotional and behavioural difficulties (SEBD), a term preferred by most professionals in education to the government's behavioural, emotional and social difficulties (BESD). Determining SEBD is a matter of the frequency, persistence, severity, abnormality and cumulative effect of the behaviour when compared to 'normal' behaviour (DfEE, 2001). There is, within even this definition, a high degree of contextuality, such that behaviours in one context may result in the ascription of the label SEBD and in another not so.

The term 'challenging behaviour' has become prevalent in the language of some educational practitioners since the nature of the behaviours deemed inappropriate are seen in terms of a 'challenge' by one or more pupils against another pupil, group of pupils or staff. Most often this is perceived in terms of an individual pupil and individual staff; the latter then describing the former as challenging. It often also conveys notions of threats to physical safety. In contrast, within academic educational literature and research the term challenging behaviour is used more precisely and is most often associated with the presence of cognitive impairment. As Porter (2003) indicates, pupils with cognitive impairments can have behaviours that are extreme, repetitive and intense; however, the pupils with cognitive impairment may have little or no awareness of the behaviour they are performing and thus are challenging to the adults attempting to intervene as there may be few ways of engaging and changing the behaviours. However, in the discourse of teachers in schools the term is used without recourse to notions of cognitive impairment, and with the implication that the child or young person concerned 'chooses' to behave in this manner.

Within the educationalist's concept of SEBD and challenging behaviour, then, there is a notion that some control over these behaviours (even if only a very little) can be exercised by the child or young person concerned, or that such possibilities can be brought to his or her attention. For the most part, there is very little or no focus on any connection between such behaviours and anti-social or criminal behaviour.

## Prevalence of SEBD

Given the problematic nature both of defining the terms and the inconsistency of their use, the numbers of pupils with SEBD in educational settings can only be estimated. Data given by official statistics are 'snapshots', which often do not allow for the vagaries and subjectivity of their collection. Comparisons over time of data should similarly be treated with caution.

Estimates of prevalence rates for SEBD in England are around 4 per cent (Cole et al., 2003), which accords with those estimated by Kauffman (2001) in the United States and Fortin and Bigras (1997) for Canada. Cooper (1996) argued for the higher figure of between 10 per cent and 20 per cent of pupils between 4 and 16 years of age, as having some degree of SEBD. He was working from a broader definition than that contained within the Code of Practice on special educational needs (DfEE, 2001) to include a number of mental health conditions that he associated with SEBD. Of pupils deemed to have SEN, such that some form of additional educational support is required and that they were on 'School Action Plus' ('School Action Plus' refers to schools asking for additional external support or help from educational, social work or health services) or a 'Statement' (a 'Statement' is a document that details the results of a formal assessment of the special educational needs of the minority of children who are put forward for a statutory assessment), those with SEBD form the second largest group (30.6 per cent) within SEN (DCSF, 2009c).

All authors acknowledge a gender imbalance associated with those deemed SEBD. Cole and colleagues (1998) established that there were ten to 12 times as many boys as girls attending specialist provision. The latest analysis indicates that the male/female ratio has fallen, with DCSF (2009c) indicating a fall to four boys to one girl being in receipt of a SEN Statement for SEBD. However, not all of these pupils attend specialist provision. A Scottish study indicated that 80 per cent of SEBD pupils were male (Lloyd and O'Regan, 1999). These figures hold similarities with gender patterns in the youth justice system. In the early 1990s there was an over-representation of some ethnic minority groups within the SEBD population as a whole, particularly those of black Caribbean origin (Parsons, 1999). However, work by Cole and colleagues (1998) indicates that this over-representation has decreased. There is clear evidence of poverty amongst those children and young people with SEBD with DCSF (2009c), indicating nearly all of these pupils are entitled to free school meals. The same analysis also indicates that they are amongst the lowest achieving students in terms of academic attainments.

## Educational provision for SEBD

In terms of provision it is difficult to be certain of the proportion of pupils with SEBD who are to be found in mainstream schools as against specialist provision. Two main forms of specialist provision are available in most, but not all, local authorities; these are pupil referral units (PRUs) (shortly to be known as short stay schools) and special schools. Though PRUs were specifically created to cater for pupils who were excluded or in danger of being excluded from mainstream schools and were not deemed to be SEBD under the Code of Practice for special educational needs (DfEE, 2001), in practice many of the pupils within this provision either had been identified as being SEBD or had not had their SEN identified and assessed before arriving in the PRU (Daniels et al., 2003). Special school provision overall has remained static in recent years, though there has been a shift away from residential towards day provision and this follows a trend in decreased numbers of special schools going back into the early 1990s. However, Ofsted (2003b) indicates that an increasing number of pupils were attending the remaining specialist schools. Daniels and colleagues (1998) found that provision for SEBD within mainstream schools was, at best, patchy, with some making provision but most not doing so. Issues of ethos, staffing and curriculum were considered major barriers in making provision. More recent changes in the national curriculum, including greater flexibility in the range of subjects and accreditation on offer, have made some impact on the provision some mainstream schools make.

## Strategies for meeting SEBD needs in mainstream schools

During the past ten years there has been a significant growth of provision within mainstream primary schools with the introduction of the social and emotional aspects of learning (SEAL) programme (DCSF, 2005) and interventions such as nurture groups (Cooper and Tiknaz, 2007) amongst many others. These strategies are beginning to transfer across into secondary schools, mainly because the Every Child Matters agenda (DfES, 2003a) has, since 2004, highlighted the need for schools to widen their vision to include issues of 'well-being' as well as academic achievement. While these are the 'latest' strategies to emerge within mainstream schools they were preceded by a large number of others; many began as local initiatives that were taken over by central government and then rolled out as nationally funded and supported strategies. All too often the funding has proved to be short term, usually lasting two years or so before the initiative is overtaken by another. Visser (2002) refers to the tendency to 're-invent wheels' when exploring some of the initiatives that have been funded. Each generation of teachers 're-discover' behaviour as being challenging. As Visser (2002) points out, teachers and the educational media repeat the following sentence, or one very like it, every seven to ten years:

> For the past 'A' a rising concern facing 'B' because of 'C' is a lack of 'D'.

Where 'A' stands for a period of time, B equals teachers or/and teaching assistants, C any recent change in educational approaches generally and D one of the following: standards, behaviour, discipline, respect or order. The reaction to these concerns is usually a search for a 'new' strategy to implement (Visser, 2002). The core of the 'new' strategy can more often than not be found in previous provision made by earlier generations of teachers. Seldom do teachers, policy makers or administrators make use of previous research that indicates what systemic changes produce changes in behaviour. More seldom still are questions raised as to the underlying principles that are key to the success of strategies and that might be useful as a 'litmus' test for suggested 'new' strategies.

## Systemic factors for successful interventions

The following sections draw upon a review of national and international reports that contain recommendations for improving behaviour in schools and upon a study by Daniels and colleagues (1998) on successful provision within mainstream schools. Table 10.1 indicates the recommendations made and shows the degree of congruence that exists across these reports. These are discussed below.

There is universal agreement on the need to have whole school policies on behaviour (see also Chapter 12). Daniels and colleagues (1998) found that a positive whole school behaviour policy is instrumental in providing a culture that fosters appropriate behaviours in schools. Whilst they indicate that it enabled a consistency of approach by staff towards inappropriate behaviour, they found that this consistency need not be total. Rather, they indicate that its implementation by key staff was the crucial aspect, alongside having the policy clearly accessible by all in the school, as well as parents.

The second most common recommendation relates to the quality of teaching and learning in the school as a whole. It is not that a particular style of teaching is required, as outlined in Lewis and Norwich (2004), nor is a specialist teaching style required. Rather, it is the case that teaching of a high quality engenders in the learner the motivation to engage

Table 10.1 Recommendations – challenging behaviour and mainstream schools

| Country | Source | Year | Whole school policies | Teaching and learning | Teacher education | Leadership | Respect of students | Additional support | Class size | Parents | Multi-agency | Specialist provision within mainstream | Physical environment |
|---|---|---|---|---|---|---|---|---|---|---|---|---|---|
| EIRE | Government Report | 2006 | ✓ | ✓ | ✓ | ✓ | ✓ | ✓ | ✓ | ✓ | ✓ | | |
| Scotland | The Educational Institute of Scotland | 2006 | ✓ | ✓ | ✓ | | | ✓ | ✓ | ✓ | ✓ | | |
| Scotland | Scottish Executive | 2006 | ✓ | ✓ | ✓ | ✓ | | | ✓ | ✓ | ✓ | | |
| Europe wide | NFER & CIDRER | 2005 | ✓ | ✓ | ✓ | | ✓ | | | | ✓ | | |
| Europe wide | Council of Europe | 2005 | ✓ | ✓ | ✓ | | | | | | | ✓ | ✓ |

| Country | Organisation | Year | | | | | | | | | |
|---|---|---|---|---|---|---|---|---|---|---|---|
| England | Office of Standards in Education (Ofsted) | 2007 | ✓ | ✓ | ✓ | | | | ✓ | | ✓ |
| England | Department for Child Schools and Families | 2009 | ✓ | ✓ | ✓ | ✓ | ✓ | ✓ | ✓ | ✓ | ✓ |
| Worldwide | The International Academy of Education | 2002 | ✓ | ✓ | ✓ | ✓ | ✓ | ✓ | ✓ | | |
| England | Department for Education and Science | 1989 | ✓ | ✓ | ✓ | ✓ | ✓ | ✓ | ✓ | ✓ | |

(Drawn from national and international reports.)

in the learning (Daniels et al., 1998). Though it might sound trite it remains true that a learner engaged in a learning task will be displaying appropriate behaviour; on-task behaviour is not challenging!

Apparent in national reports such as Underwood Report (1955), Elton Report (1989), Ofsted (2005) and Steer (2009) is the need for a greater linkage between quality teaching and behaviour in both initial teacher training and in the provision of continuing professional development (CPD). Daniels and colleagues (1998) found that schools that had an emphasis upon CPD that encapsulated a focus on both learning and behaviour were likely to experience fewer challenging behaviours.

Systemic change, however, can only provide a preventative framework within which successful interventions can flourish. This is not to downgrade their importance, rather it is to point out that, as seen in Table 10.1, their importance has been emphasised by numerous reports over a period of time, and yet there remains concern about the behaviour of pupils. There is a propensity for these reports to deliver quick, uncomplicated headline 'answers' to what are complex individual challenges. These headlines generally point to structures and systems needing change (Visser, 2002). What is required is more emphasis upon the qualitative nature of those changes and the emotional commitment of professionals to meeting the needs of pupils with SEBD. Visser (2002) first referred to the characteristics of this emotional commitment as eternal verities.

## Eternal verities

'Eternal verities' is not a term that is often seen in educational publications. In 1968 Wills used it in his closing address at a conference for those working with SEBD pupils, termed at the time as the 'maladjusted'. He referred to the need for the researcher to have faith based upon 'the unchanging and eternal verities' to survive the stresses involved in working with pupils with SEBD.

The term resonates with a personal quest for an underlying set of unifying principles within all approaches to meeting the educational needs of pupils with SEBD. I set out to find out whether there is a set of principles that are seldom enunciated, associated with good practice, which, to quote Whelan (1998), are the field's 'memory banks', subliminally passed on to each succeeding generation of teachers.

My quest has its origins in my early development as a teacher of pupils with SEBD. I faced contradictions, as I perceived them, between the various approaches put forward as ways of meeting these pupils' needs.

Some of the approaches seemed to me to be diametrically opposed to each other. As a young teacher struggling to do what was right for the pupils in my charge, which should I choose? What could ensure that the approach chosen would work? And as a provider of professional development for teachers and others working within SEBD what approaches should I espouse? What advice could be given to help educators examine the likely success of any given policy shift, 'new' initiative or change in provision?

As part of my professional development I took a year off to gain an MEd. The course provided me with the opportunity to visit a number of institutions, among them one that espoused a behavioural approach and one that had a psychodynamic basis for its work. Both were perceived at that time as schools of good practice. In one setting I felt more comfortable than in the other, but it was evident that they were both successful in meeting the needs of pupils with SEBD. Were there common underlying factors/principles/beliefs that accounted for this success? Are there eternal verities that are a part of all successful approaches? The DNA of approaches? Just as cells within the human body perform different functions but contain the same DNA, are there eternal verities to be found in all effective interventions to meet the needs of children and young people with SEBD?

## What is an 'eternal verity'?

Verities are truths that are apparent in the web and weave of approaches. They are eternal inasmuch as they are necessary to the proficiency of all approaches regardless of the time frame in which the approaches are being developed and applied. They are the strongest links between different approaches and the achievement of successful outcomes. As such, they carry values and beliefs about the human condition and the quality of life to which we, and especially pupils with SEBD, are entitled. They are rarely made explicit, often emerging implicitly from literature, discussion and research. They are observable but their quantification is seldom helpful. Having more or less of them is not so much the issue as their quality and presence within an approach. They sustain teachers and other professionals in times of stress and good practice flows from them.

The list that follows is not presented as a definitive one (see Figure 10.1). It is idiosyncratic and there is a need for further research if it is to be of use in the future. This list of eternal verities has drawn on three sources. The first is my experiences as a pedagogue in a variety

- Behaviour can change: emotional needs can be met.
- Intervention is second to prevention.
- Instructional reactions.
- Transparency in communications.
- Empathy and equity.
- Boundaries and challenge.
- Building positive relationships.
- Humour.

*Figure 10.1*   Eternal verities and working with children with SEBD

of roles, from the classroom teacher to researcher and provider of staff development programmes, and from parent to foster parent. The second is from my involvement with education in a number of research and consultancy projects. The third comes from a review of the literature, which describes the various understandings and perspectives on emotional and behavioural difficulties. Amongst these I have drawn particularly on the work of Ayers and colleagues (2000), Cooper and colleagues (2009) and Cooper (2001), Education Resources Information Centre (ERIC) (1997), Kauffman (2001), Laslett and colleagues (1998), Porter (2000) and Whelan (1998). These writers offer the reader a comprehensive view of the variety of approaches to be found in SEBD work, in both England and the United States, and thus provide a basis for seeking possible eternal verities. The work of Bowlby, Erickson, Maslow and Daniels has also informed the 'eternal verities' put forward below. This list is offered as a litmus test. It is suggested that interventions, strategies and approaches that support these verities will be successful. Where a school's ethos fails to encapsulate them, then I contend there is a much smaller chance of a successful outcome for pupils with SEBD.

## Eternal verities and working with children with SEBD

### Behaviour can change: emotional needs can be met

It may seem axiomatic that approaches are premised upon a belief that behaviour can change and emotional needs can be met. However, it is dangerous to assume that this is so. Meeting the needs of pupils with SEBD absorbs a large slice of any agency's budget, particularly in education. If approaches cannot meet needs and produce change, then should they be funded?

Behaviour is perceived by effective teachers as capable of change, whatever the source or underlying reason. There is an understanding that to be human is not to be at the mercy of instincts or genetic make-up. This is apparent even in the re-emerging medical perspectives of aspects of SEBD, such as ADHD (Cooper, 2001). Nurture, the psychosocial development and the social context of the child or young person are always viewed as central to understanding. The starting premise must be where the child currently is, and where the adult wishes the child to be. The child is seen as being able to attain control over the actions and emotional needs that have caused the emotional and behavioural difficulties.

This belief in the possibility of change provides teachers with the ability to continue to work with children and young people when so often the latter reject the attempts to meet their needs. This quality, of going 'the extra half mile', is seen as being necessary in teachers (Cole et al., 1998). As Rodway (1993) pointed out in his 1992 David Wills Lecture:

> However much a child may wound his own self-esteem... (he) cannot change the esteem in which (the teachers) hold him (if the approach is to be successful).
>
> (p. 379)

### Intervention is second to prevention

The history of nearly all approaches indicates that they have been derived from the identification of a 'challenge' presented by a group of children or young people. The difficulties are identified before the approaches are developed. The interventions seek to meet the challenge presented by the identified difficulties. Publicising the success of the intervention inevitably leads to the identification of 'fault lines' within the child's environment, be that school, home or community. Prevention strategies become apparent. At some usually early stage, aspects of the approach are highlighted as being able to contribute to the prevention of SEBD. All effective approaches underscore the proverb: 'prevention is better than cure'.

Much of the literature on classroom management, for example, is derived from studies of the approaches that make for poor classroom management. Prevention in the form of ensuring that positive strategies are in place initially in teacher training has only recently been focused upon. Approaches that ensure that preventive strategies are at least as strongly represented as intervention strategies have more possibilities of achieving successful outcomes (Visser, 2000).

### Instructional reactions

Pupils with SEBD do not always understand the relationship between their behaviours and the reactions those behaviours cause. Few children set out with malice aforethought to be the disturbed and disturbing characters many of them become. When they do, it is to achieve some gratification or status that protects their self-esteem. Effective approaches recognise this and work to consistently portray to the child what the relationship is between cause and effect, and how they can achieve different reactions that meet their needs. Just telling pupils with SEBD off or issuing sanctions for inappropriate behaviours has little effect, except perhaps to persuade the child not to get caught next time. Staff who give the child the reasons why the behaviour is inappropriate, together with alternative ways to react appropriately, achieve successful outcomes.

## Transparency in communications

A consistent finding in the research mentioned above is the degree to which clear, consistent, coherent communication is a factor in meeting the social and emotional needs of pupils with SEBD (see, for example, Cole et al., 1998; Daniels et al., 1998). A variety of approaches advocated by teachers have emphasised the importance of consistency, so that 'the team around the child' have spoken from the 'same hymn sheet' and thus provided a consistency of approach. This consistency also provides for a transparency in communications. This in turn supports the development of a caring, learning and sharing school ethos in meeting the needs of pupils with SEBD (Visser et al., 2002).

## Empathy and equity

Approaches to pupil's needs devoid of empathy seem to have had less effect than those that incorporate it. Proficient approaches encourage the development of a robust empathy with the children and young people. This is not as easy as some would make out. The case histories of most pupils with SEBD reveal significant family trauma, poverty in their range of positive experiences, a paucity of expectations, an absence of the emotional capacity to make and sustain relationships and, sadly all too often, physical, emotional and sexual abuse. Though some teachers may have personal experience of one or more of these, few have experienced them in the depth and range experienced by the pupil with SEBD.

Empathy, that ability to begin to see the world through the eyes of the child's experience, requires a degree of emotional commitment to the well-being of the child. Empathy provokes the question, which needs to be asked continuously when working with the child with SEBD, 'why do

I think this child behaved in this way and what does that mean for the approach I use?' It provides the basis upon which the pupil can begin to feel valued and understood. Being empathic should not lead to the teacher excusing the SEBD: rather it provides an understanding as to why the SEBD has occurred.

## Boundaries and challenge

All approaches within the literature speak of the need for structure, particularly of the need to provide boundaries. They recognise that the lack of self-imposition or acknowledgement of boundaries has a co-morbidity with SEBD. This is hardly surprising given that it is the constant lack of being able to behave and display emotions within boundaries that most frequently triggers the identification of a pupil as having SEBD. The boundaries need to be set by the teachers but must have a flexibility, in that it bends but never breaks (Cole et al., 1998). In other words, approaches that have a rigid structure in meeting the needs of pupils are very unlikely to be effective. As Royer (2001) points out, the inflexible approach fails because it ends up identifying all difficulties as nails because the only tool in the teacher's kit is a hammer. Bentley (1997) saw this eternal verity as being very necessary if pupils with SEBD are to avoid being further marginalised within schools and classrooms.

With flexible boundaries should go high, achievable expectations of behaviour and educational achievement (Cole et al., 1998; Daniels et al., 1998; Ofsted, 1999a). The therapeutic effect of being set challenging, achievable targets, even when initially a great deal of support is required, is noted by Wilson and Evans (1980) and others (Greenhalgh, 1994; Cooper, 1996). Ofsted (1999b) reported low expectations in relation to pupils' achievements as a contributory cause in many schools 'causing concern' or with 'serious weaknesses'.

## Building positive relationships

Bentley (1997) writes: *social networks are powerful determinants of an individual's life chances* (p. 46). He goes on to indicate that having access to a range of adults as role models is an indispensable resource for young people. Daniels (2001) and Ryan (2001) reinforce this with their view that the ability to develop genuine caring and learning relationships, and knowing where to go to make them, is an important skill for pupils to acquire if they are to be integrated members of their community. Children and young people with SEBD are not good at making and sustaining positive relationships; they constantly test out the adults they come across (Laslett, 1999). Porter (2000) indicates that, for pupils with SEBD, relationships need to provide emotional safety and protection, personal involvement and trust, and acceptance from others. Approaches that are successful emphasise the need to develop such relationships.

## Humour

As Cole and colleagues (1998), Porter (2000) and Visser (2000) point out, having a sense of humour has been seen, since the early 'pioneers' working with children and young people with SEBD, as a vital component in any approach to working with young people who present these behaviours. Humour is rarely mentioned in descriptions of approaches and yet, as one study (Cole et al., 1998) found, it is consistently placed as one of the top three characteristics of the effective pedagogue working with pupils with SEBD. Fovet (2009) provides a useful insight into the mechanisms of humour, noting that it is a complex area of human communication rooted in subjective standards making investigation difficult. He notes from his study that the receptivity of students to humour is dependent upon 'genuine' positive relationships between students and staff.

## The range of eternal verities

We work in an age where there has been an information explosion, and gone are some of the old certainties of testing the veracity of what we are told. The pattern, shape and accessibility of information is radically changing. If schools and teachers are to develop and adapt their abilities to meet the needs of pupils with SEBD, then having a set of eternal verities may provide a sound base upon which to test the information available.

Are these the only eternal verities? Greenhalgh (1999) lists six characteristics he saw as important. Laslett (1999) puts forward 17 he saw as common to the early pioneers (such as David Wills). Ofsted (1999a) indicate six features consistently associated with good practice, and Whelan (1998) three. All these accord with the eight listed above, differing in emphasis and range of terminology rather than content. There remains a lack of empirical quantitative evidence to support this qualitative consensus. Cooper and colleagues (2009), completing a review of a wide range of reported research, point to a lack of replicable evidence to support approaches (to working with children with SEBD) deemed to be good practice and delivering positive outcomes.

## Conclusions

Educationalists have long had the task of affecting the behaviour of young people in schools. The evidence base for the effectiveness of many of the approaches utilised has been seen as questionable, and in relation to meeting special education needs is at best equivocal and at worst non-existent (Dyson, 2001). The evidence base in SEBD is similarly poor. Besides the need to halt the cycle of wheel reinvention, establishing a set of eternal verities may also provide a brake on the increasing categorisation of pupils within SEBD. It will not negate the need for teachers and schools to use their independent and professional judgements (Pirrie, 2001); rather it may provide the basis upon which to make that judgement. The educationalist's central focus on teaching and learning in schools is a reminder to policy makers and agencies working with schools of where their agenda might sit in relation to this necessary focus of schools. Whilst the wider remit of schools includes responding effectively to the more extreme and problematic behaviours that are clearly criminal; in the main this is not what teachers have to focus on most of the time in most schools.

# 11
# Restorative Approaches in UK Schools

*Belinda Hopkins*

## Restorative *justice* and restorative *approaches*

Since the late 1990s there has been a growth in the use of restorative approaches (RAs) in UK schools, at the same time that there has been a wider use and interest in restorative justice (RJ) within the Youth Justice System. Restorative approaches are also growing in other areas of child welfare, such as children's residential care (Hopkins, 2009; Hayden and Gough, 2010). Schools use RAs as a response to a variety of behaviours and situations, such as addressing pupil disputes, bullying, disruptive and challenging behaviour and to inform a 'whole school approach' to managing behaviour in schools (see also Chapter 12). As we have noted elsewhere in this volume, these behaviours can be perceived as 'anti-social' and occasionally the behaviour is identified as criminal; however, for the most part the behaviours that RAs address in schools are not criminal. The latter is a key issue when transferring an approach informed by restorative *justice* into the school context, as we will explore later in this chapter.

The application of restorative philosophy and practice in school contexts in the United Kingdom has grown from isolated practice in individual schools in the late 1990s, to a widespread initiative with at least one project in over 60 local authorities in England, a country-wide, government-backed initiative in Scotland, and growing interest in Northern Ireland and Wales. There are three key, overlapping character-istics in relation to the development of services for children and young people that help to explain how and why there has been support for the development of RAs in UK schools. Firstly, concerns about child wel-fare have prompted consideration of the social, emotional, mental and spiritual needs of young people. Related to these latter concerns, the development of multi-agency and partnership working has led to the cross-fertilisation of ideas from a variety of philosophies, working practices and experiences. Secondly, changes in the practice of youth justice have included a search for new ways of responding to and preventing offending behaviour (see Chapter 1). Thirdly, there have been a number of educational initiatives set up to address a range of problem behaviours in and associated with schools, including bullying, disruptive behaviour and poor attendance. These concerns and initiatives converged and created a 'zeitgeist' for the early 2000s, which developed into a focus on the safety and welfare of children and young people, alongside concerns about anti-social behaviour and young people and a need to find effective ways of dealing with this problem. It was against this backdrop that the first Restorative Justice in Schools initiatives began.

Key policy frameworks have been influential in developing a situation in which RJ and RAs are an appropriate response to youthful conflict and wrongdoing: namely Every Child Matters (2003), Youth Matters (2005) and Care Matters (2006). Key aspects of these policy frameworks include a growing awareness of, and commitment to, the key values of inclusion, mutual respect, collaboration, joint problem-solving, open communication, accountability and trust – all values that underpin RJ philosophy and principles.

The chapter draws on research evidence on the impact RAs can have in schools, set in the context of an exploration of the underpinning values and their resonance with contemporary policy and thinking about how to respond constructively to children and young people. It is informed by experience and practice in working on RAs with over 60 local authorities and hundreds of schools.

The term 'restorative justice' was first used in criminal justice settings to describe an innovative approach to offending behaviour that places emphasis on the impact of the behaviour on those affected, the importance of developing the wrongdoer's appreciation of the harm they have caused and the provision of opportunities for them to put things right again by some kind of reparative gesture or work. In other words, RJ seeks to define accountability in terms of things being put right again rather than in terms of the punishment inflicted on the perpetrator. This approach also offers opportunities for those affected by wrongdoing to be involved in the process – getting a chance to explain how they have been affected, receiving answers to their questions ('Why me?' 'Was I somehow to blame?' 'Will it happen again?') and being involved in identifying what needs to happen for the harm they have suffered to be repaired and for them to move on. In recent years research on victim satisfaction indicates that this restorative opportunity is one of the most notable and successful outcomes of a restorative response (Shapland et al., 2007; Sherman and Strang, 2007).

In his foreword to my book *Just Schools* (Hopkins, 2004), Guy Masters describes some of what he believes are the key historical influences on what is nowadays described as 'restorative justice or practice'. Each of these past influences has certain key characteristics, which help to illustrate the essential essence of what RJ is all about. They can also be identified as influential in the model of RJ applied in the school context. The first of these has been the development of victim–offender mediation, a process that was first used by two youth justice workers in Ontario, Canada, in the 1970s. They evolved a face-to-face process, bringing those affected by anti-social behaviour together with those engaging in it, after having reached a point of desperation with two particular young men. These two had resisted all attempts to make them change their behaviour with punishments or threats of punishment. The experience of meeting the families whom they had affected by their anti-social behaviour was life-changing for the young men. The success of the initiative led to the development of victim–offender schemes all over North America and subsequently around the world (Peachey, 1989; Zehr, 1990).

The second important influence emerged from New Zealand and the traditional practice of Maori peoples in response to wrongdoing in their communities. Their approach was to sit in a circle with their community to share together what has occurred and find ways forward collectively (Consedine, 1995). This included the wider community becoming accountable for what might be behind the young person's problem behaviour, and helping to reintegrate the young person back into the community. Maori communities expressed their distress to the 'Pakeha' government about western responses to law-breaking and anti-social behaviour, which were resulting in Maori young people finding themselves, disproportionately, on the wrong side of the law and then incarcerated far from friends and family. As a result of the lobbying from the Maori community their community circle practices were developed into what has become known as the Family Group Conferencing (FGC) model. This approach to youth offending and anti-social behaviour has been enshrined in the New Zealand youth justice system since 1989 as the preferred way of dealing with any offence other than the most violent crimes (McCold, 2001).

Inspired by the New Zealand model, Sergeant Terry O'Connell from New South Wales visited New Zealand to learn more about FGCs and then, supported by John Macdonald and David Moore, developed what has become known as 'the scripted conferencing model' (Moore and O'Connell, 1994). This model has been influential on the development of RJ practice in the United Kingdom and in some areas of the United States. Much of the early training in RJ in the United Kingdom was in fact training in the use of the 'scripted conferencing model' and in some underpinning theories that had been developed retrospectively to try and understand what was happening in the restorative circle (Braithwaite, 1989; Nathanson, 1992; Johnstone, 2002, 2003; Liebmann, 2007).

The final influential approach on the way restorative practice has developed worldwide comes from Canada, where First Nation communities, especially in the Yukon, have developed sentencing circles; these involve the community in deciding the appropriate sentence and way forward for a young offender, endorsed by the judge, who also takes part. Zehr (1990) points out the value of involving the community in dealing with its own problems and the potential this offers to building positive relationships between people and communities. In fact, it has become clear that many indigenous groups around the world have some variant on community problem-solving, often with group members sitting together in a circle sharing their stories and their ideas for resolving issues that have arisen in their communities (Pranis, 2001).

In recent years the field of restorative *approaches* or *practices* in educational settings has been developing its own discourse – informed, but not dictated to, by parallel developments in youth and criminal justice fields. This chapter adds to the record about the way in which the discourse is developing and argues that restorative practitioners introducing RAs into schools are carving out new meanings for the adjective 'restorative'. They are helping schools to appreciate the contribution restorative principles and practices can make in day-to-day interactions between members of the school community, not only when things go seriously wrong. Their contention is that the more young people are encouraged to take responsibility for their behaviour towards each other early on, and the more they feel connected (see Chapter 5, 'school connectedness' research) and valued in the learning community in each classroom the less likely they will be to engage in anti-social or violent behaviour towards each other. Restorative practices do not have the monopoly on these proactive strategies, but restorative values and principles are consistent with other initiatives promoting community cohesion and pro-social skill development. This chapter makes the case for the restorative approach as a mechanism for educational reform, as opposed to simply a selection of useful techniques for addressing young people's behaviour and reducing exclusion from school. In other words, the chapter begs the question – does RJ in school settings have more in common with *social justice* or with *criminal justice*?

## Social justice or criminal justice?

There has been, in the past at least, a tendency for those who come from a criminal justice perspective (as with the police or youth offending teams) to offer RJ to schools as a new tool for dealing with serious misbehaviours that might otherwise lead to exclusion from school. The focus has been on one specific form of restorative intervention – the restorative conference – which is predicated on there being a clearly identified 'wrongdoer' and 'wronged'[1], and indeed use of the term 'restorative justice' is virtually synonymous with the process of conferencing.

Evaluations conducted from this perspective have been focused largely on the outcomes of these conferences (Youth Justice Board, 2004; Skinns et al., 2009). The performance indicators tend to include: reduction in school exclusion and in offending and re-offending behaviours and levels of satisfaction from those people participating in a conference.

In contrast to the 'youth justice agenda', many of those who come from an educational background, see RJ not so much as a tool, but as a new approach to managing relationships and behaviour, and it is the philosophy and principles that are their starting point. The intention of such people is not simply to change individuals' behaviour or provide closure for individual victims and their families, but to effect a change in whole school culture (see also Chapter 12), involving (but not limited to) the reform of an outmoded behaviour management policy based on sanctions and rewards. Whilst reduction in exclusion, improved behaviour and the satisfaction of those engaging in restorative meetings are important indicators of success, these are only part of the picture. For the reformers, other issues are also important: such as an increased sense of safety, enhanced well-being and feeling of belonging; feeling listened to and respected; improved self-esteem, emotional literacy, resilience and the development of a strong inner locus of control. All of these latter issues may be used as indicators of change and measures of success; not only with individual pupils but also in the whole school community (Barnet Youth Offending Service, 2009). It should be noted that the distinction between the intentions and perspectives of criminal justice professionals and educationalists is not always clear; some of the former are also school reformers, whilst some of the latter are drawn to RJ – in the first instance at least – in order to simply reduce their exclusion figures.

A restorative approach, adopted across a whole school community, can, claim the reformers, contribute to community cohesion and citizenship due to greater student involvement in decision-making and decisions involving their community. It can also provide a mechanism by which emotional literacy is modelled, and therefore taught, by staff even when addressing challenge, conflict and disruption (Hopkins, 2004; Hendry, 2009). Furthermore, it can strengthen an anti-bullying policy by providing strategies for dealing with bullying, violence and anti-social behaviour that are consistent with the preventative measures promoted by so many anti-bullying and violence reduction organisations (Cowie and Jennifer, 2008).

## What restorative justice means in practice

To understand what is now happening in schools where RAs are being adopted it is useful to understand some of the key ideas and theories that are informing practice. Some of the most important values and principles applied are outlined below.

## A paradigm shift

Howard Zehr has been credited with the title of 'grandfather of restorative justice' and certainly his articulation of the differences between a restorative approach and a more traditional retributive approach has informed what he described as the 'paradigm shift' in people's thinking. When he first wrote *Changing Lenses* (Zehr, 1990) and developed the notion of a paradigm shift, he was not specifying what model of practice should be used. His speculations were about the general principles: considering crime primarily as a violation of people rather than of laws; recognising that the harm caused is not simply to those directly affected but also to the victim's community of friends, family and colleagues; defining accountability not in terms of punishment but in terms of taking responsibility for the impact of one's actions on another and acknowledging one's obligation to repair that harm; identifying the need of both wrongdoer and wronged (in the criminal justice arena, the offender and the victim) to tell their story and be listened to; championing the need of those affected by an incident to be given the opportunity to find ways forward to repair the harm amongst themselves.

These basic principles inform a wide variety of practices, some of which have been developed in recent years and some of which have been part of indigenous people's practice for centuries – including family group conferencing, restorative conferencing, community problem-solving circles, victim–offender mediation and circle sentencing. In the late 1990s I adapted Zehr's paradigm (see Table 11.1), with his permission and endorsement, for the school context. It is important to acknowledge that his sharply drawn differentiation between a retributive and a restorative approach has been criticised by others (Daly, 2000) and, indeed, now qualified by Zehr himself. However, educationalists tend to find the contrast a useful insight and a starting point for change.

In recent years the paradigm shift from a retributive and authoritarian mindset[2] to a restorative mindset has been characterised by three main questions. Traditionally, by their own admission, in responding to a discipline incident teachers have first asked themselves:

What happened? (the intention being to get to the bottom of the matter and establish 'the truth'; and, if necessary, using interrogation techniques and witness statements)

Who started it? (the intention being to identify the culprit, attribute guilt and assign blame)

What needs to happen to deter and punish? (with the assumption that the threat of punishment acts as a deterrent and that the punishment itself ensures that the behaviour will not be repeated)

This style of questioning contrasts very strongly with the way a restoratively minded teacher would begin – which would be by asking themselves:

I wonder what each person involved has experienced? (in other words, what has happened from each of their perspectives?)

I wonder who has been affected by what has happened and how each person has been affected?

I wonder how those affected can be supported in finding a way forward for themselves and repairing the harm?

*Table 11.1* Old and new paradigms for thinking about behaviour management in schools

| Old paradigm: retributive approach | New paradigm: restorative approach |
| --- | --- |
| Wrongdoing often defined as breaking the school **rules**/letting the school down. | Wrongdoing defined as **harm done** to well-being of one person or a group by another or others. |
| Focus on establishing **blame or guilt**, on the past – what happened? who did it? | Focus on **problem-solving** by expressing feelings and needs and exploring how to meet them in the future. |
| **Adversarial** relationship and process – wrongdoer in conflict with a person in authority, who decides on penalty. | **Dialogue and negotiation** – everyone involved in communicating and cooperating with each other |
| **Imposition** of pain or unpleasantness to punish and deter/prevent. | **Restitution** as a means of restoring both/all parties, the goal being reconciliation and taking responsibility in future. |
| **Wrongdoing** represented as **impersonal and abstract**: individual versus school. | **Wrongdoing** recognised as **interpersonal conflicts** with opportunities for learning. |
| One **social injury replaced by another.** | Focus on **repair** of social injury/damage. |
| **People affected by wrongdoing not necessarily involved**; victims' needs often ignored; they can feel powerless. The matter dealt with by those in authority. | Encouragement of all concerned to be **involved and empowered.** |
| **Accountability** of wrongdoer defined in terms of receiving **punishment**. | **Accountability** of wrongdoer defined as: <br> – **understanding** the impact of their actions, <br> – seeing the impact as a **consequence of choices** <br> – taking **responsibility** <br> – helping to decide how to **put things right**. |

*Source*: Adapted from Hopkins (2004).

Zehr's contribution helps to clarify what educationalists mean when they use the word 'restorative'. Whilst the particular form of the restorative intervention is not specified by Zehr's paradigm, the intention is clear. To respond 'restoratively' towards wrongdoing is to have the harm caused in mind rather than the rule broken, and to seek to empower those involved to put things right.

## Restorative themes and values

In more recent years Zehr and others have been exhorting restorative practitioners to keep in mind the value base of their practice, and various countries have developed a set of principles informed by such values. In the United Kingdom, the Restorative Justice Consortium (the national charity advocating for restorative approaches across multi-agency settings) has published its own *Principles of Restorative Processes* (RJC, 2004). Key to these principles are the underpinning values, identified as: Empowerment; Honesty; Respect; Engagement; Voluntarism; Healing; Restoration; Personal accountability; Inclusiveness; Collaboration and Problem-solving. These principles and underpinning values were identified from a survey conducted for the RJC by the current author.

It has been pointed out that RJ does not have the monopoly on these values and that they have much in common with those of liberal humanism, and indeed social justice. They also overlap with the core values of many world religions (Sawatsky, 2001; Cremin, 2002). Zehr's work and the identification by practitioners around the world of the core values and principles of RJ have shaped the development of the conceptualisation of RJ in the school context.

## The social control window

Another significant contribution to the development of an educational restorative philosophy came from McCold and Wachtel (2001) in the United States, as they considered how such an approach has relevance in a wide variety of settings. They identified that the essence of a restorative approach was one that involved creating a balance between care and support on the one hand and discipline (in the sense of structure and boundaries) and control on the other. They defined this as working WITH people rather than doing things FOR them or TO them. This balance between support and control is conceptualised as the social control window, illustrated in Figure 11.1.

## Restorative practice and models of intervention

These various elements of RJ philosophy inform educational practice but they do not predicate models of intervention. When educational practitioners use the word 'restorative' they are generally referring to behaviours that are underpinned by the core restorative

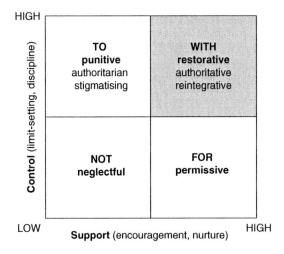

*Figure 11.1* The social control window
*Source*: Adapted from Wachtel and McCold (2001).

values and a mindset that is geared towards respect for individuals, repairing or minimising harm to relationships, and empowering those involved to find ways forward for themselves. This approach can inform behaviour and relationship development and management, leadership at various managerial levels within the school and even pedagogy. My sense is that this is the way that the word is being used by all the major theorists (who by and large are also practitioners, trainers and consultants) in the 'restorative justice in schools' field. In the United Kingdom these theorists include – Hopkins (2004, 2009), Hendry (2009) and Mahaffey and Newton (2008); in Australia – Blood (2005) and Thorsborne and Vinegrad (2002, 2004); in New Zealand – Drewery (2004); in Minnesota/USA – Riestenberg (2005); in Pennsylvania/USA – McCold and Wachtel (2002) and in Canada – Morrison (2007).

## Restorative approaches: proactive as well as reactive

Despite the introduction in the past few years of social and emotional aspects of learning (SEAL) programmes, and the widespread use of techniques like circle time to promote communication skills, a sense of belonging and self-esteem, not all educationalists working in schools have made the connection between the values that these approaches are trying to promote and encourage, and the way that they deal with discipline issues. A discipline system based on doing things TO people (laying down the rules and then using a system of sanctions and rewards to impose these rules) is diametrically opposed to the philosophy and principles underpinning programmes such as SEAL, and yet this type of system is common in schools.

What restorative educational practitioners have been trying to do is to make the necessary links so that schools can see the importance of congruence between the proactive programmes and strategies and the reactive measures taken when there are problems. This is why they have chosen to use the phrase 'restorative practices or approaches' to describe both strategies – not because the proactive strategies necessarily 'restore' broken relationships but because they are underpinned by restorative values and principles. Nevertheless, Wachtel (1999) describes all restorative practices as those that are aimed at 'restoring community in a disconnected world' – which suggests that community-building and proactive initiatives are indeed restorative in the 'repair' sense of the word.

Educational restorative theorists around the world have come to the same conclusion, based on their personal experiences working in schools and on empirical research; that for the reactive aspect of restorative practice to be successful it needs to be embedded in a 'restorative milieu' and that what is required is a 'whole school restorative approach' (Morrison, 2001, 2002, 2005b; Riestenberg, 2001; McCold and Wachtel, 2002; Thorsborne and Vinegrad, 2002, 2004; Hopkins, 2004; Blood, 2005; Hendry, 2009).

Many of us have found Morrison's (Morrison, 2005a) conceptualisation, informed by Braithwaite's (2002) work on responsive regulation, to be useful in work with schools. Morrison's model posits three levels of restorative intervention (see Figure 11.2 and a similar conceptualisation in Figure 12.2 in Chapter 12). These three levels relate to different types of need and intensity of response. The first level involves programmes and approaches relevant for the whole school community – those that build capacity in the field of relationships and problem-solving. The second level is applicable to those who become involved in conflicts and low-level disruption. The third and most serious level is for those whose behaviour risks seriously disconnecting them from the school community and from those who have been adversely affected by this behaviour.

Increasingly, the use of circles (for establishing pro-social cohesive learning communities) is seen as the key to developing a whole school restorative approach – amongst young people and also amongst staff.

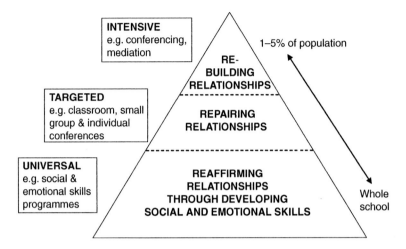

*Figure 11.2* Three levels of restorative intervention
*Source*: Morrison (2005a).

Indeed, circles become the mechanism by which all three levels of intervention can work, with some key themes and key language being used at every level, whether the circle process is one that is future-focused (to build community and an understanding that everyone needs to give of their best) or responsive, following a problem or some disruptive behaviour.

## Models for responding to harm and wrongdoing in schools

The models of practice in schools for reacting to wrongdoing and conflict are developing differently from what has been happening in criminal justice and youth justice settings because the situations that occur in schools require a far wider and more flexible set of responses – from the informal and immediate to the more formal – requiring the individual preparation of all involved. These developments have been largely teacher-led.

For example, in 2000 a school in the south-east of England became a pioneer by training a team of its staff in restorative conferencing – the first time that a group of school staff in a state school had received this training. Several years later I was fortunate enough to have the opportunity to evaluate this project as part of my doctoral research. What I found was that whilst staff had enjoyed the training, and found the paradigm shift from punitive to restorative eye-opening, they were frustrated by the fact that the model they had been given was too time-consuming and unwieldy for day-to-day use in schools (Hopkins, 2006). What they needed was a set of far more flexible skills that could be used informally, more often than not between two students with no support-ers, and sometimes even when dealing with a single student. This latter finding very much resonates with research in ten children's residential care homes (Hayden and Gough, 2010).

What was important for this pioneer school was that the teach-ers themselves were not differentiating between situations where there was a clear cut, self-acknowledged 'wrongdoer' – a pre-requisite for restorative intervention in the youth and criminal justice field – and situations that were essentially interpersonal disputes. This was also the case with care staff in the children's residential care setting (Hayden and Gough, 2010). In the wider community there is a distinction between civil cases and criminal cases. Generally speaking, unless violence is involved the criminal justice system and the police do not get involved in interpersonal disputes (such as those between neighbours[3]). Such disputes are sometimes referred to civil courts. However, in schools there is only one system – and one that takes its cues from the crimi-nal justice system as Zehr's paradigm and my adaptation indicate. This system punishes young people for using inappropriate ways to resolve their disputes even though many schools do not teach children how to resolve disputes in the first place. In other words, situations requiring mediation, and situations requiring conferencing, are both dealt with punitively unless a school has decided to embrace a restorative philos-ophy. Once they have done this, schools require an approach that they can use in both circumstances – or run the risk of being inconsistent and unfair.

In my research I found that teachers themselves began to adapt what they had learnt, finding some of the questions from the scripted model they had been taught useful in a wide range of contexts. They also found the emphasis on the affective (see Chapter 10) domain novel but useful, and it changed the way they related to students. Many of them had never thought to ask how the young people were feeling, or thought to share their own feelings in difficult situations. The exchanges enhanced the authenticity for their relationships with the young people and devel-oped mutual empathy and respect. Little by little students were coming to them spontaneously for help in sorting out their disputes – even when there was no clear-cut wrongdoer. The teachers I spoke to on this first course commented that their training would have been more useful if it had given them these more flexible approaches at the outset, and the trainer of the course himself remarked how much easier it would have been if the course had been adapted for school contexts before he had started.

The experience of the pioneer school informed the development of a training course that offered a whole school framework of restorative responses, from minor to major issues, as well as providing staff with the confidence and skill to facilitate circles for community-building and problem-solving for both their colleagues and their students. I found that it was not necessary to distinguish between mediation and conferencing – a simple model could be adapted to fit any situation a teacher came across since most cases of harm in school involve disputed responsibility. The point is that so often in school the so-called 'perpetrator' is either the one who was caught (and those unseen get away scot-free), the one who was instigating the wrongdoing on that day (whereas the previous day they may have been the so-called 'victim') or the one who caused the most harm (so that a physical blow, for example, is deemed to be the wrongdoing, whereas the insult that occasioned the blow is often ignored). Arguments over who is to blame are the bane of teachers' lives, but the process we have given them has allowed them to begin listening and clarifying a situation without the need to 'get to the bottom of it' and assign blame. The ultimate intention behind the restorative intervention is to encourage accountability on all sides (if appropriate) and to repair the harm. The process is not predicated on the condition that there is an identified 'offender' who must take responsibility for their actions and acknowledge the harm done. More often than not this is almost impossible for someone to do if they believe that the other person or people also contributed to the situation.

In schools we simply applied the restorative maxim that all rule breaking and misbehaviour can be considered to be acts that cause harm to relationships and people and as such are interpersonal conflicts – at least one person has done something that has negatively affected at least one other person. This becomes the starting point from which to try and repair the harm and reconnect those involved as far as possible so that teaching and learning can continue.

What is critical in our training is gaining a deep understanding of the issues involved at every stage of the process, so that participants appreciate that every case is different, that facilitators need to be alert, sensitive and flexible, and that the needs of the individuals coming to a restorative meeting are paramount. In some cases the risk of re-victimising a genuine victim – of bullying or assault, for example – must be a consideration. Indeed, in all but the simplest of cases (such as a minor altercation in the dinner queue, which can usually be dealt with on the spot) careful preparation beforehand, and strict adherence to national practice guidelines (Home Office, 2004) is important in restorative practice.

## Restorative approaches: key themes and key questions

In recent years I have developed my own organisation's restorative model around five main themes, which give rise to five key types of question. The themes are summarised in Table 11.2 below. These five

*Table 11.2*   Restorative approaches: key themes and key questions

| | |
|---|---|
| *Theme 1 – Unique and equally valued perspectives*<br>Everyone has the need to share their own individual perspective on a given event or situation, and we are all likely to have a unique and different take, even on a shared experience. Sharing stories is a key feature of any restorative event (Pranis, 2001). It is important for everyone to feel that their perspective is also equally valued. | Question:<br>What happened? |
| *Theme 2 – Thoughts, emotions and actions*<br>In any given circumstance our interpretation of what is happening (self-talk) can influence our emotional response and this in turn will influence our choice of action. Even though some people challenge this keystone of cognitive psychology it has been found to be useful pragmatically in restorative practice. | Questions:<br>What were you thinking at that point?......and so how were you feeling? |
| *Theme 3 – Empathy and consideration*<br>Our actions are choices that have an impact on others and negative actions often have negative impacts. Empathy can develop when considering who has been (or will be) affected by any given situation. | Question:<br>Who has been affected by what has happened and how? |
| *Theme 4 – Needs*<br>To help those involved move forward in challenging situations or after harm has been caused it is helpful for everyone involved to identify what needs they have in order to be able to move forward (Rosenberg, 1999). Once needs have been identified the strategies to meet these needs can be discussed. | Question:<br>What do you need now in order to be able to move forward? |
| *Theme 5 – Ownership and empowerment*<br>Successful agreements depend on the voluntary involvement of all those affected and the degree to which those affected feel empowered to find ways forward for themselves (Barton, 2003). | Question:<br>So what needs to happen now, bearing in mind your own needs and the needs of others involved? |

themes inform five key questions, although we have found that a wide range of active listening skills are also needed to use these five questions effectively. The five questions share much in common with questions used by many restorative practitioners, whether they use a 'scripted model' or a simple framework.

These simple themes and questions are applicable across a wide range of day-to-day interactions in school settings: in one-to-one situations involving an active listener; in conversations when both sides need to take turns in order to resolve their own interpersonal conflict; in face-to-face mediation using an impartial facilitator; in group meetings as well as formally facilitated restorative conferences. There are always multiple sides to any situation, always unmet needs that have led to things going wrong, but more often than not when everyone gets a chance to be heard and feels understood people can work together to find solutions to what were thought to be intractable problems.

In the early days of introducing RAs into school settings there was a naivety around the challenges of organisational change. Even now, those keen to introduce the approach into their area assume that training one or two individuals from each school will be enough. However, experience and research suggest that project managers and trainers need to be far more realistic about the time that change can take, the complexity of changing practice and the formidable task of changing organisational, and especially school, culture (Thorsborne and Vinegrad, 2002; Hopkins, 2006).

In broad terms, restorative practitioners in school settings are agreed that whole school change takes time – between three and five years; that the involvement of senior management is crucial, that resistance is inevitable and needs to be planned for and that the restorative principle of working WITH people rather than doing things FOR them or TO them applies as much to HOW the change is implemented as it does to WHAT is being aspired to as an eventual outcome (Hopkins, 2006; Kane et al., 2007).

## Restorative approaches in schools – evaluation and research

Compared with a lot of approaches to behaviour management, restorative *justice* has received a great deal of attention. Much of this evidence focuses on the criminal justice system, 'victim' satisfaction and reductions in recidivism. In an era of evidence-based practice and a search for 'what works' (see also Chapter 12), the fact that there are positive and authoritative reviews of the impact of RJ, should give encouragement to those advocating the adoption of such practices in schools (see also the systematic review on anti-bullying initiatives by Farrington and Ttofi, 2009, and Chapter 12). Overall, a systematic review of the use of RJ within the criminal justice system, conducted by Sherman and Strang (2007), found that RJ works differently at different times with different people but that:

> there is far more evidence on RJ, with more positive results, than there has been for most innovations in criminal justice that have ever been rolled out in the country.
>
> (p. 8)

Less research has been conducted into RAs in school settings, although there is a well-supported belief that RAs in schools can make a positive impact on school climate and the health and well-being of both staff and students, as well as reducing the need for exclusion as a result of offending or anti-social behaviour, bullying, disruption or challenging behaviour.

The first major national research project involving schools in the United Kingdom was conducted by the Youth Justice Board (YJB, 2004). Starting in two schools in the London borough of Lambeth in 2000, it was extended to eight other areas in 2001. In total, nine YOTs, covering 26 schools (20 secondary and six primary) were involved, each taking a different approach to the introduction of restorative practices. The overall aims were to reduce offending, bullying and victimisation, and to improve attendance. The research was inconclusive about the impact of RAs in relation to these key performance indicators and concedes that these issues are, in any case, influenced by multiple causes, as well as other ongoing interventions. The research conclusions are fairly complex, emphasising that change in schools takes time:

> Restorative justice is not a panacea for problems in schools but, if implemented correctly, it can improve the school environment, enhance learning and encourage young people to become more responsible and empathetic. The pupil surveys showed no statistically significant effects on attitudes across the study, but there were some important improvements in pupils' attitudes in schools that had implemented RJ in a way that involved the whole school. The interview data found that, with only a few exceptions, staff believed that their school had benefited from RJ approaches. They felt that RAs had

helped to improve the school, and results were stronger for schools that had implemented restorative approaches across the whole school.

(p. 15)

In common with research on school effectiveness (Reynolds et al., 1996) one of the key findings was that the role of the head teacher was vital if the initiative was to be successful. On the other hand, high levels of satisfaction with the process were expressed by pupils, who also generally perceived the process as fair. In the great majority of conferences agreements were reached and adhered to.

My own doctoral research (Hopkins, 2006) focused on the implementation of RAs in schools, as experienced by staff who had been trained in a wide range of restorative skills and by the project managers responsible for the initiative. The impact of the training on the trainees and on their job satisfaction was not a specific focus of the research, but the experience of using RAs with young people were recorded as positive by all trainees, who attested to improved confidence in dealing with challenging issues, improved listening skills and improved relationships with their students.

My research identified factors that could militate against successful implementation of RAs in schools, such as lack of sufficient investment in both time and money, so that too much was expected of too few people. In my three case studies (a single school, a cluster of schools and a local authority initiative) the importance of sufficient time being made for training and for opportunities to hold restorative meetings, for ongoing skill development covering a wide range of day-to-day situations, for regular support and for senior management endorsement were all highlighted.

Another piece of research on the implementation of RAs in the United Kingdom was conducted by a team of researchers from Glasgow and Edinburgh universities (Kane et al., 2007). Their findings highlighted what schools in their research (from three pilot authorities) identified as important for successful implementation of RAs:

- High-quality training and ongoing support for staff
- Positive modelling, direction and commitment from school management
- Inclusion of all school staff in awareness of RAs, not only teachers
- Flexible adaptation of RAs to map on to a school's identified needs

- Need for both whole school approaches and more focused intervention
- Recognition that there is more than one model of successful development
- Involvement of parents was recognised as important but was still limited in practice
- Emphasis on compatibility of RAs with other developments
- Recognition that RAs involve values, skills and processes

A more recent update on this research conducted by Lloyd and McCluskey (2008) identified some further developments in schools where restorative practice is becoming more firmly embedded. These developments included a number of issues largely relating to embedding the approach more widely: as in, across primary as well as secondary schools; across local authorities; using the approach to resolve conflicts between staff, as well as with children and young people; and in work with the community. In this study too there was a recognition of the need for a better connection between RAs and other initiatives and approaches, such as emotional literacy.

Other promising findings have emerged from restorative initiatives conducted in Ireland (Mc Garrigle et al., 2006), Hull (Mirsky, 2009), Barnet (Barnet Youth Offending Service, 2009) and Bristol (Skinns et al., 2009) However, there is undoubtedly a need for more research to understand the ways in which a restorative approach can be used and to identify its potential for addressing a number of issues in and around schools, including bullying, violence reduction, community cohesion, conflict resolution, citizenship, mental health and well-being, as well as in enhancing student voice.

## Conclusions

This chapter has considered the development of RAs as they apply in educational settings in the United Kingdom from the perspective of a researcher/practitioner. It must be admitted that there is still much work to be done. Some projects are being instigated by Local Authority Behaviour Support Teams who, whilst enthusiastic, are frustrated at the challenges they meet when introducing restorative practices into individual schools. Elsewhere, small numbers of school staff have been trained and struggle to implement the approach in the face of cynicism and resistance from colleagues. Despite this, some schools are, after several years of patience and perseverance, proudly calling themselves 'restorative schools' and are serving as an inspiration to those just beginning this transformation. Some local authorities are recognising the importance of 'joined-up' thinking and aspiring to become 'restorative authorities'.

Available research evidence is encouraging, but points up many challenges in developing RAs in schools. Perhaps in any case the most important issue is whether the values inherent in RAs fit contemporary schools. There is no doubt in this writer's mind that RAs, applied systematically and consistently across a whole school, can make a significant contribution to community cohesion, develop a more positive school climate, increase a sense of belonging and improve relationships between all members of the school community. These approaches therefore have a significant contribution to make in tackling everyday problem behaviours, as well as more serious behaviours that may be viewed as 'anti-social' or may be criminal. If the unmet needs leading to anti-social behaviour and crime can be addressed at very early stages, proactively as well as reactively in these less serious situations, there could be a real chance that some forms of these behaviours will become less widespread.

## Endnote

This chapter is an adapted and extended version of an article that was originally published in the *International Journal of Restorative Justice* in 2008, supplemented by sections of my doctoral thesis. I am grateful to the journal's editor John Charlton for giving me permission to adapt this article.

## Notes

1. I am fiercely opposed to the use of the labels 'offender' and 'victim' in school contexts as such terms totalise people and apply a label that can become difficult to escape. Furthermore, the roles are very often interchangeable – it depends on the timing of the intervention.
2. The paradigm shift is often regarded as changing from retributive to restorative but in my research I discovered that for teachers the far more challenging shift in mindset and behaviour is one involving letting go of power and control, however benevolent the intention.
3. Although, interestingly, now that many police officers have been trained in restorative conferencing, they have been adapting their skills to use in neighbourhood conflicts and community conflicts in a comparable way to teachers.

# 12
## Schools as a Response to Crime, Anti-Social and Problem Behaviour

*Carol Hayden*

### Responding to problem behaviour in schools

This chapter concludes the book with a broader consideration about schools as a response to crime, anti-social and criminal behaviour. Most chapters in this book have emphasised that problem behaviours in schools are relatively rarely anti-social, or criminal. However, the *connection* between some problem behaviours and the development of anti-social and criminal behaviour is fully acknowledged. Further-more, some actions that are criminal do occur in and around the school site. This book has explored a range of perspectives on the issue, although throughout there has been some tension between the focus of educationalists and that of criminologists. The last three chapters have detailed specific responses to problem, anti-social and criminal behaviour in schools. They have explored different aspects of what the focus of any response in schools should be: safety and crime prevention, through Safer Schools Partnerships (SSPs); better understanding and response to special educational needs, specifically social, emotional and behavioural difficulties (SEBD); and resolving interpersonal conflict through restorative approaches (RAs). This final chapter considers some of the key research evidence about a range of other interventions that focus on (or relate to) problem behaviour and schools, including whole school approaches, work with families and the individual work involved with 'mentoring' children. The chapter also considers questions about what schools are for and arguments about their role in crime prevention. A crime prevention role is not always made explicit, for reasons that we will consider at the end of this chapter. Although the argument about the need for schools to have a role in crime prevention might be easy to make, how schools put this into practice is another matter. There are inevitable tensions in relation to the time available to do this, as well as in the potential for 'net widening' (Cohen, 1985), unless all parties are clear about what they are trying to achieve and why.

SSPs may seem like an obvious response to anti-social and criminal behaviour in schools; they clearly embrace the wider emphasis on safety and other aspects of the Every Child Matters (ECM) agenda already referred to (DfES, 2003a). They offer a particular model of partnership, working between the criminal justice and education systems, and, as such, necessarily bring the police into schools. Briers and Dickmann (see Chapter 9) present a case for these partnerships in Britain, drawing on comparative research in the United States. SSPs are a relatively new phenomenon in the United Kingdom and as yet there is little evidence about whether they are a good use of police time and other resources. Their effectiveness in actually preventing crime is, as yet, unclear.

Visser (Chapter 10) offers the view of an educationalist, focusing instead on SEBD as a recognised special educational need. This conception of particular forms of problem behaviour as relating to a special educational need raises questions about the morality of labelling some behaviours as 'anti-social'. Indeed, critics of anti-social behaviour orders (ASBOs) have argued that in some cases the behaviours identified in the order arise out of a special educational need and are not necessarily under the control of the individual who has been given the order (Bright, 2005). Visser puts forward 'eternal verities' (or well-evidenced 'truths') about how to respond to the needs of children with SEBD. His chapter clearly moves away from a focus on crime and anti-social behaviour and helps to illustrate the different remit of educationalists and those in the criminal justice system. Crime prevention can sit uneasily within the broader understanding of what schools are for, particularly from the point of view of people who primarily see themselves as educationalists.

Restorative justice (RJ), or restorative *approaches* (RAs) as they are often referred to in schools (see Hopkins, Chapter 11), offer a model for conflict resolution both within schools and between members of the school and wider community. In contrast to the more explicit link to the criminal justice system in SSPs, Hopkins argues that schools are uncomfortable with the emphasis on 'justice', 'victims' and 'offenders' (or 'perpetrators') in traditional RJ approaches, illustrating the problem of transporting an approach that originated in the criminal justice system into a mainstream service such as schools. The evidence base for RJ approaches is much better than for other ways of responding to problem behaviour, and in the main is positive.

The difference and tensions between 'affective' and 'effective' school-ing are at the heart of the debate about responding to problem behaviour. Traditionally, research on *effective* schools has focused on cognitive measures, such as achievements in a range of taught subjects that are recognised and certificated. Evidence about *affective* schools tends to focus on behaviour and attitudes and how these in turn relate to socially desirable outcomes (such as reduced rates of offend-ing) as well as academic achievement. However, research that tries to link the affective and the effective outcomes from schooling shows that these are not always in accordance with each other (Knuver and Brandsman, 1993). In what is regarded as a landmark study (referred to elsewhere in this volume), Rutter and colleagues (1979) provided evidence about how schools operate in ways that make a difference to pupils. Their study showed that cognitively effective schools were also effective for non-cognitive (or 'affective') outcomes such as the per-centage of 'delinquent' pupils. In the decades following this study there have been numerous attempts to research specific aspects of the mech-anisms behind the different outcomes from schools – although much of it has focused on academic achievement. We know that pupil back-ground characteristics are related to both cognitive and non-cognitive outcomes: socio-economic status, gender and ethnicity are all important in these respects (as detailed in Chapter 4).

In sum, *effective* schools are primarily those that produce a high level of academic achievement, whilst *affective* schools are places where chil-dren are happy to come and behave in a positive and pro-social way. The key question is whether schools can do both: that is, can schools be effective in both the cognitive and affective domains? This is a question that brings us to another: what are schools for?

## What are schools for?

Contemporary educational policy measures school effectiveness primar-ily on cognitive outcomes (academic achievement and other credentials) whilst at the same time acknowledging the importance of affective aspects. Nevertheless, the central purpose of going to school is to be 'educated' or 'to learn', in the broadest senses of these terms, and the main remit of schools is teaching and learning. However, we acknowl-edge in Chapter 3 that schools have always had a broader remit than this; at the most basic level they help keep young people out of trouble by occupying them and by promoting pro-social values in a range of ways. Contemporary schools operate as part of children's services and within the broader framework of the five main outcomes specified in the ECM agenda (see Chapter 3). Pertinent to the focus of this text, these five outcomes include *staying safe* and *making a positive contribution* (in relation to the latter it is specified *not engaging in anti-social and criminal behaviour*).

Bloom's taxonomy (in Fitz-Gibbon, 2000, p. 7) characterises schools as having three broad goals: cognitive, affective and behavioural. *Cognitive* goals are to do with academic learning. *Affective* goals relate to happiness, aspirations and satisfaction with school. *Behavioural* goals include regular attendance, paying attention in class and pro-social behaviour. Fitz-Gibbon (2000) notes how parents are often reported to be equally interested in affective and behavioural goals, as well as cognitive attainment. The ideal school would maximise opportunities for these goals, recognising that one affects another. Furthermore, all of these goals interrelate with well-known protective factors against criminal involvement. We also saw in Chapter 5 that young people who are happy and 'connected' to school are more likely to behave in 'acceptable' ways: by attending and achieving at school, and by having aspirations for a law-abiding future.

The wider role for schools that has developed in recent years in Britain (especially since ECM) means that schools are subject to many major social (as well as academic) aspirations, with crime prevention being just one of these. However, there is an under-articulated aspect to all of this – the real issue is how to change what goes on in schools with the lowest academic results, which are usually associated with the poorest areas (and pupils), which are in turn associated with more problematic, anti-social and criminal behaviour. For teachers, their central purpose is compromised by young people who do not attend, attend erratically and/or behave in a disruptive or problematic way when they are in school. These latter problems are unevenly spread; some schools have to pay a great deal of attention to getting young people into school and behaving in a way where they can be taught and learn in large groups *before* they can address academic achievement. The response of teachers and schools to this situation can vary – for some it can lead to them embracing external or additional support – such as SSPs – for others it can lead to a sense that there are too many (and competing) demands to cope with. The movement of teachers away from poorer (and more 'difficult') schools and towards more affluent (and less 'difficult') schools is well documented (Smithers and Robinson, 2005) and adds to the difficulties of schools that have the greatest issues with problem behaviour.

The expectations about the role and purpose of teachers and schools is central to the debate about crime prevention and can be forgotten by other professionals working with children, as well as policy makers. In particular, there is a lack of honesty about whether this role really is for *all* schools, or only those in 'challenging' circumstances. It is pertinent to ask how much time parents want their children to spend on initiatives that may well have desirable social purposes, but are targeted at the most troubled and troublesome young people in schools.

## Schools and crime prevention

Schools in the United Kingdom are already seen as part of the wider crime prevention project, at least in terms of policy. Within SSPs and elsewhere in the education service some of the language more commonly used in the criminal justice system has already entered schools in relation to pupil behaviour. For example, combating 'hate crime' is used to cover equal opportunities issues, as well as in relation to broader work on police and community relations and within attempts to make schools safer places (Thorpe, 2006). However, it is also clear that there is some debate and difference of opinion about how (and whether) to use specific criminal justice terminology in relation to children's behaviour in school. Some police forces include bullying within their definition of hate crime (such as Tameside police), others separate the two terms. Some police forces (such as Thames Valley police) make a distinction between bullying and criminal behaviour (using terms such as 'assault', 'theft' and 'criminal damage' in relation to certain behaviours); they advise that the police should be called to schools to deal with these instances when they occur (Hall and Hayden, 2007). The Home Office, on the other hand, views hate crime as a criminal offence (Home Office, 2006a, para. 1). However, the recognition that many 'crimes' in schools are minor and that many incidents would be better dealt with by school disciplinary systems is evident in jointly agreed guidance and Home Office Counting Rules. Since 2007, guidance issued jointly by the Department for Children Schools and Families (DCSF) and Association of Chief Police Officers (ACPO), provides that:

> police officers attending school premises may become aware of incidents that would amount to a minor crime in law. The guidance allows for an officer not to record a crime provided it is not serious and the school, child and parent/responsible adult agrees to this; and that it should be dealt with via the school's disciplinary procedure.
>
> (Millard and Flatley, 2010, p. 4 referring to Home Office
> Counting Rules for Recorded Crime)

This guidance allows discretion on the part of the officer/officers when getting involved with incidents in school. As yet there is little evidence about how this works in practice, as discussed in Chapter 9. Certainly, the external pressure to perform on police (Martin, 2003) could mean that this guidance is not always followed.

Support for the role of schools in relation to crime prevention comes from a variety of academic commentators and disciplines (more often outside education than within it) and has been a central feature of youth social policy in the United Kingdom since the late 1990s. School and educational factors are often cited as part of the well-known list of 'risk' and 'protective' factors for future criminality (Farrington, 1996). According to Farrington, risks specifically relating to schooling include low intelligence and school failure, and hyperactivity/impulsivity/attention deficit. More broadly, Farrington notes that the prevalence of offending by pupils varies greatly between schools, although the mechanisms at work alongside the social mix of pupils attending schools are not sufficiently understood. Outside the school, other risk factors relate to poor socio-economic circumstances and community influences, poor parenting and family conflict and low levels of parental supervision, as well as individual temperament. Many of these factors have in turn been found to be associated specifically with truancy and school exclusion (Graham and Bowling, 1995; Hayden, 2001). Protective factors identified by Farrington (1996) include: resilient temperament; warm affectionate relationship with at least one parent; parents who provide effective supervision; pro-social beliefs; consistent discipline and parents who maintain a strong interest in their child's education. McCarthy and colleagues (2004, pp. ix–x) caution against a simplistic interpretation of the concept of risk, noting that risks are *context-dependent and vary over time and with different circumstances*. In particular, children vary in their resilience to difficult circumstances. Children with a stronger sense of attachment to other people, with a more positive outlook on life, more plans for the future and more control over their lives are more likely to demonstrate resilience (Hayden, 2007).

The high prevalence of youth offending and victimisation found in and surrounding schools in surveys and official statistics (see Chapter 6) suggests the conclusion that primary crime prevention in the form of universal programmes in schools are an obvious component in the overall fight against crime. Schools as universal service providers have the difficult task of ensuring effective targeting of help whilst avoiding the potentially negative impact of what might be seen as labelling. Sutton and colleagues (2004) conclude that preventative services should be presented and justified in terms of children's existing needs and problems, rather than in relation to any future risk of criminality.

Crime prevention policies and measures may be carried out at the individual, situational or structural level, and are carried out by many different agencies. Schools can play a role on all levels. At the level of the individual, schools can enhance pro-social behaviour, personal achievement and the sense of being part of a wider community, as well as the opportunity to lead a productive and law-abiding life. Schools can promote parental interest and involvement in their child's education and achievement. In other words, schools can help to enhance many of the well-known 'protective factors' against criminal involvement. Furthermore, schools can provide the opportunity for social advancement and, as such, they are a vehicle for a route out of poverty and lack of opportunity and the temptation to follow a 'criminal career'. On the other hand, schools are also a site where criminal, anti-social and abusive behaviour can occur, both from within and outside the community. Schools thus have to guard against 'outsiders' as well as develop a safe and orderly community within the school environment.

Research evidence on persistence and desistance of 'anti-social behaviour' (as defined in psychological terms by Rutter and colleagues, 1998) would indicate that the more serious and persistent forms can be detected as early as age 3, in the form of oppositional and hyperactive behaviour. The distinction is made between 'adolescent-limited' and 'life course persistent' anti-social behaviour. However, it is emphasised that 'nothing is cast in stone' and a range of life events and other opportunities and circumstances can play a part in helping anti-social behaviour to continue or cease (Rutter et al., 1998, p. 307). Schools could be said to occupy this difficult terrain – they can help to ameliorate and reduce problem behaviour or in the worst circumstances they may emphasise and entrench their significance. The explicit involvement of schools in crime prevention programmes might be seen as further evidence of the 'net-widening' already referred to, or, alternatively, evidence of attempts at 'nipping problems in the bud'. There is clearly the potential for schools to occupy both positions simultaneously.

Overall, schools clearly have wide *potential* for enhancing protective factors against criminal involvement. Schools can help foster positive and 'pro-social behaviour' (used in a psychological sense, as the other end of the continuum from 'anti-social behaviour') by providing opportunities for a sense of personal achievement, school 'connectedness' and 'inclusion' in a community. Schools already provide positive opportunities for the great majority of young people, many of whom have committed a minor criminal offence and some of whom are at risk of more extensive criminal involvement. Schools are encouraged to involve and interest parents and carers in their children's education (thereby enhancing a protective factor against criminality); in policy terms this is often seen as a self-evidently 'good thing'. We will now turn to some of the key evidence about specific types of intervention or programmes.

## Reviewing the evidence

Research 'evidence' is not a value-free notion in relation to what evidence may support particular approaches to a problem, and, indeed, what approaches may be politically acceptable. The 'What Works' argument (see Davies et al., 2000) has privileged certain types of evidence over others, such as specifically randomised control trials (RCTs) and other forms of experimental research. This argument has some validity in relation to the evaluation of intervention programmes or particular approaches to reducing problem behaviours in schools. The Campbell Collaboration (http://www.campbellcollaboration.org/) is an easily accessible web-based location for systematic reviews of a range of interventions, including those based in and around schools. However, as has been argued elsewhere (Hayden, 2007), this evidence (although growing) doesn't answer all of our questions, and other forms of evidence are important. In particular, the context of an individual school is crucial when considering whether a specific approach or intervention would 'work' (or at least 'work' better than other approaches). Furthermore, there are other considerations when working with children – many of which relate to values and beliefs about the role of schools, teachers and other adults – when faced with problem behaviour.

## Whole school approaches and school-based approaches

As Visser highlights in Chapter 10, there is near universal agreement about the need for whole school policies on behaviour in schools. For adults working in schools, policies necessarily have to be translated into practical approaches to managing and responding to problem behaviour. Whole school approaches have developed since the Elton Report (DES/WO, 1989) in Britain. Although the focus of any whole school approach (WSA) is ultimately about how people understand and relate to each other within the school, many also reach out to parents and the wider community. The specific focus (or terminology used) varies. For example, Violence in Schools Training Action (VISTA) (a European project focused on the prevention of violence in schools) characterises a WSA in the following way:

> A successful WSA approach to the promotion of non-violence not only addresses violent behaviour it also improves the climate and ethos of the school, improves relationships among staff, children and young people and parents, it also supports the emotional health and well-being and learning potential of children and young people, and all adult members of the school community.
>
> (VISTA, 2006, p. 4)

There is general agreement from researchers that a WSA necessarily includes work at different levels: the individual, the classroom, school-wide; as well as work with the community around the school. The active involvement of young people as well as adults is encouraged (Greene, 2006). Furthermore, any approach to problem behaviour has to be continually reviewed and developed in the knowledge that aggressive and problem behaviours cannot be eliminated.

There are numerous well-known 'whole school' and more targeted approaches to managing behaviour and reducing conflict in schools in Britain, such as 'Assertive Discipline' (see Canter and Canter, 2001), 'Circle Time' (see Mosley and Doyle, 2005), 'Team-Teach' (see Hayden and Pike, 2005), as well as RAs (already explored in more depth in Chapter 10). Specific problem behaviours, such as bullying, have produced hundreds of evaluations and a variety of methods and programmes (see Farrington and Ttofi, 2009). Indeed, schools in Britain are awash with different programmes and interventions aimed at tackling various types of problem behaviour. Whilst systematic reviews of specific types of programme are freely available on the Campbell Collaboration website, their findings may seem complex to the practitioner. Furthermore, the available evidence and associated approaches depend not only on a very clear problem definition by a school, but also on an appropriate adaptation to a specific context (Pawson and Tilley, 2004). In relation to the latter point it is important to note that much of the available evidence, on the Campbell Collaboration website, is from the United States and may not be appropriate in other cultural contexts.

Figure 12.1 illustrates the different levels of response to problem behaviour within schools in the United Kingdom. Whole school approaches are the overall context for children; at the 'universal' level this will help create a school ethos and climate and can be crucial

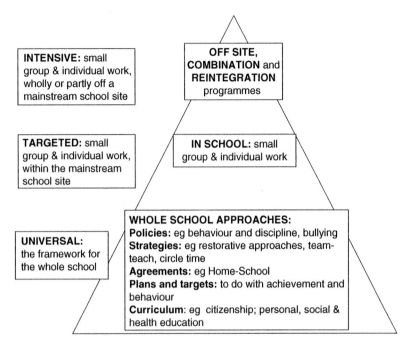

*Figure 12.1*   Responses to problematic pupil behaviour in schools

in promoting positive behaviour. The promotion of a WSA is apparent in a raft of policies, agreements and strategies that are expected in all schools in Britain: such as behaviour and discipline, anti-bullying, anti-harassment and equal opportunities policies; and Home-School agreements and particular strategies or approaches to realising these policies and agreements (such as RAs). The use of the curriculum to promote pro-social values, for example through citizenship education, and through teaching and learning strategies, are yet another part of what all schools are expected to do. Individual pupils have 'targets' they are trying to achieve in relation to their behaviour (as well as in relation to academic learning) and some have individual plans for behavioural and social reasons. In school, more intensive support is provided for individual and small groups of pupils based on an assessment of their educational and social needs. Other provision is partly or wholly provided off the mainstream school site: these provisions focus on the most problematic or vulnerable children. We might conceptualise responses to pupil behaviour as becoming more and more targeted and intense, as the focus is on the minority of pupils who present the most problematic behaviour in school. Figure 12.1 deliberately echoes Figure 11.2 on the use of RAs in schools (Chapter 11) by illustrating how a particular approach can be adapted and used with different levels of need and as a WSA.

There are a number of major reviews of research on school-based programmes. For example, a meta-analysis of 165 studies of school-based prevention activities (to do with pupil behaviour) analysed the evidence available about the impact of activities, ranging from individual counselling or behaviour modification programmes, to change the way schools are managed. The analysis shows that school-based practices appear to be effective in relation to certain behaviours: reducing drug and alcohol use, school drop out and attendance problems. In common with findings from prisons research, cognitive behavioural programmes have been found to be consistently positive in effect. Non-cognitive behavioural counselling, social work and other therapeutic interventions showed consistently negative effects in this review (Wilson et al., 2001).

Wilson and Lipsey (2006a, 2006b) conducted systematic reviews on social information processing programmes in schools. These are programmes designed to improve social behaviour by teaching cognitively based problem-solving skills. Wilson and Lipsey (2006b) noted that programmes that address social-information-processing difficulties tend to be structured and have detailed lesson plans, which make them attractive to schools. They are delivered by classroom teachers or school psychologists and can be used in different formats (group or individual) and settings (classrooms or out-of-class school facilities). They reviewed 73 studies of universally delivered social-information-processing programmes in school settings and 43 programmes for selected or targeted pupils. They found positive effects overall in both reviews. These programmes were less effective with young people who had special educational needs, but they were more effective with mainstream pupils, particularly with 'higher risk' pupils who had not yet developed serious problems.

'Bullying' behaviour in and connected to schools deserves a particular mention, as this particular group of behaviours has received a great deal of attention in many countries (see, for example, Smith et al., 1999). Farrington and Ttofi (2009) note, however, that American research is generally targeted at school violence and peer victimisation (rather than 'bullying'). Although it is well recognised that bullying behaviour can happen anywhere, the particular circumstances of the school, as well as adult responsibilities towards children in this setting, has tended to provide the strongest focus for research on children. Indeed, Cawson and colleagues (2000) have argued that the term 'bullying' is often seen as intrinsic to the school setting, rather than as a description of the behaviours themselves. Research focused on bullying highlights the important differences between this form of aggressive behaviour and other such behaviours: namely the power imbalance between bully and victim, as well as repeat victimisation. All schools in Britain must have a policy to prevent all forms of bullying, and a wide range of initiatives and resources have been committed to combating bullying. School policies must set out strategies to be followed, backed up by systems to ensure effective implementation, monitoring and review. Policies must comply with the Human Rights Act 1998 and the Race Relations Act 2000. Schools are not *directly* responsible for bullying off their premises, but do have a common law 'duty of care' towards their pupils (Smith, 2002b, p. 4). Over a decade ago, a survey of 307 schools in England and Wales by Douglas and colleagues (1999) indicated almost universal awareness of the existence of bullying in schools, from the head teachers responding.

Farrington and Ttofi (2009) have conducted a systematic review and meta-analysis of the effectiveness of programmes designed to reduce bullying and victimisation. They found 622 reports, of which 89 met the selection criteria in terms of research quality. These 89 reports related to 53 different intervention programmes. The effect size could be calculated for 44 studies in all. This showed that that on average bullying reduced by 20–23 per cent (and victimisation by 17–20 per cent) following the introduction of these various programmes. This review detailed the different elements of the programmes, concluding that the most effective were the use of videos as anti-bullying materials and disciplinary methods. 'Work with peers' was reported to be associated with an *increase* in victimisation. Programmes of longer duration and higher intensity, based on the work of Olweus (widely recognised as the pioneer of anti-bullying programmes in schools), and with older children were found to be more effective. Furthermore, this review concluded with support for RAs that set out to repair relationships and bring together bullies, victims and other children. Basing programmes on appropriate theories of bullying and victimisation is advocated:

> [D]efiance theory is useful because it places emphasis on improving bonding to the sanctioner, shame management, and legitimate, respectful sanctioning of anti-social behaviour.
>
> (Farrington and Ttofi, 2009, p. 73)

The relevance of defiance theory to RAs adds to arguments for using this approach in responding to bullying, as well as to other problem behaviours in schools.

## Working with families

Working with families in relation to promoting positive behaviour and engagement with education comes in many forms. The preventative aspect is especially evident at the pre-school stage and in the early years of primary school in Britain. This preventative end of the spectrum is the main focus of the current chapter. As children reach the age of criminal responsibility their behaviour can result in various orders and contracts for parents – such as parenting contracts and orders, school attendance and supervision orders, as well as fines and even imprisonment (these have been covered in Chapters 2, 3 and 8). It is common for various organisations, interest groups and the media to call for some issue to do with children's behaviour to be addressed by 'parenting programmes' and initiatives in schools. Yet the behavioural expectations that are presented as the norm may be at odds with sub-cultural differences and realities; this means that some schools may be at odds with the dominant norms of the communities they serve. 'Involving' or eliciting the support of parents in their child's education, as supporters of the school and so on, is another strand to this broader issue of working with families.

Early intervention, in the sense of early intervention in a child's life, necessarily involves the family. There is a considerable body of research in the United Kingdom, as well as Europe and the United States, which examines early interventions in the lives of children. On the other hand, very few interventions have been rigorously evaluated. Birth cohort and other longitudinal research studies in the United Kingdom provide useful information about life course trajectories, adding to our understanding of risk and protective factors from the early years through to adulthood. The focus of most early intervention programmes is on children and families in need and high-risk circumstances and, usually, pre-school children or children in the first years of primary school. There are also prevention programmes targeted at pregnant women. Research has established associations between low birth weight, maternal smoking or alcohol consumption during pregnancy and later health, education and behaviour problems (Sutton et al., 2004). The risks to children in adverse circumstances are numerous and varied, ranging from the likelihood of low achievement at school, poor employment prospects and welfare dependency, to drug misuse and involvement in criminal activity.

'Conduct disorder' is a frequent diagnosis for children who behave in a problematic way. One longitudinal research study in England has focused specifically on the potential financial benefit of intervening early by estimating the costs of not intervening with conduct-disordered children. This study, published in the *British Medical Journal* in 2001, followed 142 10-year-old children into adulthood, grouping them into three categories: 'no problems', 'conduct problems' and 'conduct disorder'. Data were gathered on six key areas of their lives: the provision of special education; foster and residential care; relationship breakdown, health and crime; state benefits in adulthood. The mean comparative costs (at the time this study was completed) by the age of 28 years were: £7423 for those with 'no problems'; £24,324 for those with 'conduct problems' and £70,019 for those with 'conduct disorders' (Scott et al., 2001). Scott and colleagues estimated the specific costs in relation to offending at £1200 for the police to identify a young offender and £2500 for a successful prosecution, with the *weekly* cost of a place in a secure unit at £3450.

Some well-known and well-evidenced early intervention programmes, such as High/Scope and Head Start, developed in the United States, are focused on children from poorer families and are primarily educational in their focus. The principles behind High/Scope are based on a pre-school programme that emphasises active learning and a child-centred approach in which children learn through a sequence of activities (plan-do-review) that are guided by adults in a play environment. The longitudinal research shows positive benefits in the lives of children in a range of ways; the most striking of which relates to achievement, motivation and social behaviour. Longer term benefits included: higher levels of educational attainment, lower rate of teenage pregnancy, reduced need for special education, lower welfare payments and more tax paid because of higher rates of employment, as well as lower rates of crime and drug misuse. The 'savings' to the public purse have been calculated as in the region of $7 for every $1 of expenditure, with the largest proportion (65 per cent) of this saving coming from savings in the criminal justice system (Schweinhart and Weikart, 1980).

Whilst the financial arguments for early intervention are persuasive we should remember that not everything can be given a financial cost: for example, children may be happier as a result of particular help, or adults may feel better able to work with or look after a child with very difficult behaviour. There are also potentially three key problems with targeting early intervention too explicitly and too narrowly: one is ethical, with the potential for labelling young children as potential delinquents; a second is the fact that there is movement in and out of the group of children with conduct problems; a third is the need to provide services that will gain the trust and participation of parents. Both McCarthy and colleagues (2004) and Sutton and colleagues (2004) highlight the different types of risk present and the responses needed in relation to children of different ages, as well as the way in which particular risk and protective factors fluctuate over time.

We have already seen that some outcome measures, such as longer term cost-benefit analyses, as in High/Scope, can take a considerable time to establish. Other interventions, such as Head Start, were seen as a disappointing in the early stages (Westinghouse Learning Corporation, 1969), then later pronounced effective, because of what might be termed 'sleeper effects' (McKey et al., 1985). That is, the benefits of some interventions might not be immediately apparent, emerging some years after a programme was experienced. Head Start was a pre-school programme for disadvantaged children, which begun as a summer programme in the United States in 1965 with over half a million predominantly African-American children. It quickly expanded and included white children in the following year. It was designed to close the gap between these children and their more advantaged peers. Head Start encompassed a variety of initiatives including High/Scope. Early evidence suggested that short-term gains in test scores for Head Start children faded out after a few years in primary school, although Head Start had wider objectives than raising test scores. The later positive outcomes from Head Start were found in relation to educational attainment, anti-social behaviour, use of special education services and track records in relation to employment and offending behaviour (McKey et al., 1985). Research by Garces and colleagues (2002) examined a Panel Survey of Income Dynamics, which included a question about participation in Head Start. They found that participation in Head Start is associated with a significantly increased probability of completing high school and attending college, as well as higher earnings in one's early 20s for white participants. The most significant difference for African-Americans who participated in Head Start was that they were less likely to have been booked for or charged with a crime. Differences in achievement levels between ethnic groups attending Head Start have been explained by structural factors, such that the African-American children attended lower quality schools than white children (Currie and Thomas, 2000).

The influence of High/Scope and Head Start can be seen in the development of Sure Start in the United Kingdom. The first wave of Sure Start projects began in 1999, starting in neighbourhoods with a high proportion of children living in poverty. Key to the way Sure Start worked was a focus on a more integrated approach to service provision in the early years (DCSF, 2010). The findings from the evaluation are complex but contain enough positive indications for funding to continue at the time of writing. For example, a randomised control trial (within 11 Sure Start areas) of the Webster-Stratton Incredible Years parenting programme, focused on children at risk of conduct disorder, showed significant improvements in the intervention group, confirming other evaluations of this approach (Hutchings et al., 2007). On the other hand, Belsky and colleagues (2006) found that at area level (Sure Start areas, compared with areas without Sure Start) differences in impact were small and varied according to the degree of deprivation. Sure Start areas had beneficial effects on non-teenage mothers (better parenting, better social functioning in children) and adverse effects on children of teenage mothers (poorer social functioning) and children of single parents or parents who did not work (lower verbal ability). Sure Start partnerships led by health services were slightly more effective than those led by other services (such as education or social services).

The FAST (or Families and Schools Together) programme was developed in the United States in 1988 by McDonald (2010) as an approach to helping children identified as 'at risk' of failure to achieve in school. The FAST programme has been implemented in 45 states in the United States, in several sites in Australia, and also in Austria, Canada, Germany and Russia. Although FAST was developed to serve children who had been identified as 'at risk of failure' by their teachers, it is now recommended as a universal programme that involves a once-a-week contact over a period of eight weeks. An ongoing reunion process of monthly multi-family meetings of 'FAST graduates' over a period of two years may be run by the families with the support of a team (called FASTWORKS). A Campbell Collaboration review is underway (Soydan et al., 2005).

## Work with individual young people

Once children are in secondary schools there tends to be a range of ways problem behaviour is managed – from a WSA, which may be adapted to targeted and intensive small group and individual work that may occur both on and off the school site (See Figure 12.1) and small group approaches. Some children may have individual education programmes that may in part (or totally) be delivered off the school site. In addition, children may have individual counselling or therapy, either on or off the school site (the availability of school-based programmes is very variable and often dependent on short-term and additional funds). We will consider here one of the well-known one-to-one approaches to working with the more problematic young people, who are variously characterised as 'at risk' of getting into further trouble and/or 'disaffected' from school.

Mentoring is one of the most commonly used interventions with young people who show problematic behaviour. Mentoring is focused on teenagers, rather than younger children. It is also one of the well-evidenced interventions and has been the subject of a number of reviews. Mentoring has been characterised as involving an interaction between two people of unequal status over an extended period of time. The mentor has the knowledge, skill, ability or experience that should benefit the person being mentored, who in turn is in a position to imitate or benefit from the mentor (Tolan et al., 2008). At the time of writing, the systematic review, for the Campbell Collaboration, by Tolan and colleagues, is the most recent analysis of the evidence. They conclude that:

> This analysis of 39 studies on four outcomes measuring delinquency or closely related outcomes suggests mentoring for high-risk youth has a modest positive effect for delinquency, aggression, drug use, and achievement. However, the effect sizes varied by outcome with larger effects for delinquency and aggression than for drug use and achievement. (............) While these findings support viewing mentoring as a useful approach for interventions to lessen delinquency risk or involvement, due to limited description of content of mentoring programs and substantial variation in what is included as part of mentoring efforts detracts from that view. The valuable features and most promising approaches can not be stated with any certainty.
>
> (p. 5)

In other words, mentoring looks to be a good idea at the most problematic end of the continuum – in relation to the behaviour of young people – but the precise mechanism(s) that may be effective are not clearly evidenced. (Compare this to the Farrington and Ttofi 2009 review on bullying interventions that clearly specifies the mechanisms at work.) Knowing which mechanisms are effective is important because some types of mentoring are not effective (and could be harmful). Overall, there is evidence that a strong personal relationship between mentor and mentee is important, with the one-to-one relationship providing opportunities for imitation, gaining advice, pleasurable recreational activities that show care and interest in the mentee, and emotional support, information, and advocacy through this one-to-one relationship. Such opportunities are thought to foster healthy development and divert children from getting into trouble and having negative attitudes (Tolan et al., 2008, p. 6).

## Schools as a response to crime and anti-social behaviour

This final chapter highlights some of the important considerations concerning what schools are for and what they might be able to do in relation to reducing problematic behaviour. This latter issue has a broader relevance to the prevention of anti-social and criminal behaviour. Simply, feeling connected to school, achieving and having aspirations tends to protect young people from involvement in anti-social and criminal behaviour. Parents can help by supporting their children and their school and mentors can be used with young people who need additional support or lack the necessary support. We also know a lot about effective approaches to managing or responding to problematic behaviour. So what more do we need to know and do?

A key problem for schools and teachers is the sheer volume of competing calls on their time, in relation to their capacity to respond. In particular (as noted elsewhere in this volume) schools have an uneasy task if they make their crime prevention role explicit. Their potential in this respect is at once self-evident but also open to contention, misinterpretation and even potential misuse. Whilst some aspects of crime prevention (such as CCTV) and security measures may seem necessary against intruders, vandals and arsonists, they might also be open to other uses (see Chapter 3). Equally, the role of police in schools may be open to role conflict and move into crime detection, rather than prevention.

In terms of their role and potential in crime prevention, schools have to balance a number of competing priorities. None of the competing priorities shown in Figure 12.2 are necessarily mutually exclusive but they are nevertheless priorities about which it is difficult to arrive at a consensus. For schools in general (rather than only schools in the most deprived areas) to achieve a better balance in relation to these priorities we would need a fundamental rethink about their funding, staffing and

| The majority: no or minor criminal involvement | ←→ | The minority: persistent and prolific offenders (especially for reintegration programmes) |
|---|---|---|
| Victims | ←→ | Perpetrators |
| Academic achievement | ←→ | Social inclusion |
| The current cohort of children and young people | ←→ | The needs of parents and the wider community |
| Schools as welcoming and open places | ←→ | Risk reduction |
| Schools as a fortress against the community | ←→ | Schools in and of the community |

*Figure 12.2*   Competing priorities for schools
*Source*: Hayden (2005, p. 160).

evaluation. The role and potential of schools in relation to addressing problematic behaviour is a given – it is essential to the job of teaching and learning.

This book has, in the main, argued that tackling anti-social and criminal behaviour is a narrower and more specific remit than tackling problem behaviour. The bigger questions remain: such as, to what extent do we as a society want to see *schools in general* prioritising a crime prevention role? Or, should this crime prevention role only be prioritised where there is no choice – that is, in the minority of schools where circumstances make this focus essential?

# References

Anti-Bullying Alliance (ABA) (2007) *Survey Finds One in Three Bullied Outside School.* 15 November, www.anti-bullyingalliance.org.uk (accessed 23.2.2008).

Archer, L. and Francis, B. (2007) *Understanding Minority Ethnic Achievement; Race, Gender, Class and Success.* London: Routledge.

Arnot, M. (2004) 'Male working class identities and social justice', In N. Dolby and G. Dimriadis (eds) with Paul Willis *Learning to Labour in New Times.* London: Routledge/Falmer.

Arson Prevention Bureau (2002) *School Arson: Education Under Threat.* London: Arson Prevention Bureau.

Arthur, R. (2005) 'Punishing parents for the crimes of their children', *Howard Journal of Criminal Justice*, 44(3), pp. 233–253.

Ashworth, A. (2004) 'Social control and "Anti-Social Behaviour": The subversion of human rights?', *Law Quarterly Review*, 120, pp. 263–291.

Astor, R.A, Guerra, N. and Van Acker, R. (2010) 'How can we improve school safety research?', *Educational Researcher*, 39(1), pp. 69–78.

ATL/Teacher Support Network (2008) *Working in education is bad for your health and stress levels: ATL/Teacher Support Network Survey*, http://teachersupport.info/news/press-releases/Working-in-education-is-bad-for-your-health.php (accessed 4.8.2009).

Audit Commission (1996) *Misspent Youth.* London: Audit Commission.

Avon and Somerset Constabulary (2002) *What Is Schools Liaison?* Bristol: Avon and Somerset Constabulary.

Aye Maung, N. (1995) *Young People, Victimisation and the Police.* Home Office Research Study No. 140. London: HMSO.

Ayers, H., Clarke, D. and Murray, A. (2000) *Perspectives on Behaviour: A Practical Guide to Effective Interventions for Teachers.* London: David Fulton.

Bailey, R. (2009) 'Well-being, happiness and education', *British Journal of the Sociology of Education*, 30(6), pp. 795–802.

Ball, S.J. (1981) *Beachside Comprehensive. A Case Study of Secondary Schooling.* Cambridge: Cambridge University Press.

Ball, C. and Connolly, J. (2000) 'Educationally disaffected young offenders', *British Journal of Criminology*, 40, pp. 594–616.

Balls, E. (2009) 'Safer schools partnerships', *Written Ministerial Statements*, 11 May, http://www.publications.parliament.uk/pa/cm200809/cmhansrd/cm090511/wmstext/90511m0001.htm (accessed 26.9.2010).

Bansel, P., Davies, B., Laws, C. and Linnell, S. (2009) 'Bullies, bullying and power in the context of schooling', *British Journal of the Sociology of Education*, 30(1), pp. 59–69.

Barker, B. (2008) 'School reform policy in England since 1988: Relentless pursuit of the unattainable', *Journal of Education Policy*, 23(6), pp. 669–83.

Barnet Youth Offending Service (2009) *Restorative Approaches in Primary Schools*. Barnet, London, http://www.transformingconflict.org/Barnet%20007098_RA%20Evaluation%20A4%20Booklet%20final%20version%20%20%282%29.pdf (accessed 9.1.2011).

Barton, C. (2003) *Restorative Justice – The Empowerment Model*. Sydney: Hawkins Press.

Basini, A. (1981) 'Urban schools and "Disruptive Pupils": A study of some ILEA support units', *Educational Review*, 33(3), pp. 191–205.

Baumeister, R.F. and Leary, M.R. (1995) 'The need to belong: Desire for interpersonal attachments as a fundamental human motivation', *Psychological Bulletin*, 117, pp. 497–529.

BBC (1995) *Youth Gang Stabs Head Teacher to Death*. BBC News, 8 December.

BBC (2000) *Parents Back Corporal Punishment*. BBC News, 7 January.

Beck, U. (1992) *Risk Society: Towards a New Modernity*. New Delhi: Sage.

Beckman, A. and Cooper, C. (2004) ' "Globalisation", the new managerialism and education: Rethinking the purpose of education in Britain', *Journal for Critical Education Policy Studies*, 2(2), September, http://www.jceps.com/print.php?articleID=31 (accessed 28.7.2009).

Beinart, S., Anderson, B., Lee, S. and Utting, D. (2002) *Youth at Risk? A National Survey of Risk Factors, Protective Factors and Problem Behaviours Among Young People in England, Scotland and Wales*. London: Communities that Care.

Belsky, J., Melhuish, E., Barnes, J., Leyland, A.H., Romaniuk, H. and National Evaluation of Sure Start Research Team (2006) 'Effects of sure start local programmes on children and families: Early findings from a quasi-experimental, cross sectional study', *BMJ*, 332(7556), 24 June, https://www.ncbi.nlm.nih.gov/pmc/articles/PMC1482335/ (accessed 27.5.2010).

Bentley, T. (1997) *Learning to Belong*. Demos Collection, Issue 12, pp. 44–46.

Berger, R.R. (2002) 'Expansion of police power in public schools and the vanishing rights of students', *Social Justice*, 29, pp. 119–130.

Berridge, D., Brodie, I., Pitts, J., Porteous, D. and Tarling, R. (2001) *The Independent Effects of Permanent Exclusion from School on the Offending Careers of Young People*. Home Office Research Findings No. 71. London: Home Office.

Bhabra, S., Dinos, S. and Ghate, D. (2006) *The National Evaluation of on Track, Phase Two: Young People, Risk and Protection: A Major Study of Secondary Schools in on Track Areas*. Brief No. RB728. London: DfES.

Bhabra, S., Hill, E. and Ghate, D. (2004) *Safer School Partnerships: National Evaluation of the Safer School Partnerships Programme*. London: Youth Justice Board for England and Wales/DfES.

Blair, T. (2005) 'Our citizens should not live in fear', *The Observer*, 11 Sunday, http://www.guardian.co.uk/politics/2005/dec/11/labour.prisonsandprobation (accessed 20.8.2010).

Blaya, C. (2006) 'School violence and the professional socialisation of teachers: The lessons of comparatism,' *Journal of Educational Administration*, 41(6), pp. 650–668.

Blishen, E. (1969) *The School That I'd Like*. Harmondsworth: Penguin.

Blood, P. (2005) 'The Australian context – Restorative practices as a platform for cultural change in schools', *XIV World Congress of Criminology: Preventing Crime and Promoting Justice: Voices for Change*. Philadelphia, PA.

Blyth, E. and Milner, J. (1994) 'Exclusion from school and victim-blaming', *Oxford Review of Education*, 20(3), pp. 293–306.

Bottoms, A.E. (1983) 'Neglected features of contemporary penal systems', In D. Garland and P. Young (eds) *The Power to Punish*. Aldershot: Gower.

Boulton, M.J., Trueman, M. and Murray, L. (2008) 'Association between peer victimization, fear of future victimization and disrupted concentration on class work among junior school pupils', *Journal of Educational Psychology*, 78, pp. 473–489.

Bowles, S. and Gintis, H. (1976) *Schooling in Capitalist America*. London: Routledge and Kegan Paul Ltd.

Bowles, S. and Gintis, H. (2002) 'Schooling in capitalist America revisited', *Sociology of Education*, 75(1), pp. 1–18.

Bowles, R., Reyes, M.G. and Pradiptyo, R. (2005) *Safer Schools Partnerships*. London: Youth Justice Board.

Boxford, S. (2006) *Schools and the Problem of Crime*. Cullompton: Willan.

Braithwaite, J. (1989) *Crime, Shame and Reintegration*. Cambridge: Cambridge University Press.

Braithwaite, J. (2002) *Restorative Justice and Responsive Regulation*. Oxford: Oxford University Press.

Briers, A.N. (2003) 'School-based police officers: What can the UK learn from the USA?', *International Journal of Police Science and Management*, 5(2), pp. 129–142.

Briers, A.N. (2004) *Safer School Communities. Working in Partnership with School Based Officers*. London: Middlesex University Press.

Briers, A.N. and Dickmann, E.M. (2009) 'International comparative perspective of police in schools resulting from a Fulbright Alumni Initiative Award', *International Journal of Police Science and Management*, September, pp. 130–140.

Bright, M. (2005) 'Children with autism the target of Asbos', *The Observer*, 22 May, p. 7.

Brown, B. (2006) 'Understanding and assessing school police officers: A conceptual and methodological comment', *Journal of Criminal Justice*, 34(6), November–December, pp. 591–604.

Brown, J. (2007) 'Time, space and gender: Understanding problem behaviour in young people', *Children in Society*, 21, pp. 98–110.

Brown, J. and Munn, P. (2008) ' "School violence" as a social problem: Charting the rise of the problem and the emerging specialist field', *International Studies in Sociology of Education*, 18(3–4), pp. 219–230.

Brown, S. (2005) *Understanding Youth Crime*. Buckingham: Open University Press.

Brownlee, I. (1998) 'New labour, new penology? Punitive rhetoric and the limits of new managerialism in criminal justice policy', *Journal of Law and Society*, 25(3), pp. 313–335.

Buckley, S. and Maxwell, G. (2007) *Respectful Schools: Restorative Practices in Education. A Summary Report*. Wellington: Office of the Children's Commissioner and The Institute of Policy Studies, School of Government, Victoria University.

Burke, R.H. (1998) 'The socio political context of zero tolerance policing strategies', *Policing*, 21(4), pp. 666–682.

Burney, E. (1999) *Crime and Banishment: Nuisance and Exclusion in Social Housing*. Winchester: Waterside Press.

Burney, E. (2005) *Making People Behave: Anti-Social Behaviour Policy and Politics*. Cullompton: Willan.

Burney, E. and Gelsthorpe, L. (2008) 'Do we need a naughty step? Rethinking the parenting order after ten years', *The Howard Journal of Criminal Justice*, 47(5), pp. 470–483.

Byrne, B. (2009) 'Not just class: Towards an understanding of the whiteness of middle class schooling choice', *Ethnic and Racial Studies*, 32(3), pp. 424–441.

Cabinet Office (2008) *Aspiration and Attainment Amongst People in Deprived Communities. Analysis and Discussion Paper*. London: Cabinet Office/Social Exclusion Task Force.

Cameron, M. and Morrison, I. (2008) *Engaging Men through Learning Centres*. Phase Two Final Report. Inverness: the North Forum for Widening Participation in Higher Education.

Canter, L. and Canter, M. (2001) *Assertive Discipline. Positive Behaviour Management for Today's Classroom* (3rd edition). Bloomington, IN: Solution Tree.

Carlen, P. Gleeson, D. and Wardhaugh, J. (1992) *Truancy. The Politics of Compulsory Schooling*. Buckingham: Open University Press.

Case, S. (2007) 'Questioning the "evidence" or risk that underpins evidence-led youth justice interventions', *Youth Justice*, 7(2), pp. 91–105.

Casella, R. (2006) *Selling us the Fortress: The Promotion of Techno-Security Equipment for Schools*. New York: Routledge.

Cassidy, S. (2002) 'Toughest schools to get full-time police presence', *The Independent*, 30 April, http://www.independent.co.uk/news/education/education-news/toughest-schools-to-get-fulltime-police-presence-658618.html (accessed 29.8.2010).

Catch 22 (2009) *Your Experiences of Crime*, Survey Results, http://www.catch-22.org.uk/index.asp?m=242&t=Publications (accessed 8.7.2010).

Cawson, P. (2002) *Child Maltreatment in the Family: The Experience of a National Sample of Young People*. London: NSPCC.

Cawson, P., Wattam, C., Brooker, S. and Kelly, G. (2000) *Child Maltreatment in the United Kingdom: A Study of the Prevalence of Child Abuse and Neglect*. London: NSPCC.

Cladis, M.S. (1999) 'Durkheim and foucault on education and punishment', In M.S. Cladis (ed.) *Durkheim and Foucault: Perspectives on Education and Punishment*. Oxford: Durkheim Press Ltd.

Cohen, A.K. (1955) *Delinquent Boys: The Culture of the Gang*. Glencoe, IL: The Free Press.

Cohen, S. (1972) *Folk Devils and Moral Panics*. London: MacGibbon and Kee Ltd.

Cohen, S. (1973) 'Property destruction: Motives and meanings', In C. Ward (ed.) *Vandalism*. London: The Architectural Press.

Cohen, S. (1979) 'The punitive city: Notes on the dispersal of social control', *Contemporary Crises*, 3(4), pp. 339–363.

Cohen, S. (1985) *Visions of Social Control*. Cambridge: Polity Press.

Cole, T., Daniels, H. and Visser, J. (2003) 'Patterns of provision for pupils with behavioural difficulties in England: A study of government statistics and support plan data', *Oxford Review of Education*, 29(2), pp. 187–205.

Cole, T., Visser, J. and Upton, G. (1998) *Effective Schooling for Pupils with Emotional and Behavioural Difficulties*. London: David Fulton.

Consedine, J. (1995) *Restorative Justice: Healing the Effects of Crime*. Lyttelton: Ploughshares Publications.

Cooper, P. (1996) 'Giving it a name: The value of descriptive categories in educational approaches to emotional and behavioural difficulties', *Support for Learning*, 4, pp. 146–159.

Cooper, P. (2001) *We Can Work It Out: What Works in Educating Pupils with Social, Emotional and Behavioural Difficulties Outside Mainstream Classrooms*. Barkingside: Barnardo's.

Cooper, C. (2004) 'Surviving the British school system: A toolbox for change', In R. Meighan (ed.) *Damage Limitation: Trying to Reduce the Harm Schools do to Children*. Nottingham: Educational Heretics Press.

Cooper, P. and Tiknaz, Y. (2007) *Nurture Groups in School and at Home*. London: Jessica Kingsley.

Cooper, P. Jacobs, B. and Martin, M. (2009). *Caring to make a Difference: Educating Children and Young People with Social, Emotional and Behavioural Difficulties*. Dublin: National Council for Special Education.

Council of Europe (2002) 'Local partnerships for preventing and combating violence at school', *Final Declaration Adopted at the Close of the Conference*. Strasbourg, France, 2–4 December.

Covell, K., Howe, R.B. and McNeil, J.K. (2008) ' "If there's a dead rat, don't leave it". Young children's understanding of their citizenship rights and responsibilities', *Cambridge Journal of Education*, 38(3), pp. 321–339.

Cowie, H. and Jennifer, D. (2008) *New Perspectives on Bullying*. Buckingham: Open University Press.

Cowie, H. and Oztug, O. (2008) ' "Pupils" perceptions of safety at school', *Pastoral Care in Education*, 26(2), pp. 40–44.

CPAG (2009) *2 Skint 4 School: Time to End the Classroom Divide*. London: Child Poverty Action Group, http://www.cpag.org.uk/2skint4school/details.htm (accessed 10.8.2009).

CPAG, Child Poverty Action Group (2010) *2 Skint 4 School*. London: Child Poverty Action Group, http://www.cpag.org.uk/2skint4school/details.htm (accessed 10.9.2010).

Crawford, A. (1997) *The Local Governance of Crime: Appeals to Community and Partnership*. Oxford: Clarendon Press.

Crawford, A. (2009) 'Governing through anti-social behaviour: Regulatory challenges to criminal justice', *British Journal of Criminology*, 49(6), pp. 810–831.

Cremin, H. (2002) 'Pupils resolving disputes: Successful peer mediation schemes share their secrets', *Support for Learning*, 17(3), pp. 138–144.

Crozier, G. (1997) 'Empowering the powerful: A discussion of the interrelation of government policies and consumerism with social class factors and the impact of this upon parent interventions in their children's schooling', *British Journal of Sociology of Education*, 18(2), pp. 187–200.

Crozier, G. (1999) 'Is it a case of "We know when we're not wanted"? The parents' perspective on parent-teacher roles and relationships', *Educational Research*, 41(3), pp. 315–328.

CtC, Communities that Care (2005) *Findings from the Safer London Youth Survey 2004*. London: Communities that Care.

Currie, J. and Thomas, D. (2000) 'School quality and the long-term effects of head start', *Journal of Human Resources*, Fall, 35(4), pp. 755–774.

Dale, R., Esland, G. and MacDonald, M. (1976) *Schooling and Capitalism: A Sociological Reader.* London: Routledge and Kegan Paul, in association with the Open University Pess.

Daly, K. (2000) 'Revisiting the relationship between retributive and restorative justice', In H. Strang and J. Braithwaite (eds) *Restorative Justice: Philosophy to Practice.* Dartmouth: Ashgate.

Daniels, H. (2001) 'Activity theory and knowledge production: Twin challenges for the development of schooling for pupils who experience EBD', *Emotional and Behavioural Difficulties*, 6(2), pp. 113–124.

Daniels, H., Cole, T., Sellman, E., Sutton, J., Visser, J. with Bedward, J. (2003) *Study of Young People Permanently Excluded from School.* Research Report RR 405. London: DfES.

Daniels, H., Visser, J., Cole., T. and de Reybekill, N. (1998) *Emotional and Behavioural Difficulties in Mainstream Schools.* Research Report RR 90. London: DfEE.

Danish Crime Prevention Council (1998) *SSP Co-operation. Basis and Organization.* Copenhagen, Denmark: Danish Crime Prevention Council.

Davies, P., Shqiponje, T., Hutton, D., Adnett, N. and Coe, R. (2008) 'Socioeconomic background, gender and subject choice in secondary schooling', *Educational Research*, 50(3), pp. 235–248.

Davies, S.M., Nutley, M. and Smith, P.C. (eds) (2000) *What Works? Evidence-Based Policy and Practice in Public Services.* Bristol: The Policy Press.

DCSF, Department for Children Schools and Families (2005) *Social and Emotional Aspects of Learning: Improving Behaviour, Improving Learning.* London: DCSF.

DCSF (2007a) *The Children's Plan: Building Brighter Futures.* London: DCSF.

DCSF (2007b) *Raising Expectations: Staying in Education and Training Post-16.* London: DCSF.

DCSF (2008a) *Ensuring Children's Right to Education: Guidance on the Legal Measures Available to Secure Regular School Attendance.* London: DCSF.

DCSF (2008b) *Improving the Attainment of White Working Class Boys; a Study of a Small Sample of Successful Secondary Schools.* London: DCSF.

DCSF (2009a) *Your Child, Your Schools, Our Future: Building a 21st Century Schools System.* London: DCSF.

DCSF (2009b) *Permanent and Fixed Period Exclusions from Schools and Exclusion Appeals in England, 2007/08*, SFR 18/2009, 30 July. London: DCSF.

DCSF (2009c) *Children with Special Educational Needs 2009: An Analysis.* London: DCSF.

DCSF (2009d) *Safer School Partnership Guidance*, http://www.teachernet.gov.uk/_doc/13566/8250-DCSF-Safer%20School-3.pdf (accessed 26.9.2010).

DCSF (2010) *Sure Start Children's Centres*, http://www.dcsf.gov.uk/everychildmatters/earlyyears/surestart/whatsurestartdoes/ (accessed 16.7.2010).

Debarbieux, E. (2006) 'Violence in School: A few orientations for a worldwide scientific debate', *International Journal on Violence and School*, 2(December), On-line journal, http://www.ijvs.org/3-6224-Article.php?id=19&tarticle=0 (accessed 10.1.2011).

Dedel Johnson, K. (2005) *School Vandalism and Break-Ins.* Problem-Specific Guides Series No. 35. Washington, DC: US Department of Justice, DfEE.

Dennis, N. (ed.) (1997) *Zero Tolerance: Policing a Free Society.* London: IEA.

DES, Department for Education and Skills (2001) *2000/2001 Statistics of Education: Pupil Absence and Truancy from Schools*. London: DfES.

DES/WO (1978) *Special Educational Needs. Report of the Committee of Enquiry into the Education of Handicapped Children and Young People*. Chairman: Mrs HM Warnock. London: Her Majesty's Stationery Office.

DES/WO, Department for Education and Science/Welsh Office (1989) *Discipline in Schools. Report of the Committee of Inquiry Chaired by Lord Elton*. London: HMSO.

DfE, Department for Education (1992) *Exclusions – A Discussion Paper*. London: DfE.

DfE (2010a) *Permanent and Fixed Period Exclusions from Schools and Exclusion Appeals in England, 2008/09*, S FR 22/2010 29 July. London: DfE, http://www.dcsf.gov.uk/rsgateway/DB/SFR/s000942/SFR22_2010.pdf (accessed 3.9.2010).

DfE (2010b) *Pupil Absence in Schools in England. Including Pupil Characteristics: 2008–09*, March. London: DfE, http://www.dcsf.gov.uk/rsgateway/DB/SFR/s000946/SFR25-2010.pdf (accessed 3.9.2010).

DfE (2010c) *Youth Cohort Study & Longitudinal Study of Young People in England: The Activities and Experiences of 18 year olds: England 2009*. BO1/2010, 22 July. London: DfE.

DfE (2010d) Nick gibb to the reform conference. *Speech*, http://www.education.gov.uk/news/speeches/ng-reform-conference (accessed 22.7.2010).

DfEE, Department for Education and Employment (1996) *Improving Security in School*. London: HMSO.

DfEE (2001) *Code of Practice on the Identification and Assessment of Special Educational Needs*. London: DfEE.

DfES, Department for Education and Skills (2003a) *Every Child Matters*. A Green Paper presented to Parliament September 2003, Cm5860. London: DfES.

DfES (2003b) *Youth Cohort Study: The Activities of 17 Year Olds: England and Wales 2003*. SFR 35/2003. London: DfES.

DfES (2005) *Behaviour and Attendance Strand Toolkit unit 10: Links with Partners and Other Agencies*. Key Stage 3 National Strategy. London: DfES.

DfES (2006) *Learning Behaviour Principles and Practice: What Works in Schools, Section 2 of the Report of the Practitioners on School Behaviour and Discipline chaired by Alan Steer*. London: DfES.

DfES/Home Office (1997) *School Security, Dealing with Trouble Makers*. London: DfES.

Dickmann, E.M. (1999) *The Culture of School Resource Officers – An Ethnographic Study*. Dissertation (unpublished). Colorado State University, Fort Collins, CO.

Dinkes, R., Kemp, J. and Baum, K. (2009) *Indicators of School Crime and Safety: 2009* (NCES 2010-012/NCJ 228478). Washington, DC: National Center for Education Statistics; Washington, DC: Institute of Education Sciences, U.S. Department of Education, and Bureau of Justice Statistics, Office of Justice Programs.

Douglas, N., Warwick, I., Kemp, S., Whitty, G. and Aggleton, P. (1999) 'Homophobic bullying in secondary schools in England and Wales – teachers' experiences', *Health Education*, 99(2), pp. 53–60.

Drakeford, M. and McCarthy, K. (2000) 'Parents, responsibility and the new youth justice', In B. Goldson (ed.) *The New Youth Justice* (pp. 96–114). Lyme Regis: Russell House Publishing.

Drewery, W. (2004) 'Conferencing in schools: Punishment, Restorative Justice, and the productive importance of the process of conversation', *Journal of Community and Applied Social Psychology*, 14(2004), pp. 332–344.

Dunne, M. and Gazeley, L. (2008) 'Teachers, social class and underachievement', *British Journal of Sociology of Education*, 29(5), pp. 451–63.

DuRant, R.H., Krowchuk, D.P., Kreiter, S., Sinal, S.H. and Woods, C.R. (1999) 'Weapon carrying on school property among middle school students', *Archives of Pediatrics and Adolescent Medicine*, 153(1), January, pp. 21–24.

Dyson, A. (2001) 'Special need education as the way to equity: An alternative approach', *Support for Learning*, 16(3), pp. 99–104.

Edwards, T. (2008) 'A sociology for our times?', *British Journal of Sociology of Education*, 29(4), pp. 369–379.

Elton Report (1989) *Discipline in Schools: Report of Committee of Enquiry Chaired by Lord Elton*. London: H.M.S.O.

ERIC, Education Resources Information Centre (1997) 'Common features of school wide behaviour management', *ERIC Research papers* 1(1), http://www.ericdigests.org (accessed 3.9.2010).

Evans, G. (2007) *Educational Failure and Working Class White Children in Britain*. Basingstoke: Palgrave Macmillan.

Farrington, D. (1996) *Understanding and Preventing Youth Crime*. York: York Publishing Services Ltd./Joseph Rowntree Foundation.

Farrington, D.P. (2002) 'Developmental criminology and risk-focussed prevention', In M. Maguire, R. Morgan and R. Reiner (eds) *The Oxford Handbook of Criminology* (3rd edition). Oxford: Oxford University Press.

Farrington, D.P. and Ttofi, M.M. (2009) *School-Based Programs to Reduce Bullying and Victimization*. 6. The Campbell Collaboration, http://www.campbellcollaboration.org/library.php.

Farrington, D.P. and Welsh, B.C. (2007) *Saving Children from a Life of Crime: Early Risk Factors and Effective Interventions*. Oxford: Oxford University Press.

Feeley, M.M. and Simon, J. (1992) 'The new penology: Notes on the emerging strategy of corrections and its implications', *Criminology*, 30(4), pp. 452–474.

Felson, R.B. and Staff, J. (2006) 'Explaining the academic performance-delinquency relationship', *Criminology*, 44(2), pp. 299–320.

Fitz-Gibbons, C. (2000) 'Education: realising the potential', In S.M. Davies, M. Nutley and P.C. Smith (eds) *What Works? Evidence-Based Policy and Practice in Public Services*. Bristol: The Policy Press.

Fitzgerald, M. and O'Connor, L. (2005) *Safer School Partnerships in the London Borough of Southwark: An Implementation and Impact Study*. Research Report. Roehampton: University of Surrey.

Flint, J. (ed.) (2006) *Housing, Urban Governance and Anti-Social Behaviour*. Bristol: The Policy Press.

Flint, J. and Nixon, J. (2006) 'Governing neighbours: Anti-social behaviour orders and new forms of regulating conduct in the UK', *Urban Studies*, 43(5/6), pp. 939–955.

Flood-Page, C., Campbell, S., Harrington V. and Miller, J. (2000) *Youth Crime: Findings from the 1998/99 Youth Lifestyles Survey*. Home Office Research Study 209, London: Home Office.

Fortin, L. and Bigras, M. (1997) 'Risk factors exposing young children to problems', *Emotional and Behavioural Difficulties*, 2(1), pp. 3–14.

Foucault, M. (1977) *Discipline and Punish: The Birth of the Prison*. London: Penguin.

Fovet, F. (2009) 'The use of humour in classroom interventions with students with social, emotional and behavioural difficulties', *Emotional and Behavioural Difficulties*, 14(4), pp. 275–289.

France, A. (2008) 'Risk factor analysis and the youth question', *Journal of Youth Studies*, 11(1), pp. 1–15.

Freire, P. (1994) *Pedagogy of Hope*. London: Continuum Publishing.

Furedi, F. (1997) *Culture of Fear: Risk Taking and the Morality of Low Expectation*. London: Cassell.

Furedi, F. (2009) *Wasted: Why Education Isn't Educating*. London: Continuum Publishing.

Furlong, A. and Cartmel, F. (1997) *Young People and Social Change: Individualization and Risk in Late Modernity*. Buckingham: Open University Press.

Furniss, C. (2000) 'Bullying in schools: It's not a crime – is it?', *Education and the Law*, 12(1), pp. 9–29.

Garces, E., Thomas, D. and Currie, J. (2002) 'Longer-term effects of head start', *The American Economic Review*, September, pp. 999–1012.

Garfinkel, H. (1956) 'Conditions of successful degradation ceremonies', *American Journal of Sociology*, 61(5), pp. 420–424.

Garland, B., Lecocq, C. and Philippot, P. (2007) 'School violence and teacher professional disengagement', *British Journal of Educational Psychology*, 77, pp. 465–477.

Garland, D. (1996) 'The limits of the sovereign state: Strategies of crime control in contemporary society', *British Journal of Criminology*, 36(4), pp. 445–471.

Garland, D. (2001) *The Culture of Control: Crime and Social Order in Contemporary Society*. Oxford: Oxford University Press.

Gaskell, C. (2008) ' "But they just don't respect us": Young people's experiences of (dis)respected citizenship and the New Labour Respect Agenda', *Children's Geographies*, 6(3), pp. 223–238.

Ghate, D. and Hazell, N. (2002) *Parenting in Poor Environments: Stress, Support and Coping*. London: Jessica Kingsley.

Giddens, A. (1999) *Runaway World: How Globalization is Reshaping Our Lives*. London: Profile.

Gill, M. and Hearnshaw, S. (1997) *Personal Safety and Violence in Schools*. DfEE Research Report RR21. London: DfEE.

Gillborn, D. and Kirton, A. (2000) 'White heat: Racism, under-achievement and white working-class boys', *International Journal of Inclusive Education*, 4(4), pp. 271–288.

Gillborn, D. and Mirza, H. (2000) *Mapping Race, Class and Gender Educational Inequality*. London: Institute of Education.

Gillies, D. (2008) 'Quality and equality: The mask of discursive conflation in education policy texts', *Journal of Education Policy*, 23(6), pp. 685–699.

Gillies, V. (2005) 'Raising the "Meritocracy": Parenting and the individualization of social class', *Sociology*, 39(5), pp. 835–853.

Gillis, J.R. (1974) *Youth and History: Tradition and Change in European Age Relations, 1770–Present*. London: Academic Press.

Gilmore, L. and Boulton-Lewis, G. (2009) ' "Just Try Harder and You Will Shine": A study of 20 lazy children', *Australian Journal of Guidance and Counselling*, 19(2), pp. 95–103.

Giroux, H.A. (2001) *Theory and Resistance in Education. Towards a Pedagogy for the Opposition.* Westpoint, CT: Bergin and Garvey, an imprint of Greenway Publishing Group Inc.

Giroux, H.A. (2003) *The Abandoned Generation: Democracy Beyond the Culture of Fear.* New York: Palgrave Macmillan.

Goggins, E.O., Newman, I., Waechter, D. and Williams, B.G. (1994) 'Effectiveness of police in schools: Perceptions of students, teachers, administrators and police officers', *Journal of School Research and Information*, 12, pp. 16–22.

Goldson, B. and Jamieson, J. (2002) 'Youth crime, the "parenting deficit" and state intervention: A contextual critique', *Youth Justice*, 2(2), pp. 82–99.

Goodenow, C. (1993) 'The psychological sense of school membership amongst adolescents: Scale development and educational correlates', *Psychology in the Schools*, 30, pp. 79–90.

Gordon, R. (2000) 'Criminal business organizations, street gangs and "Wanna Be" groups: A vancouver perspective', *Canadian Journal of Criminology and Criminal Justice*, 42(1), pp. 39–60.

Gottfredson, D. (2001) *School and Delinquency.* New York: Cambridge University Press.

Graham, J. and Bowling, B. (1995) *Young People and Crime.* Home Office Research Study 145. London: Home Office.

Green, F.G. (2008) 'Bullying in school', *Safer Schools News*, 18, http://www.keystosaferschools.com/Newsletter_Vol.18.htm (accessed 27.11.2008).

Greenaway, D. and Haynes, M. (2003) 'Funding higher education in the UK: The role of fees and loans', *Economic Journal*, 113, pp. 150–166.

Greene, M.B. (2006) 'Bullying in schools: A plea for a measure of human rights', *Journal of Social Issues*, 62(1), pp. 63–79.

Greenhalgh, P. (1994) *Emotional Growth and Learning.* London: Routledge.

Greenhalgh, P. (1999) 'Integrating the legacy of David Wills in an era of target setting', *Emotional and Behavioural Difficulties*, 4(1), pp. 46–53.

Grimshaw, R. with Berridge, D. (1994) *Closing Children's Homes.* London: National Children's Bureau.

Hales, J., Neveill, C., Pudney, S. and Tipping, S. (2009) *Longitudinal analysis of the Offending, Crime and Justice Survey 2003–06.* Research Report 19. November. London: Home Office.

Hall, N. and Hayden, C. (2007) 'Is "Hate Crime" a relevant and useful way of conceptualising some forms of school bullying?', *International Journal on School Violence*, 3(April), pp. 3–24.

Hallam, S., Rogers, L., Rhamie, J., Shaw, J. with Rees, E., Haskins, H., Blackmore, J. and Hallam, J. (2007) 'Pupil's perceptions of an alternative curriculum: Skill force', *Research Papers in Education*, 22(1), pp. 43–63.

Hallsworth, S. and Young, T. (2008) 'Gang talk and gang talkers: A critique', *Crime Media Culture*, 4(2), pp. 175–195.

Harber, C. (2001) 'Schooling and violence in South Africa: Creating a safer school', *Intercultural Education*, 12(3), pp. 261–272.

Harber, C. (2004) 'Schooling can seriously damage your health: Education for violence, education for peace', In R. Meighan (ed.) *Damage Limitation: Trying to Reduce the Harm Schools Do to Children.* Nottingham: Educational Heretics Press.

Harber, C. (2008) 'Perpetrating disaffection: Schooling as an international problem', *Educational Studies*, 34(5), pp. 457–467.

Harris, A. and Ranson, S. (2005) 'The contradiction of education policy: Disadvantage and achievement', *British Educational Research Journal*, 31(5), pp. 571–587.

Hayden, C. (1997) *Children Excluded from Primary School*. Buckingham: Open University Press.

Hayden, C. (2000) 'Exclusion from school and the generation or maintenance of social exclusion', In G. Walveren, D. van Veen, C. Parsons and C. Day (eds) *Education and Social Exclusion. Authoritarianism, Laissey-Faire or some Third Way?* Amsterdam: EERA (European Educational Research Association) Children and Youth at Risk Network.

Hayden, C. (2001) 'Social exclusion and exclusion from school in England', In J. Visser, H. Daniels and T. Cole (eds) *Emotional and Behavioural Difficulties in Mainstream Schools*. International Perspectives on Inclusive Education, Volume 1. London: JAI/Elsevier Science.

Hayden, C. (2005) 'Crime prevention: The role and potential of school', In J. Winstone and J. Pakes (eds) *Community Justice. Issues for Probation and Criminal Justice*. Cullompton, Devon: Willan Publishing.

Hayden, C. (2007) *Children in Trouble*. Basingstoke: Palgrave Macmillan.

Hayden, C. (2009) 'Deviance and violence in schools: A review of the evidence in England', *International Journal of Violence and School*, 9, On-line journal, http://www.ijvs.org/3-6224-Article.php?id=74&tarticle=0 (accessed 10.1.2011).

Hayden, C. (2010) 'Crime, anti-social behaviour and schools', keynote at *SEBDA International Conference: Transforming Troubled Lives*. Keble College, Oxford, UK, 14–17 September.

Hayden, C. and Blaya, C. (2001) 'Violence and aggression in english schools', In E. Debarbieux and C. Blaya (eds) *Violence in Schools. Ten Approaches in Europe*. Issey-les-Moulineaux: ESF editeur.

Hayden, C. and Dunne, S. (2001) *Outside Looking In: Families' Experiences of Exclusion from School*. London: The Children's Society.

Hayden, C. and Gough, D. (2010) Implementing a Restorative Justice approach in children's residential care. Bristol: Policy Press.

Hayden, C. and Martin, T. (1998) 'Safer cities and exclusion from school', *Journal of Youth Studies*, 1(3), pp. 315–331.

Hayden, C. and Pike, S. (2005) 'Including "positive handling strategies" within training in behaviour management – the "Team-Teach" approach', *Emotional and Behavioural Difficulties*, 10(3), pp. 173–188.

Hayden, C., Williamson, T. and Webber, R. (2007) 'Schools, pupil behaviour and young offenders: Using postcode classification to target behaviour support and crime prevention programmes', *British Journal of Criminology*, 47(2), pp. 293–310.

Hayward, G., Stephenson, G. and Blyth, M. (2004) 'Exploring effective educational interventions for young people who offend', In R. Burnett and C. Roberts (eds) *What Works in Probation: Developing Evidence-Based Practice* (pp. 88–108). Willan: Cullompton.

Hendrick, H. (2006) 'Histories of youth crime and justice', In B. Goldson and J. Muncie (eds) *Youth Crime and Justice*. London: Sage.

Hendry, R. (2009) *Building and Restoring Respectful Relationships at School – a Guide to using Restorative Practice*. Abingdon: Routledge.

Hirsch, D. (2007) *Experiences of Poverty and Educational Disadvantage*. York: Joseph Rowntree Foundation.

Hirschfield, P.J. (2008) 'Preparing for prison? The criminalization of school discipline in the USA', *Theoretical Criminology*, 12(1), pp. 79–101.

Hodgson, P. and Webb, D. (2005) 'Young people, crime and school exclusion: A case of some surprises', *Howard Journal of Criminal Justice*, 44(1), pp. 12–28.

Holt, A. (2008) 'Room for resistance? Parenting Orders, disciplinary power and the production of "the bad parent"', In P. Squires (ed.) *ASBO Nation: The Criminalisation of Nuisance*. Bristol: Policy Press.

Holt, A. (2009a) '(En)Gendering responsibilities: Experiences of parenting a "Young Offender"', *The Howard Journal of Criminal Justice*, 48(4), pp. 344–356.

Holt, A. (2009b) 'Managing "spoiled identities": Parents' experiences of compulsory parenting support programmes,' *Children and Society*, http://onlinelibrary.wiley.com/doi/10.1111/j.1099-0860.2009.00255.x/abstract (accessed 7.9.2010), ifirst published 6 August 2009.

Holt, A. (2010a) 'Disciplining "problem parents" in the youth court: Between regulation and resistance', *Social Policy and Society*, 9(1), pp. 89–99.

Holt, A. (2010b) 'Managing "spoiled identities": Parents' experiences of compulsory parenting support programmes', *Children and Society*, (DOI: 10.1111/j.1099-0860.2009.00255.x).

HM Government (2008) *Youth Crime Action Plan 2008*. London: COI.

HMICA, Her Majesty's Inspector of Court Administration (2003) *Streets Ahead, A Joint Inspection of the Street Crime Initiative*. London: HMSO.

Home Office (1997) *No More Excuses*, Cm.3809. London: HMSO.

Home Office (2002) *Narrowing the Justice Gap*. Justice Gap Task force. London: Home Office.

Home Office (2004) *Best Practice Guidelines for Restorative Practitioners and Their Case Supervisors and Line Managers*. London: HMSO.

Home Office (2006a) *Crime and Victims – Hate Crime*, www.homeoffice.gov.uk/crime-victims/reducing-crime/hate-crime/ (accessed 10.4.2010).

Home Office (2006b) *Respect Action Plan*. London: Home Office.

Home Office (2008) *Offending Crime and Justice Survey*, http://www.homeoffice.gov.uk/rds/offending_survey.html (accessed 30.3.2010).

Hood, S. (1999) 'Home-school agreements: A true partnership?', *School Leadership and Management*, 19(4), pp. 427–440.

Hope, A. (2009) 'CCTV, school surveillance and social control', *British Educational Research Journal*, 35(6), pp. 891–907.

Hopkins, B. (2004) *Just Schools*. London: Jessica Kingsley Publishers.

Hopkins, B. (2006) *Implementing a Restorative Approach to Behaviour and Relationship in Schools – The Narrated Experiences of an Educationalist*. PhD thesis. School of Education. Reading: University of Reading.

Hopkins, B. (2009) *Just Care – Restorative Justice Approaches*. London: Jessica Kingsley Publishers.

Horgan, G. (2007) *The Impact of Poverty on Young Children's Experience of School*. York: Joseph Rowntree Foundation.

HSE, Health and Safety Executive (2008) *Health and Safety at Work 2007/8*. Sudbury: Health and Safety Executive.

Hudson, B. (2003) *Justice in the Risk Society*. London: Sage.

Hughes, G. (2002) 'Crime and disorder reduction partnerships: The future of community safety?', In G. Hughes, E. McLaughlin and J. Muncie (eds) *Crime Prevention and Community Safety: New Directions*. London: Sage.

Hutchings, J., Bywater, T., Daley, D., Gardner, F., Whitaker, C., Jones, K., Eames, C. and Edwards, R.T. (2007) 'Parenting intervention in Sure Start services for children at risk of developing conduct disorder: Pragmatic randomised controlled trial', *BMJ*, 334(678), 31 March, http://www.bmj.com/cgi/content/abstract/334/7595/678 (accessed 27.5.2010).

Hyman, I.A. and Perone, D.C. (1998) 'The other side of school violence: Educator policies and practices that may contribute to student misbehavior', *Journal of School Psychology*, 36, pp. 7–27.

Illich, I. (1971) *Deschooling Society*. New York: Harper & Row.

Jamieson, J. (2005) 'New labour, youth justice and the question of respect', *Youth Justice*, 5(3), pp. 180–193.

Johnson, I.M. (1999) 'School violence: the effectiveness of a school resource officer program in a southern city', *Journal of Criminal Justice*, 27(2), pp. 173–192.

Johnson, R. (1976) 'Notes on the schooling of the english working class, 1780–1950', In R. Dale et al. (eds) *Schooling and Capitalism*. London/Henley: Routledge and Kegan Paul/Open University Press.

Johnstone, G. (2002) *Restorative Justice – Ideas, Values, Debates*. Cullompton, Devon: Willan Publishing.

Johnstone, G. (2003) *A Restorative Justice Reader*. Cullompton, Devon: Willan Publishing.

Jones, T. and Newburn, T. (2007) *Policy Transfer and Criminal Justice: Exploring US Influence over British Crime Control Policy*. Maidenhead: Open University Press.

Joseph Rowntree Foundation (2009) *Contemporary Social Evils*. Bristol: Policy Press.

Kane, J., Lloyd, G., McCluskey, G., Riddell, S., Stead, J., Weedon, E., Maguire, R. and Hendry, R. (2007) *Restorative Practices in Three Scottish Councils: Final Report of the Evaluation of the First Two Years of the Pilot Projects 2004–2006*. Edinburgh: Scottish Government.

Kauffman, J. (2001) *Characteristics of Emotional and Behavioural Disorders of Children and Youth* (7th edition). Upper Saddle River, NJ: Merrill Prentice Hall.

Kelly, P. (2003) 'Growing up as risky business? risks, surveillance and the institutionalized mistrust of youth', *Journal of Youth Justice Studies*, 6(2), pp. 165–180.

Klein, M.W., Weerman, F.M. and Thornberry, T.P. (2006) 'Street gang violence in Europe', *European Journal of Criminology*, 3, pp. 413–437.

Knuver, A.W.M. and Brandsman, H.P. (1993) 'Cognitive and affective outcomes in school effectiveness research', *School Effectiveness and School Improvement*, 4(3), pp. 189–204.

KPMG (2004) *Government Office for London Evaluation of the Safer Routes to School Pilot Scheme*, July. London: KMPG.

Lambert, R.D. and McGinty, D. (2002) 'Law enforcement officers in schools: Setting priorities', *Journal of Educational Administration*, 40(3), p. 258.

Laslett, R. (1999) 'Respecting the past: Regarding the present', *Emotional and Behavioural Difficulties*, 3(1), pp. 5–11.

Laslett, R., Cooper, P., Maras, P., Rimmer, A. and Law, B. (1998) *Emotional and Behavioural Difficulties Since 1945*. Maidstone: AWEBD.

Lawrence, J., Steed, D. and Young, P. (1984) *Disruptive Children: Disruptive Schools?* Orpington: Croom Helm.

Levitt, S. (2004) 'Understanding why crime fell in the 1990s: Four factors that explain the decline and six that do not', *Journal of Economic Perspectives*, 18(1), pp. 163–190.

Lewis, A. and Norwich, B. (2004) *Special Teaching for Special Children*. London: McGraw-Hill Education.

Liebmann, M. (2007) *Restorative Justice: How It Works*. London: Jessica Kingsley Publishers.

Lindsay, G., Davies, H., Band, S., Cullen, M., Cullen, S., Strand, S., Hasluck, C., Evans, R. and Stewart-Brown, S. (2008) *Parenting Early Intervention Pathfinder Evaluation*. RW054. London: Department for Children Schools and Families.

Lindstrom, P. (2001) 'School violence: A multi-level perspective', *International Review of Victimology*, 8(2), pp. 141–158.

Lister, D. (2006) 'Children (but not women) first: New Labour, child welfare and gender', *Critical Social Policy*, 26(2), pp. 315–335.

Lloyd, G. and McCluskey, G. (2008) *Restorative Practice Pilots and Approaches in Scotland – Follow Up*. Edinburgh: Scottish Government.

Lloyd, G. and O'Reyan, A. (1999) 'Education for social exclusion? Issues to do with effectiveness of educational provision for young women with SEBD', *Emotional and Behavioural Difficulties*, 4(2), pp. 38–46.

Loader, I. (1996) *Youth, Policing and Democracy*. Basingstoke: Palgrave Macmillan.

Lou, N. (2008) *Understanding the Role of School-Based Police Officers. Police and School Relations in a UK Setting: A Cultural Perspective*. MA dissertation (unpublished). London: Kings College.

Loveday, B. (1999) *The Impact of Performance Culture in Criminal Justice Agencies: The Case of the Police and the Crown Prosecution Service*. Occasional Paper no. 9. Portsmouth: Institute of Criminal Justice, University of Portsmouth.

Lucey, H. and Reay, D. (2000) 'Identities in transition: Anxiety and excitement in the move to secondary school', *Oxford Review of Education*, 26(2), pp. 191–205.

Maguin, E. and Loeber, R. (1996) 'Academic performance and delinquency', *Crime and Justice: A Review of Research*, 20, pp. 145–264.

Mahaffey, H. and Newton, C. (2008) *Restorative Solutions*. Nottingham: Inclusive Solutions.

Mannheim, H. (1965) *Comparative Criminology*. London: Routledge/Kegan Paul.

Margo, J., Dixon, M., Pearce, N. and Reed, H. (2006) *Freedom's Orphans: Raising Youth in a Changing World*. London: IPPR.

Martin, D. (2003) 'The politics of policing: Managerialism, modernisation and performance', In R. Matthews and J. Young (eds) *The New Politics of Crime Control*. Cullompton, Devon: Willan.

Martin, D. Chatwin, C. and Porteous, D. (2007) 'Risky or at risk? young people, surveillance and security', *Criminal Justice Matters*, 68, Summer, pp. 27–28.

Martin, D., Mackenzie, N. and Healy, J. (2008) *Secondary School Teachers Experience of Violence in the Workplace*. ESRC Final Research Report. Swindon: ESRC.

Martino, W., Kehler, M.D. and Weaver-Hightower, M.N. (2009) *The Problem with Boys' Education: Beyond the Backlash*. London/New York: Routledge.

May, D. (1975) 'Truancy, school absenteeism and delinquency', *Scottish Educational Studies*, 7, pp. 97–107.

McAra, L. (2004) *Truancy, School Exclusion and Substance Misuse*. Edinburgh: Centre for Law and Society, http://www.law.ed.ac.uk/cls/esytc/findings/digest4.pdf (accessed 12.10.2009).

McAra, L. and McVie, S. (2005) 'The usual suspects, street-life, young people and the police', *Criminal Justice*, 3(1), pp. 5–36.

McCarthy, P., Laing, K. and Walker, J. (2004) *Offenders of the Future? Assessing the Risk of Children and Young People Becoming Involved in Criminal or Antisocial Behaviour*. DfES Research Report RR545. London: DfES.

McCold, P. (2001) 'Primary restorative justice practices', In A. Morris and G. Maxwell (eds) *Restorative Justice for Juveniles*. Oxford: Hart.

McCold, P. and Wachtel, T. (2002) 'The worst school I've ever been to: Empirical evaluations of a restorative school and treatment milieu', *Dreaming of a New Reality, The Third International Conference on Conferencing, Circles and other Restorative Practices*. Minneapolis, MN.

McCormack, I. (2005) *Getting the Buggers to Turn up*. London: Continuum Books.

McCrystal, P., Higgins, K. and Percy, A. (2007) 'Exclusion and marginalisation in adolescence: The experience of school exclusion on drug use and antisocial behaviour', *Journal of Youth Studies*, 10(1), pp. 35–54.

McDonald, L. (2010) *Families and Schools TOGETHER Inc. Founder Biography*, http://www.familiesandschools.org/about/founder-biography.php (accessed 16.7.2010).

Mc Garrigle, M., Meade, K. and Santa-Maria Morales, A. (2006) *Pilot implementation of Restorative Practices in Post-Primary Schools in theNorthwest Region*. Galway: National University of Ireland, http://transformingconflict.org/Pilot-Implementation-of-restorative-practices-in-Northwest-Ireland.doc (accessed 9.1.2011).

McGraw, K., Moore, S., Fuller, A. and Bates, G. (2008) 'Family, peer and school connectedness in final year secondary school students', *Australian Psychologist*, 43(1), pp. 27–37.

McIntyre-Bhatty, K. (2008) 'Truancy and coercive consent: Is their an alternative?', *Educational Review*, 60(4), pp. 375–390.

McKey, H.R., Condelli, L., Ganson, H., Barrett, B., McConkey, C. and Palntz, M. (1985) *The Impact of Head Start on Children, Families and Communities. Final report of the Head Start Evaluation, Synthesis and Utilisation Project*. The Head Start Bureau. Administration for Children, Youth and Families, Office of Human Development Services, US Department of Health and Human Services, Washington, DC.

McManus, M. (1989) *Troublesome Behaviour in the Classroom. A Teacher's Survival Guide*. London: Routledge.

McNeely, C.A., Nonnemaker, J.M. and Blum, R.W. (2002) 'Promoting school connectedness: Evidence from the National Longitudinal Study of Adolescent Health', *Journal of School Health*, 72(4), April, pp. 138–146.

McNeish, D. and Roberts, H. (1995) *Playing it Safe: Today's Children at Play*. Ilford: Barnardos.

Meighan, R. (ed.) (2004) *Damage Limitation: Trying to Reduce the Harm Schools Do to Children*. Nottingham: Educational Heretics Press.

Millard, B. and Flatley, J. (eds) (2010) *Experimental Statistics on Victimisation of Children Aged 10 to 15: Findings from the British Crime Survey for the Year Ending*

*December 2009. England and Wales*, 17 June, Home Office Statistical Bulletin 11/10. London: Home Office.

Millie, A. (2009a) *Anti-Social Behaviour*, Maidenhead: Open University Press.

Millie, A. (2009b) *Securing Respect: Behavioural Expectations and Anti-Social Behaviour in the UK*. Bristol: Policy Press.

Millie, A., Jacobson, J., McDonald, E. and Hough, M. (2005) *Anti-Social Behaviour Strategies: Finding a Balance*. Bristol: The Policy Press.

Ministère de la Sécurité publique, Quebec (2002) *Réflexion sur les enjeux de la présence policière en milieu scolaire*. Conseil consultative québecois en prevention de la criminalité. Quebec: Canada.

Mirsky, L. (2009) *Restorative Practices Forum*, 12 January, pp. 1–2 Hull, UK: Toward a Restorative City, http://www.iirp.org/pdf/Hull.pdf (accessed 9.1.2011).

Moore, D.B. and O'Connell, T.A. (1994) 'Family conferencing in Wagga Wagga', In G. Johnstone (ed.) *A Restorative Justice Reader*. Cullumpton, Devon: Willan Publishing.

Morgan, R. (2007) 'They smoke, drink and behave badly. Will we never learn?', *Sunday Independent*, 16 September.

MORI (2004) *MORI Youth Survey 2004*. London: Youth Justice Board.

MORI (2006) *MORI Five-Year Report: An Analysis of Youth Survey Data*. London: Youth Justice Board.

MORI (2010) *Evaluation of Campus Police Officers in Scottish School*. Edinburgh: Scottish Government.

Morita, Y. (2002) 'Violence in school: A Japanese approach', In E. Debarbieux and C. Blaya (eds) *Violence in Schools and Public Policies*. Paris: Elsevier Science.

Morrison, B. (2001) 'The School System:developing its capacity in the regulation of a civil society', In H. Strang and J. Braithwaite (eds) *Restorative Justice and Civil Society*. Cambridge: Cambridge University Press.

Morrison, B. (2002) 'Bullying and victimisation', *Trends and Issues in Crime and Criminal Justice*. 219, pp. 1–6.

Morrison, B. (2005a) 'Building safe and healthy school communities: Restorative justice and responsive regulation', *Building a Global Alliance for Restorative Practices and Family Empowerment, Part 3'*, the IIRP's Sixth International Conference on Conferencing, Circles and other Restorative Practices. Penrith, New South Wales, Australia.

Morrison, B. (2005b) 'Restorative justice in schools', In E. Elliott and R.M. Gordon (eds) *New Directions in Restorative Justice*. Cullompton, Devon: Willan.

Morrison, I. (2007) *Engaging Men through Learning Centres*. Final Report. Inverness: The North Forum for Widening Participation in Higher Education.

Morrison, I. (2008) *Engaging Men: Learning Centres in the Highlands and Islands of Scotland*. Paper presented to the International Conference on Learning, University of Chicago, Chicago, IL, 3–6 June.

Morrison, R. (2009) 'Feral kids should watch out: I've had enough', *The Times* [online], 8 April 2009, http://www.timesonline.co.uk/tol/comment/columnists/richard_morrison/article6052880.ece (accessed 16.12. 2009).

Morss, J. (1996) *Growing Critical: Alternatives to Developmental Psychology*. London: Routledge.

Mortimore, P., Sammons, P., Stoll, L., Lewis, D. and Echo, K. (1988) *School Matters: The Junior Years*. Wells: Open Books.

Mosley, J. and Doyle, J. (eds) (2005) Circle *Time. A Practical Book of Circle Time Lesson Plans.* Trowbridge: Positive Press.

Muncie, J. (2002) 'A new deal for youth, early intervention and correctionalism', In G. Hughes, E. McLaughlin and J. Muncie (eds) *Crime Prevention and Community Safety: New Directions.* London: Sage.

Muncie, J. (2004) *Youth and Crime.* London: Sage.

Muncie, J. (2006) 'Governing young people: Coherence and contradiction in contemporary youth justice', *Critical Social Policy*, 26(4), pp. 770–793.

Munn, P., Johnstone, M., Sharp, S. and Brown, J. (2007) 'Violence in schools: Perceptions of secondary teachers and head teachers over time', *International Journal of Violence and Schools.* 3(April), On-line journal, http://www.ijvs.org/ 3-6224-Article.php?id=31&tarticle=0 (accessed 10.1.2011).

Munn, P., Sharp, S., Lloyd, G., Macleod, G., McCluskey, G., Brown, J. and Hamilton, L. (2009) *Behaviour in Scottish Schools 2009.* Edinburgh: Scottish Government.

Murray-Harvey, R. and Slee, P.T. (2006) '"Australian and Japanese school students" experiences of school bullying and victimisation: Associations with stress, support and school', *International Journal on Violence and School*, 2(December), On-line journal, http://www.ijvs.org/3-6224-Article.php?id=28& tarticle=0 (accessed 10.1.2011).

NAHT, National Association of Head Teachers (2000) *Managing Security: Personnel.* NAHT Professional Management Series, PM018. London: NAHT.

NAHT (2008) *Security Headaches.* National Association of Head Teachers website, 12 June, http://www.naht.org.uk/welcome/resources/library/features/ security-headaches (accessed 22.2.2011).

NAHT (2010) *Boycott Schools List – A 'Badge of Honour' Says Mick Brookes*, NAHT, 6 July, http://www.naht.org.uk/welcome/resources/key-topics/assessment/ ks2-tests-in-2011/ (accessed 10.9.2010).

NAO (2005) *Improving School Attendance in England.* London: The Stationary Office.

NAS/UWT, National Association of Schoolmasters, Union of Women Teachers (2004) *Evaluation of the Behaviour Improvement Programme. A Final Report by the Perpetuity Group.* Birmingham: NAS/UWT, http://www.nasuwt.org.uk/consum/ groups/public/@education/documents/nas_download/nasuwt_000620.pdf (accessed 27.9.2010).

Nathanson, D.L. (1992) *Shame, Pride, Affect, Sex, and the Birth of Self.* New York: W.W. Norton.

Neill, S.R. St. J. (2008) *Disruptive Pupil Behaviour: Its Causes and effects: A Survey Analysed for the National Union of Teachers.* Warwick: Institute of Education, University of Warwick.

Nixon, J. and Parr, S. (2009) 'Family intervention projects and the efficacy of parenting interventions', In M. Blyth and E. Solomon (eds) *Prevention and Youth Crime: Is Early Intervention Working?* Bristol: Policy Press.

O'Beirne, M., Denney, D. and Gabe, J. (2004) 'Fear of violence as an indicator of risk in probation work', *British Journal of Criminology*, 44, pp. 113–126.

O'Connor, L. (2001) *ACPO Drugs Sub Committee.* Roehampton: Roehampton Institute, University of Surrey.

OECD, Organisation for Economic Cooperation and Development (2008) *Jobs for Youth: United Kingdom.* Paris: OECD Publishing.

Ofsted (1999a) *Principals into Practice: Effective Education for Pupils with EBD.* London: Ofsted.

Ofsted (1999b) *Lessons Learnt from Special Measures.* London: Ofsted.

Ofsted (2003a) *Yes He Can; Schools Where Boys Write Well.* HMI 505. London: Ofsted.

Ofsted (2003b) *Annual Report of Her Majesty's Chief Inspector for Schools: Standards and Quality in Education 2002/03.* London: Ofsted.

Ofsted (2005) *Managing Challenging Behaviour.* London: Ofsted.

O'Keefe, D. (1993) *Truancy in English Schools.* A Report Prepared For DfEE. London: HMSO.

Oliver, C. and Candappa, M. (2003) *Tackling Bullying: Listening to the Views of Children and Young People.* RR400. Nottingham: DfES Publications.

Olweus, D. (1993) *Bullying at School: What We Know and What We Can Do.* Oxford: Blackwell.

Osler, A. and Starkey, H. (2005) 'Violence in schools and representations of young people: A critique of government policies in France and England', *Oxford Review of Education*, 31(2), pp. 195–215.

Pain, R. (2003) 'Youth, age and the representation of fear', *Capital & Class*, 60, pp. 151–171.

Parr, S. and Nixon, J. (2008) 'Rationalising family intervention projects', In P. Squires (ed.) *ASBO Nation: The Criminalisation of Nuisance.* Bristol: Policy Press.

Parsons, C. (1999) *Education, Exclusion and Citizenship.* London: Routledge.

Paterson, L. and Iannelli, C. (2007) 'Social class and educational attainment: A comparative study of England, Wales and Scotland', *Sociology of Education*, 80(October), pp. 330–358.

Pawson, R. and Tilley, N. (2004) *Realist Evaluation.* Paper funded by the British Cabinet Office. This paper develops ideas from the well-known book – Pawson, R. and Tilley, N. (1995) *Realistic Evaluation.* London: Sage.

Peachey, D.E. (1989) 'The kitchener experiment', In M. Wright and B. Galaway (eds) *Mediation and Criminal Justice.* London: Sage Publications.

Pearson, G. (1983) *Hooligan: A History of Respectable Fears.* Basingstoke: Macmillan.

Phillips, F. (2008) 'Lame Justice for feral kids keeps us living in fear', *The Mirror* [online], 20 January, http://www.mirror.co.uk/news/columnists/phillips/2008/01/20/lame-justice-for-feral-kids-keeps-us-living-in-fear-115875-20292672/ (accessed 16.12.2009).

Pirrie, A. (2001) 'Evidenced-based practice in education: the best medicine', *British Journal of Educational Studies*, 49(2), pp. 124–136.

Pitts, J. (2008) *Reluctant Gangsters. The Changing Face of Youth Crime.* Cullumpton: Willan Publishing.

Plowden Committee (1967) *Children and Their Primary Schools.* The Plowden Report. London: HMSO.

Porteous, D., Chatwin, C., Martin, D. and Goodman, A. (2007) 'Young victims of street crime in an east London Borough', *Community Safety Journal*, 6(3), pp. 29–35.

Porter, J. (2003) *Challenging Behaviour and learning Difficulties: A Context for Understanding Challenging Behaviour.* Birmingham: University of Birmingham.

Porter, L. (2000) *Behaviour in Schools: Theory and Practice for Teachers.* Buckingham: Open University Press.

Potts, A. (2006) 'Schools as dangerous places', *Educational Studies*, 32(3), pp. 319–330.

Povey, D. (ed.), Coleman, K., Kaiza, P. and Roe, S. (2009) *Homicides, Firearms Offences and Intimate Violence 2007/*08, 22 January, 02/09, http://www. homeoffice.gov.uk/rds/pdfs09/hosb0209.pdf (accessed 6.1.2010).

Pranis, K. (2001) 'Telling our stories and changing our lives', *The Texas Mediator*, 16(3), pp. 1–4.

Pratt, J.D. (1983) 'Folk-lore and fact in truancy research: Some critical comments on recent developments', *British Journal of Criminology*, 23(4), pp. 336–353.

Reay, D. and Ball, S. (1997) ' "Spoilt for choice": The working class and educational markets', *Oxford Review of Education*, 23(1), pp. 89–101.

Regan, B. (2007) 'Campaigning against neo-liberal education in Britain', *Journal for Critical Education Policy Studies*, 5(1), May, http://www.jceps.com/index. php?pageID=article&articleID=82 (accessed 28.7.2009).

Reid, K. (2003) 'A strategic approach to tackling school absenteeism and truancy: The PSCC scheme', *Educational Studies*, 29(4), pp. 351–371.

Reissman, C. (1993) *Narrative Analysis.* London: Sage.

Resnick, M.D., Bearman, P.S. and Blum, R.W. (1997) 'Protecting adolescents from harm: Findings from the National Longitudinal Study on Adolescent Health', *JAMA*, 278, pp. 823–832.

Reynolds, D., Sammons, P., Stoll, L., Barber, M. and Hillman, J. (1996) 'School effectiveness and school improvement in the United Kingdom', *School Effectiveness and School Improvement*, 7(2), pp. 133–158.

Rich, E. and Evans, J. (2009) 'Now I am Nobody, see me for who I am: The paradox of performativity', *Gender and Education*, 21(1), pp. 1–16.

Richardson, H. (2008) *Turning Success into Failure*, BBC News, 9 June, http:// news.bbc.co.uk/1/hi/education/7440040.stm, 30th April 2009 (accessed 7.1.2010).

Ridge, T. (2009) *Living with Poverty. A Review of the Literature on Children's and Families' Experiences of Poverty.* Norwich: Her Majesty's Stationary Office.

Riestenberg, N. (2001) *In-School Behavior Intervention Grants – Final Report 1999–2001.* Roseville, MN: Minnesota Dept. of Children, Families & Learning.

Riestenberg, N. (2005) *PEASE Academy: The Restorative Recovery School*, http:// www.safersanerschools.org/articles.html?articleId=516 (accessed 10.1.2011).

Riley, D. (2007) 'Anti-social behaviour: Children, schools and parents', *Education and the Law*, 19(3/4), pp. 221–236.

RJC, Restorative Justice Consortium (2004) *Principles of Restorative Processes.* London, http://www.restorativejustice.org.uk/?Resources:Best_Practice: Principles (accessed 10.1.2011).

Robinson, J.A. and Hawpe, L. (1986) 'Narrative thinking as a heuristic process', In T. R. Sarbin (ed.) *Narrative Psychology: The Storied Nature of Human Conduct* (pp. 111–125). New York: Praeger.

Rodger, J.J. (2008) *Criminalising Social Policy. Anti-Social Behaviour and Welfare in a De-Civilised Society.* Cullumpton/Devon: Willan.

Rodway, S. (1993) 'Children's rights: Children's needs. Is there a conflict?', *Therapeutic Care*, 2(2), pp. 375–391.

Roffey, S. (2004) 'The home-school interface for behaviour: A conceptual framework for co-constructing reality', *Educational and Child Psychology*, 21(4), pp. 95–108.

Roker, D., Devitt, K. and Holt, A. (2007) 'Children's move to secondary school: what do parents need at this time?', In D. Roker and J. Coleman (eds.) *Working with Parents of Young People: Research, Policy & Practice* (pp. 80–102). London: Jessica Kingsley.

Roper, M. (2002) 'Kids first: Approaching school safety', In E. Pelser (ed.) *Crime Prevention Partnerships. Lessons from Practice*. Pretoria: Institute for Security Studies.

Rosenberg, M. (1999) *Nonviolent Communication*. Encinitas, CA: PuddleDancer Press.

Rowe, S. and Ashe, J. (2008) *Young People and Crime: Findings from the 2006 Offending Crime and Justice Survey*. 15 July 09/08, http://www.homeoffice.gov.uk/rds/pdfs08/hosb0908.pdf (accessed 6.1.2010).

Royer, E. (2001) 'The education of students with EBD: One size does not fit all', In J. Visser, H. Daniels and T. Cole (eds) *International Perspectives on Inclusive Education: Emotional and Behavioural Difficulties in mainstream Schools*. Amsterdam: JAI.

Rubenstein, D. (1969) *School Attendance in London 1870–1901*. Hull: Hull University Press.

Rutter, M., Giller, H. and Hagell, A. (1998) *Antisocial Behaviour by Young People*. Cambridge: Cambridge University Press.

Rutter, M., Maughan, B., Mortimore, P. and Ouston, J. (1979) *Fifteen Thousand Hours. Secondary Schools and Their Effects on Children*. Shepton Mallet: Open Books Publishing Ltd.

Ryan, C., Mathews, F. and Banner, J. (1994) *Community Project to Fight Violence in Schools: A Model Partnership between the Police and Schools*. Canada: Central Toronto Youth Services.

Ryan, K. (2001) *Strengthening the Safety Net: Home Schools Can Help Youth with Emotional and Behavioural Needs*. Burlington, VT: School Research, University of Vermont.

Salmivalli, C. (1999) 'Participant role approach to school bullying: Implications for interventions', *Journal of Adolescence*, 22(4), pp. 453–459.

Sammons, P. (2008) 'Zero tolerance of failure and new labour approaches to school improvement in England', *Oxford Review of Education*, 34(6), pp. 651–664.

Sandford, R.A., Duncombe, R. and Armour, K.M. (2008) 'The role of physical activity/sport in tackling youth disaffection and anti-social behaviour', *Educational Review*, 60(4), pp. 419–435.

Sawatsky, J. (2001) 'A shared just peace ethic: Uncovering restorative values', *Conciliation Quarterly*, 20(3), pp. 2–4.

Schweinhart, I. and Weikart, D. (1980) *Young Children Grow Up: The Effects of the Perry Pre-School Program on Youths Through Age 15*. Monographs of the High/Scope Educational Research Foundation, No.7. Yspsilanti, MI.

Scott, S., Knapp, M., Henderson, J. and Maughan, B. (2001) 'Financial cost of social exclusion: Follow-up study of antisocial behaviour into adulthood', *British Medical Journal*, 323(191), 28 July. On-line journal, www.bmj.bmjjournals.com.

Seager, A. (2009) 'The lost generation: surge in joblessness hits young Under 25s feel the brunt of recession as unemployment hits 14 year high', *The Guardian*, http://www.guardian.co.uk/business/2009/aug/13/surge-in-joblessness-hits-young (accessed 13.8.2009).

Shapland, J., Atkinson, A., Atkinson, H., Chapman, B., Colledge, E., Dignan, J., Howes, M., Johnstone, J., Robinson, G. and Sorsby, A. (2007) *Restorative Justice: The Views of Victims and Offenders*. Ministry of Justice Research Series 3/07. London: Ministry of Justice.

Sharp, C., Aldridge, J. and Medina, J. (2006) *Delinquent Youth Groups and Offending Behaviour: Findings from the 2004 Offending, Crime and Justice Survey*. Home Office Online Report 14.06. London: Home Office.

Sharp, C., Blackmore, J., Kendall, L., Greene, K., Keys, W., Anna Macauley, A., Schagen, I. and Yeshanew, T. (2003) *Playing for Success. An Evaluation of the Fourth Year*. Research Report RR402. London: DfES.

Sharp, C., Kendall, L., Bhabra, S., Schagen, I. and Duff, J. (2001) *Playing for Success: An Evaluation of the Second Year*. Research Brief 291. London: DfES.

Shaw, M. (2004) *Police Schools and Crime Prevention: A Preliminary Review of Current Practices, Director – Analysis and Exchange*. Draft of Discussion paper, http://www.crime-preventionintl.org/publications/pub_110_1.pdf.

Sherman, L.W. and Strang, H. (2007) *Restorative Justice: The Evidence*. London: The Smith Institute.

Simon, J. (2007) *Governing Through Crime*. Oxford: Oxford University Press.

Simmons, J. et al. (2002) Crime in England and Wales 2001/2002. Home Office Statistical Bulletin Issue 7/02. London: Home Office.

Skinns, L., Du Rose, N. and Hough, M. (2009) *Restorative Approaches in Schools*. London: Restorative Solutions.

Smith, D.J. (2004) *The Links Between Victimization and Offending*. Edinburgh: Centre for Law and Society, University of Edinburgh.

Smith, D.J. and Bradshaw, P. (2005) *Gang Membership and Teenage Offending*. The Edinburgh Study of Youth Transitions and Crime, No. 8. Edinburgh: Centre for Law and Society, University of Edinburgh.

Smith, D.J. and Ecob, R. (2007) 'An investigation of causal links between victimization and offending in adolescents', *British Journal of Sociology*, 58(4), pp. 633–659.

Smith, D.J. and McVie, S. (2003) 'Theory and method in the Edinburgh study of youth transitions and crime', *British Journal of Criminology*, 43, pp. 169–195.

Smith, D.J., McVie, S., Woodward, R., Shute, J., Flint, J. and McAra, L. (2001) *The Edinburgh Study of Youth Transitions and Crime: Key Findings at ages 12 and 13*. Edinburgh: University of Edinburgh, Centre for Law and Society, http://www.law.ed.ac.uk/cls/esytc/findreport/wholereport.pdf (accessed 14.10.2009).

Smith, J. (2007) ' "Ye've got to ave balls to play this game sir!" Boys, peers and fears: The negative influence of school-based "cultural accomplices" in constructing hegemonic masculinities', *Gender and Education*, 19(2), pp. 179–198.

Smith, P.K. (2002a) 'School bullying, and ways of preventing it', In E. Debarbieux and C. Blaya (eds) *Violence in Schools and Public Policies*. Paris: Elsevier Science.

Smith, P.K. (co-ordinator) (2002b) *Bullying. Don't Suffer in Silence – An Anti-Bullying Pack for Schools*. London: DfES.

Smith, P.K. (ed.) (2003) *Violence in Schools: The Responses in Europe*. London: Routledge/Falmer, Taylor and Francis Group.

Smith, P.K. and Myron-Wilson, R. (1998) 'Parenting and school bullying', *Clinical Child Psychology and Psychiatry*, 3(3), pp. 405–417.

Smith, P.K. and Sharp, S. (1994) *School Bullying: Insights and Perspectives*. London: Routledge.

Smith, P.K., Cowie, H., Olafsson, R.F. and Liefooghe, A.P.D. (2002) 'Definitions of bullying: A comparison of terms used and age and gender differences, in a fourteen-country international comparison', *Child Development*, 73(4), pp. 1119–1133.

Smith, P.K., Mahdavi, J., Carvalho, M., Fisher, S., Russell, S. and Tippett, N. (2008) 'Cyberbullying: Its nature and impact in secondary school pupils', *Journal of Child Psychology and Psychiatry*, 49(4), pp. 376–385.

Smith, P.K., Morita, J., Junger-Tas, D., Olweus, D., Catalano, R. and Slee, P.T. (eds) (1999) *The Nature of School Bullying: A Cross-National Perspective*. London: Routledge.

Smith, R. (2007) *Youth Justice. Ideas, Policies, Practice* (2nd edition). Cullompton, Devon: Willan.

Smithers, A. and Robinson, P. (2005) *Teacher Turnover, Wastage and Movements between Schools*. Research Report 640. London: DfES.

Solomon, E. and Garside, R. (2008) *Ten Years of Labour's Youth Justice Reforms: An Independent Audit*. London: Centre for Crime and Justice Studies, Kings College London University.

Soydan, H., Nye, C., Chacón-Moscoso, S., Sánchez-Meca, J. and Almeida, C. (2005) *Families and Schools Together (FAST) for Improving Outcomes of School-Aged Children and Their Families*. The Campbell Collaboration, www.campbell. collaboration.org.

Squires, P. (1990) *Anti-Social Policy, Welfare, Ideology and the Disciplinary State*. Hemel Hempstead: Harvester-Wheatsheaf.

Squires, P. (2006a) 'New labour and the politics of anti-social behaviour', *Critical Social Policy*, 26(1), pp. 144–168.

Squires, P. (ed.) (2006b) *Community Safety: Critical Perspectives on Policy and Practice*. Bristol: The Policy Press.

Squires, P. (ed.) (2008) *ASBO Nation, the Criminalisation of Nuisance*. Bristol: Policy Press.

Squires, P. and Stephen, D.E. (2005) *Rougher Justice: Young People and Anti-Social Behaviour*. Cullompton, Devon: Willan.

Standing, H. and Nicolini, D. (1997). *Review of Workplace-Related Violence*. London: Health & Safety Executive, 6.

Stanko, E.A. (ed.) (2003) *The Meanings of Violence*. London: Routledge.

Steer, A. Sir (Chair) (2005) *Learning Behaviour. The Report of The Practitioners' Group on School Behaviour and Discipline*. Nottingham: DfES.

Steer, A. Sir (Chair) (2009) *Learning Behaviour: Lessons Learned. A Review of Behaviour Standards and Practices in Our Schools*. Nottingham: DfES.

Steffgen, G. (2009) 'Deviant behaviour and violence in Luxembourg schools', *International Journal of Violence and Schools*, 10(December), pp. 54–70, www. icjvs.com.

Steffgen, G and Ewen, N. (2007) 'Teachers as Victims of School Violence- the Influence of Strain and School Culture,' *International Journal on Violence and School*, 3(April), On-line journal, www.icjvs.com.

Stephen, D.E. (2006) 'Community safety and young people: 21st century *homo sacer* and the politics of injustice', In P. Squires (ed.) *Community Safety: Critical Perspectives on Policy and Practice*. Bristol: Policy Press.

Stephen, D.E. (2008) 'The responsibility of respecting justice: An open challenge to Tony Blair's successors', In P. Squires (ed.) *ASBO Nation: The Criminalisation of Nuisance*. Bristol: Policy Press.

Stephen, D.E. (2009) 'Time to stop twisting the knife: A critical commentary on the rights and wrongs of criminal justice responses to problem youth in the UK', *Journal of Social Welfare and Family Law*, 31(2), pp. 193–206.

Stephen, D.E. and Squires, P. (2003) ' "Adults don't realise how sheltered they are". A contribution to the debate on youth transitions from some voices on the margins', *Journal of Youth Studies*, 6(2), pp. 145–164.

Stephen, D.E. and Squires, P. (2004) 'They're still children and entitled to be children. Problematising the institutionalised mistrust of marginalised youth in Britain', *Journal of Youth Studies*, 7(3), pp. 351–369.

Stephen, D.E., O'Connell, P. and Hall, M. (2008) ' "Going the extra mile", "fire-fighting", or "*laissez-faire*"? Re-evaluating personal tutoring relationships within mass higher education', *Teaching in Higher Education*, 13(4), pp. 449–460.

Stephenson, M. (2007) *Young People and Offending: Education, Youth Justice and Social Inclusion*. Cullompton: Willan.

Sutton, C., Utting, D. and Farrington, D. (2004) *Support from the Start: Working with Young Children and their Families to Reduce the Risks of Crime and Anti-Social Behaviour*. DfES Research Report 524. London: DfES.

Sutton, L. (2002) 'Police/school/kids – A safety partnership'. Paper presented at the *The Role of Schools in Crime Prevention Conference*, Melbourne, Victoria, Australia, 30 September–1 October.

Teacher Support Network (2005) *Violence Forces Teachers to Consider Quitting*. http://www.teachersupport.info/index.cfm?p=3393 (accessed 4.05.2006).

Teacher Support Network (2007) *Report on Violence and Disruption in Schools: The Impact on Teacher Wellbeing*. London: Teacher Support Network.

Teachernet (2009) *Parental Responsibility Data: Data on Penalty Notices, Fast-Track to attendance, Parenting Orders and Parenting Contracts Cumulative Data for Period September 2004–August 2008*, http://www.teachernet.gov.uk/wholeschool/behaviour/pcspospns/prdata (accessed 7.06.2010).

Teachernet (2010) *Safer Schools Partnerships – Aims*. http://www.teachernet.gov.uk/wholeschool/behaviour/sspg/definition/aims (accessed 26.9.2010).

The Equalities Review (2007) *Fairness and Freedom: The Final Report of the Equalities Review*. London: The Equalities Review/Cabinet Office.

Thomas, G. and Glenny, B. (2000) 'Emotional and behavioural difficulties; bogus needs in a false category', *Discourse: Studies in the Cultural Politics of Education*, 21(2), pp. 283–298.

Thorpe, L. (2006) 'Police Tackle Hate Crime in Schools', *Chard and Illminster News*, 13 September.

Thorsborne, M. and Vinegrad, D. (2002) *Restorative Practices in Schools*. Buderim: Marg Thorsborne.

Thorsborne, M. and Vinegrad, D. (2004) *Restorative Practices in Classrooms*. Buderim, Queensland: Marg Thorsborne.

Tolan, P., Henry, D., Schoeny, M. and Bass, A. (2008) *Mentoring Interventions to Affect Juvenile Delinquency and Associated Problems*, Review 16. The Campbell Collaboration. http://www.campbellcollaboration.org/library.phpll.

Townsend, M. and Revill, J. (2008) 'Knife scanners at school gates to curb attacks', *The Observer*, 20 January.

Tubbs, N. (1996) *The New Teacher*. London: David Fulton Publishers.

TUC/MORI (2001) *Half a Million Kids Working Illegally*. 21 March. London: TUC.

Underwood Report (1955) *Report of the Committee on Maladjusted Children*. London: H.M.S.O.

U.S. Department of Justice (2001) *Guide to Using School COP to Address Student Discipline and Crime Problems*. Washington, DC: Office of Community Oriented Policing Services.

Valentine, G. (2004) *Public Space and the Culture of Childhood*. Aldershot: Ashgate.

Vincent, C. and Tomlinson, S. (1997) 'Home-School Relationships: "The swarming of disciplinary mechanisms"?', *British Educational Research Journal*, 23(3), pp. 361–377.

Visser, J. (2000) *Managing Behaviour in Classrooms*. London: David Fulton.

Visser, J. (2002) 'Eternal Verities: The strongest links', *Emotional and Behavioural Difficulties*, 7(2), pp. 68–84.

Visser, J. (2003) *A Study of Children and Young People Who Present Challenging Behaviour*. London: Ofsted.

Visser, J. (2006) 'Keeping violence in perspective', *International Journal on Violence and School*, May, On-line journal, http://ww.ijvs.org.

Visser, J. and Zenib, J. (2009) 'ADHD: A scientific fact or factual opinion? A critique of the veracity of attention deficit hyperactivity disorder', *Emotional and Behavioural Difficulties*, 14(2), pp. 127–140.

Visser, J., Cole, T. and Daniels, H. (2002) 'Inclusion for the difficult to include', *Support for Learning*, 17(1), pp. 23–26.

VISTA, Violence in Schools Training Action (2006) *A Resource for Practitioners and Policy-Makers and All those Working with Children and Young People Affected by School violence*, www.vista-europe.org.

Von Hirsch, A. and Simester, A.P. (2006) *Incivilities, Regulating Offensive Behaviour*. Oxford: Hart.

Vulliamy, G. and Webb, R. (2000) 'Stemming the tide of rising school exclusions: Problems and possibilities', *British Journal of Education Studies*, 48, pp. 119–133.

Wachtel, T. (1999) Safer saner schools – Restoring community in a disconnected world *Reshaping Australian Institutions Conference: Restorative Justice and Civil Society*, Canberra: Australia National University.

Wachtel, T. and McCold, P. (2001) 'Restorative justice in everyday life', In H. Strang and J. Braithwaite (eds) *Restorative Justice and Civil Society*. Cambridge: Cambridge University Press.

Waddington, P.A.J., Badger, D. and Bull, R. (2006) *The Violent Workplace*. Cullompton, Devon: Willan.

Waiton, S. (2008) *The Politics of Anti-Social Behaviour: Amoral Panics*. London: Routledge.

Watkins, C., Mauther, M., Hewitt, R., Epstein, D. and Leonard, D. (2007) 'School violence, school differences and school discourses', *British Educational Research Journal*, 33(1), pp. 61–74.

Weerman, F.M. (2005) 'Identification and self-identification: Using a survey to study gangs in The Netherlands', In S.H. Decker and F.M. Weerman (eds) *European Street Gangs and Troublesome Youth Groups: Findings from the Eurogang Research Programme*. Walnut Creek, CA: AltaMira Press.

Westinghouse Learning Corporation (1969) *The Impact of Head Start: An Evaluation of the Effects of Head Start on Children's Cognitive and Affective Development*. Report to the Office of Economic Opportunity. Washington, DC: Clearing House for Federal, Scientific and Technical Information.

Whelan, R.J. (1998) *Emotional and Behavioural Disorders: A 25-year Focus*. Denver: Love Publishers.

Whitty, G. and Wisby, E. (2007) 'Whose voice? An exploration of the current policy interest in pupil involvement in school decision-making', *International Studies in Sociology of Education*, 17(3), pp. 303–319.

Wilkinson, R. and Pickett, K. (2010) *The Sprit Level: Why Equality is Better for Everyone*. London: Penguin.

Wilkstrom, P.H and Butterworth, D.A. (2006) *Adolescent Crime: Individual Difference and Lifestyles*, Cullompton, Devon: Willan.

Willig, C. (2008) *Introducing Qualitative Methods in Psychology: Adventures in Theory and Method* (Second edition). Buckingham: Open University Press.

Willis, P. (1977) *Learning to Labour*. Westmead: Saxon House.

Wilson, D., Sharp, C. and Patterson, A. (2006) *Young People and Crime: Findings from the 2005 Offending, Crime and Justice Survey*. London: Home Office.

Wilson, D.B., Gottfredson, D.C. and Najaka, S.S. (2001) 'School-based prevention of problem behaviours: A meta-analysis', *Journal of Quantitative Criminology*, 17(3), pp. 247–272.

Wilson, J.Q. and Kelling, G.L. (1982) 'Broken Windows', *Atlantic Monthly*, March, pp. 29–38.

Wilson, M. and Evans, K. (1980) *Education for Disturbed Pupils*. Schools Council Working Paper 65. London: Methuen.

Wilson, S.J. and Lipsey, M.W. (2006a) *The Effects of School-Based Social Information Processing Interventions on Aggressive Behavior, Part I: Universal Programs*. 5. The Campbell Collaboration, www.campbell.collaboration.org.

Wilson, S.J. and Lipsey, M.W. (2006b) *The Effects of School-Based Social Information Processing Interventions on Aggressive Behavior, Part 2: Part II: Selected/Indicated Pull-out Programs*. 6. The Campbell Collaboration, www. campbell.collaboration.org.

Wolke, D., Woods, S., Bloomfeld, F. and Karstadt, L. (2000) 'The Association between direct and relational bullying and behaviour: Problems among primary school children', *Journal of Child Psychology and Psychiatry*, 41(8), pp. 989–1002.

Woolley, H. (2009) 'Every child matters in public open spaces', In A. Millie (ed.) *Securing Respect: Behavioural Expectations and Anti-Social Behaviour in the UK*. Bristol: Policy Press.

Wright, A. and Keetley, K. (2003) *Violence and Indiscipline in Schools*. Leicester: Perpetuity Press.

YJB (2004) *National Evaluation of the Restorative Justice in Schools Programme*. London: YJB.

YJB (2007) *Groups, Gangs and Weapons*. London: Youth Justice Board.

YJB (2009a) *Youth Survey 2008: Young People in Mainstream Education*. London: YJB.

YJB (2009b) *Youth Survey 2008: Young People in Pupil Referral Units*. London: YJB.

Young, J. (2007) *The Vertigo of Late Modernity*. London: Sage.

Young Voice (2008) *Effective Approaches to Anti-Bullying Practice in Schools*, http://www.young-voice.org/ (accessed 3.4.2008).

Youth Taskforce (2008) *Youth Taskforce Action Plan: Give Respect, Get Respect – Youth Matters*. London: DCSF.

Zehr, H. (1990) *Changing Lenses*. Scottdale, PA: Herald Press.

Zeira, A., Astor, R.A. and Benbenishty, R. (2004) 'School violence in Israel: Perceptions of homeroom teachers', *School Psychology International*, 25(2), pp. 149–166.

# Index